W9-ASI-300

JOHN OWEN ON THE CHRISTIAN LIFE

JOHN OWEN ON THE CHRISTIAN LIFE

Sinclair B. Ferguson

THE BANNER OF TRUTH TRUST

THE BANNER OF TRUTH TRUST
3 Murrayfield Road, Edinburgh EH12 6EL
PO Box 621, Carlisle, Pennsylvania 17013, USA

*

© Sinclair B Ferguson 1987
First published 1987
ISBN 0 85151 503 7

*

Typeset in 11/12pt Linotron Baskerville
at The Spartan Press Ltd, Lymington, Hants
and printed and bound in Great Britain
at Oxford University Press, Oxford

In Memory
of my parents
ROBERT and EMMA
FERGUSON
and my brother
KENNETH

CONTENTS

Contents

INTRODUCTION

In 1904, James Moffatt published an anthology entitled *The Golden Book of John Owen*. Its author (then only thirty-three, but already destined for fame through his later translation of the Bible) had discovered a spiritual penetration and power in the writings of the Puritans which he did not find paralleled in the contemporary church.

Moffatt compiled a series of quotations from Owen's *Works* and provided a brief biographical sketch. In his Preface, he wrote:

Apart from one or two treatises still read by a too scanty retinue, John Owen's collected works have been dropped into the cells of oblivion. An anthology is apt to reflect the arbitrary taste of the anthologist, and it is prone to be scrappy, especially in the case of continuous authors; but, so far as I am able to judge, an anthology is the one chance, or at least the best chance, of rescuing John Owen for the memory and attention of the twentieth century.[1]

It would have been impossible for the young James Moffatt to imagine that such a pessimistic view of the future of Owen's *Works* would be proved so wrong within the life-time of the next generation. Yet, wrong it has proved to be, for Owen's *Works* are today to be found throughout the English-speaking world, reprinted and re-read. Perhaps there are more readers of Owen's *Works* today than at almost any time since his death.

This study of Owen's teaching is an expression of that rediscovery of Owen and the direct result of it. My personal interest in him as a teacher and theologian began in my late teenage years when I first read some of his writings. Like others, before and since, I found that they dealt with issues which contemporary evangelical literature rarely, if ever, touched. Owen's penetrating exposition opened up areas of need in my own heart, but also correspondingly profound assurances of grace in Jesus Christ. It was only later that I

[1] J. Moffatt (ed.), *The Golden Book of John Owen*, London, 1904, p. xii.

[x]

realized why his work spoke so powerfully to a teenager: some of his material had been preached first to teenage undergraduates in the University of Oxford. Ever since those first encounters with his *Works*, I have remained in his debt.

These pages are an attempt to repay that debt, and the fulfilment of a long-held desire to make Owen a little more accessible to those less familiar with the riches of his work and those who do not have the time to make their way through the millions of words he penned. It is intended in part as something of a 'Reader's Guide to John Owen', providing a framework to his works and a conducted tour of much of his teaching.

I also hope that this study will provide more than an index to Owen. It is intended to stand in its own right as a study of God's grace in the lives of his people. My own reading of Owen has convinced me that everything he wrote for his contemporaries had a practical and pastoral aim in view – the promotion of true Christian living. That view is confirmed by the words of Owen's assistant, David Clarkson, in the course of his funeral sermon after Owen's death: 'It was his great Design to promote Holiness in the Life and Exercise of it among you,' he said to the congregation. To an age in which holiness has become a neglected theme in evangelical teaching, Owen speaks with great power.

John Owen on the Christian Life is also a study in pastoral theology. It contains theology, and that of the most demanding kind. But it is theology with a practical purpose – helping men and women in their need and sin, and showing the riches of God's grace in Christ. My hope is that these pages will promote spiritual growth, and give help and encouragement to those who share, as Owen did, in the leading and guiding of the people of God. Any other use of his writings Owen would not willingly have countenanced.

In view of this, technical discussions and criticism have largely been avoided. In a few places they appear in order to explain why Owen writes as he does. Readers who have little interest in such material can easily move on to the next stage of the theme without losing the gist of Owen's teaching. Footnote references abound, however, to serve as signposts for those who want to pursue further what Owen has to say on a particular theme.

It remains only to express my gratitude to those who have made this study possible. Among them must be included the publishers, to whom the revival of interest in Owen's writings owes a very great deal. In particular I would like to express my thanks to Mervyn Barter, Humphrey Mildred and Iain Murray whose friendship I have enjoyed while this work has been in preparation. I am grateful to S. M. Houghton and William Brailsford for their assistance with proof-reading. I am also deeply indebted to my friend John Muether, Librarian of Westminster Seminary, for graciously supplying the indices. My wife, Dorothy, who has shared her life with this study almost as long as she has shared it with me, has, more than anyone else, encouraged me to finish it. Its completion is a token of my gratitude and love for her.

Chiefly I wish to record my gratitude to the Covenant God whose grace and faithfulness John Owen so richly expounded. In the joys and sorrows of life during the years of preparing these pages, not one of his promises has failed. To have known the pastoral ministry of John Owen during these years (albeit in written form) has been a rich privilege; to have known Owen's God an even greater one. My prayer is that some of the material in these pages will help readers (as Owen would himself have desired) to serve the Triune God more faithfully.

Sinclair B Ferguson
Westminster Theological Seminary
Philadelphia, U.S.A.

I need not tell you of this who knew him, that it was his great Design to promote Holiness in the Life and Exercise of it among you: But it was his great Complaint, that its Power declined among Professors. It was his Care and Endeavour to prevent or cure spiritual Decays in his own Flock: He was a burning and a shining Light, and you for a while rejoyced in his Light. Alas! it was but for a while; and we may Rejoyce in it still.

> David Clarkson,
> *A Funeral Sermon on the Much Lamented Death of the Late Reverend and Learned Divine John Owen, D.D..*

John Owen and his Christian Life

John Owen was born at Stadham, or Stadhampton, near Oxford, in the year 1616. The second son of Henry Owen, the local Puritan vicar, John had three brothers, William, Henry and Philemon,[1] and one sister, whose Christian name is unrecorded but whose married name was Singleton.

Almost nothing is known of the intimate details of the Owen household. In a rare comment on his upbringing, Owen later wrote that his father was 'a Nonconformist all his days, and a painful labourer in the vineyard of the Lord'.[2] When he was about ten, he went to a small grammar school in the parish of All Saints, Oxford, in preparation for his entrance to Queen's College at the age of twelve. He matriculated in Oxford University on 4 November 1631, which required his subscribing to the Thirty-Nine Articles, and graduated B.A. on 11 June 1632.

While receiving his grounding in grammar, rhetoric, and philosophy, and taking part in the required academic debates, he apparently found time to throw the javelin and compete in the long jump! He also played the flute. Owen reputedly disciplined himself during this period to take only four hours of sleep each night. Already, as a teenager, he was sowing the

---

[1] William became a clergyman in Oxfordshire, Henry an army major. Philemon became an army captain, and was killed in Ireland in 1649.

[2] *The Works of John Owen*, ed. W. H. Goold, XXIV vols., Edinburgh, 1850–53, (reprinted, London, 1965–68), XIII. 224. Goold's edition consists of XVII volumes of Owen's *Works* plus VII volumes containing his *Commentary on Hebrews*. In the reprint, Owen's Latin writings in vols. XVI and XVII have been omitted, and the English material in vol. XVII transferred to vol. XVI. On the few occasions this affects the footnotes, the reference in the *reprinted* edition is given in brackets.

seeds of both the academic learning and the ill health which were to characterize his later years. He is reported to have said in adulthood that he would have sacrificed his learning in exchange for better health. On 27 April 1635 he graduated M.A., and soon afterwards was ordained deacon, and began the seven-year course for the degree of B.D.

Those were difficult times for a young man who had inherited his father's Puritan convictions, and was beginning to hold them for himself. In 1628 Charles I had forbidden debates over such controversial matters as election and predestination, the very themes which, for Owen and his friends, lay at the heart of the gospel. As the influence of William Laud and the High Church Party increased, it became clear to Owen that remaining in the University was an impossibility,[1] and so, having already 'taken orders', after two years he left Oxford in favour of becoming chaplain and tutor in the household of Sir Robert Dormer of Ascot. This was the most satisfactory way for a conscientious man to avoid a clash with the ecclesiastical authorities, and it also provided an opportunity for private thought and theological study. Later Owen moved to the house of John, Lord Lovelace, at Hurly in Berkshire. Lovelace was a Royalist, and when the 'King's War' broke out, Owen moved to London, in 1642.

Although already holding Puritan convictions, the young Owen appears to have lacked assurance of his salvation. An early anonymous biography (1720) suggests he was in a state of melancholy for a period of some five years. But, now in London, he went to hear the renowned Edmund Calamy preach at Aldermanbury Chapel. To his intense disappointment a substitute preacher entered the pulpit and preached on Matthew 8.26. From that sermon onwards Owen experienced the love of God shed abroad in his heart,[2] and enjoyed a new assurance that he was a child of God. Despite all his efforts he was never able to discover the identity of the man whose preaching had delivered him from the 'spirit of bondage' (Rom. 8.15).

[1] W. Orme, *Memoirs of the Life, Writings and Religious Connexions of John Owen, D.D.*, London, 1820, p. 13.
[2] IX.606–9.

John Owen and his Christian Life

i. *The Beginnings of his Ministry*

In March 1642 Owen began his career as an author, with the publication of *A Display of Arminianism*.[1] It is a strongly polemical treatise and bears the hallmarks of the author and his times. He was immediately thrust before the public gaze. The work itself was dedicated to the Committee of Religion,[2] which consequently conferred on him the living of Fordham in Essex, some five miles from Colchester. Already opposed to the outward formalities of contemporary ministerial life, he signed the church register 'John Owen, *Pastor.* Ann.Dom. July 16:1643'. It was a simple indication of his dislike of the expression 'parson'.[3]

Shortly afterwards he married his first wife, Mary Rooke. She was to bear him eleven children, the first of them in 1644. But only one, a girl, survived into adulthood, and she, having contracted marriage unhappily, returned to her parents and shortly afterwards died of consumption.[4] Owen's few references to his home life indicate the common tensions of every family. In a letter to John Thornton, for example, he writes:

Our musk melons are ripe, witnes that I have sent you, I would have sent more but you know Matthew.[5]

Matthew was his son, and obviously had a taste for melons!

On his settlement at Fordham, Owen soon demonstrated his deep sense of pastoral responsibility. Orme states that on one occasion he bewailed the fact that so few people seemed to be genuinely helped by his ministry,[6] and expressed his opinion that John Bunyan's preaching gifts were worth more than all of his own learning.[7] Nevertheless, his own preaching drew

[1] X.5ff.

[2] Appointed by the House of Lords, March 12, 1640, its duty was to examine all doctrinal and disciplinary innovations.

[3] Peter Toon, *God's Statesman: The Life and Work of John Owen*, Exeter, 1971, p. 17.

[4] Orme states that she married Roger Knyaston, 'a Welsh gentleman', *op. cit.*, p. 36.

[5] *Correspondence of John Owen*, ed. Peter Toon, London 1969, p. 135. Matthew died in 1665.

[6] Orme, *op. cit.*, p. 118.

[7] A. Thomson, *Life of Dr. Owen, Works* I.xcii.

influential congregations, and throughout the course of his life was helpful to many people.[1] Perhaps overawed by the learning and spiritual insight of their young pastor, the people mistakenly felt that it was unnecessary to express their appreciation of his ministry. Perhaps they appreciated him too little. Whatever the reason, there is no doubt about Owen's pastoral concern for them. It appears in the Catechisms he prepared specifically for their instruction and published in 1645.[2]

Earlier, in 1643, Owen had already published a significant study entitled *The Duty of Pastors and People Distinguished*.[3] He held to a mild form of presbyterianism, and was opposed to the supposed anarchy of congregationalism. But this viewpoint was soon to be changed.

ii. *The Congregationalist*

By 1646 the ministry at Fordham was drawing to a close, in rather unusual circumstances. Owen had been appointed to the charge when the rector's living had been sequestered through desertion. On the death of the former rector, the appointment of the incumbent now reverted from the Committee on Religion to the patron. Having no great liking for Owen, he appointed another successor. Shortly before leaving, Owen (still only 32) was invited to preach before Parliament, on 29 April 1646.[4] Later in the year he moved to Coggeshall, to occupy the distinguished pulpit of St Peter's where the brothers John and Obadiah Sedgwick (a member of the Westminster Assembly) had successively ministered, to a congregation of some two thousand people.

This geographical shift paralleled an inner development which had taken place in Owen's thinking. He was now, at least in embryo, a congregationalist by conviction. He describes his

---

[1]David Clarkson, *A Funeral Sermon on the Much Lamented Death of the Late Reverend and Learned Divine John Owen, D.D.* (printed with Anon., *The Life of John Owen*, lix–lxxv), London, 1720, p. lxxii. Orme, *op. cit.*, p. 118 refers to two testimonies to Owen's influence recorded in John Rogers, *Bethshemesh, or The Tabernacle for the Sun*, London, 1653, Book II, ch. 6.

[2]I.465ff.

[3]XIII.3ff.

[4]The sermon is printed in *Works* VIII.2ff.

change of mind in *A Vindication of the Treatise on Schism*,[1] in which he reflects on what he had previously written in *The Duty of Pastors and People Distinguished*:

I was then a young man myself, about the age of twenty-six or twenty-seven years. The controversy between Independency and Presbytery was young also, nor, indeed, by me clearly understood, especially as stated on the congregational side. The conceptions delivered in the treatise were not (as appears in the issue) suited to the opinion of the one party nor of the other, but were such as occurred to mine own naked consideration of things, with relation to some differences that were then upheld in the place where I lived. Only, being unacquainted with the congregational way, I professed myself to own the other party, not knowing but that my principles were suited to their judgment and profession, having looked very little farther into those affairs than I was led by an opposition to Episcopacy and ceremonies. Upon a review of what I had there asserted, I found that my principles were far more suited to what is the judgment and practice of the congregational men than those of the presbyterian. Only, whereas I had not received any farther clear information in these ways of the worship of God, which since I have been engaged in, as was said, I professed myself of the presbyterian judgment, in opposition to democratical confusion; and, indeed, so I do still, and so do all the congregational men in England that I am acquainted withal. So that when I compare what then I wrote with my present judgment, I am scarce able to find the least difference between the one and the other; only, a misapplication of names and things by me gives countenance to this charge. Indeed, not long after, I set myself seriously to inquire into the controversies then warmly agitated in these nations. Of the congregational way I was not acquainted with any one person, minister or other; nor had I, to my knowledge, seen any more than one in my life. My acquaintance lay wholly with ministers and people of the presbyterian way. But sundry books being published on either side, I perused and compared them with the Scripture and one another, according as I received ability from God. After a general view of them, as was my manner in other controversies, I fixed on one to take under peculiar consideration and examination, which seemed most methodically and strongly to maintain that which was contrary, as I thought, to my present persuasion. This was Mr. Cotton's book of the Keys. The examination and confutation hereof, merely for my own particular satisfaction, with what diligence and sincerity I was able, I engaged in. In the

[1] XIII.209ff.

[5]

pursuit and management of this work, quite beside and contrary to my expectation . . . I was prevailed on to receive that and those principles which I had thought to have set myself in an opposition unto.[1]

Thus persuaded of the 'congregational way', Owen gathered a church along these lines in Coggeshall, while continuing to exercise his parish ministry in St Peter's.

iii A Wider Sphere of Influence

Already an author, and now a preacher of some repute, events in the 'Second Civil War' soon brought Owen before the public eye in a yet more significant capacity. In June 1648 General Fairfax besieged Colchester. Owen was invited to preach to his troops. As a result he became a personal friend of many of the officers, including Cromwell's son-in-law, Henry Ireton, whose funeral oration, *The Labouring Saint's Dismission to Rest*,[2] he later preached in 1651. The Colchester sermon, on Habakkuk 3.1–9, was published in expanded form, and dedicated to General Fairfax, 'as a small mite of that abundant thankfulness, wherein all peace-loving men of this county stand obliged unto you'.[3]

It is difficult for us to imagine the political crises of these days. Within months King Charles I had been accused of treason, tried, found guilty, and sentenced to death. He was executed on Wednesday, January 30, 1649; his crime that of levying war on the nation. Parliament called on Owen, still only thirty-two years old, to preach before them the next day, along with John Cordell, the minister of All Hallows in Lombard Street, London. Owen spoke from Jeremiah 15.19–20.[4] His sermon was 'an appropriate message in a difficult hour'.[5] It was one of the most signal tokens of the esteem in which he was already held that, although young in years, the Commons should look to him on such an occasion for spiritual wisdom and guidance.

[1]XIII.222–3.   [2]VIII.345–363.   [3]VIII.73.   [4]VIII.128ff.
[5]Toon, *God's Statesman*, p. 34. The sermon was later condemned by the University of Oxford on July 21, 1683 a month before Owen's decease, and was ordered to be burned, Orme, *op. cit.*, p. 96. Later, Parliament reversed the score by ordering the public hangman to burn the decree! Orme, *op. cit.*, p. 97.

Owen again preached before the Members of Parliament in April of the same year, taking as his text Hebrews 12.27. In its published form his sermon took on the apocalyptic title, *The Shaking and Translating of Heaven and Earth*,[1] although, in Owen's exegesis, the heaven and earth of the passage were interpreted as the great political powers of the world.[2] This sermon was, in part, the means of his introduction to Oliver Cromwell, and the beginning of an important relationship to both of them, characterized by mutual respect and a consequently proportionate rupture in their friendship when Cromwell later appeared to be on the brink of accepting the crown.

The first encounter was, to say the least, direct: Owen had gone to pay his respects to General Fairfax, and while waiting for him to arrive, Cromwell and some fellow army officers appeared. According to the witnesses, Cromwell, recognizing the preacher of the previous day, placed his hands on Owen's shoulders, and said, 'Sir, you are the person I must be acquainted with'. Owen carefully replied: 'That will be much more to my advantage than to yours'. 'We shall soon see that', replied Cromwell.[3] It was his intention to ask Owen to accompany him to Ireland, as a chaplain, and, at the same time, to investigate the affairs of the University of Dublin. Owen had no way out. His younger brother was a standard bearer in the army, and furthermore, Cromwell wrote to the Coggeshall congregation for permission to relieve them temporarily of their pastor. Their immediate reluctance was soon overcome by Cromwell's command! So Owen accompanied the twelve thousand psalm-singing, Bible-reading Puritan soldiers to descend upon Ireland, 'Like the hammer of Thor'.[4]

Nothing need here be said of the terrible massacre at Drogheda, and the days of slaughter which lie buried in the roots of the uneasy relationship which has existed between Westminster and Dublin since then. The best that can be said is

---

[1] VIII.244ff.
[2] VIII.245; IX.131ff.
[3] I.xlii.
[4] I.xliii.

that Cromwell did not step beyond the bounds of the rules of war and siege warfare of his times.[1]

Cromwell is reported to have viewed the whole event as a 'terrible necessity'. Nevertheless, the holocaust stirred something within the depths of Owen's soul, and on his return he pleaded with Parliament for mercy to follow this 'justice':

How is it that Jesus Christ is in Ireland only as a *lion staining all his garments with the blood of his enemies*; and none to hold him out as a *lamb sprinkled with his own blood to his friends*?[2]

He longs that

the Irish might enjoy Ireland so long as the moon endureth, so that Jesus Christ might possess the Irish . . . I would there were for the present one gospel preacher for every walled town in the English possession in Ireland. The land mourneth, and the people perish for want of knowledge. . . . The tears and cries of the inhabitants of Dublin after the manifestations of Christ are ever in my view.[3]

In March of the same year (1650) Owen was appointed an official preacher in Whitehall, with a salary of £200. But later he was again on the move, this time to Scotland, where the army had been sent primarily as a protective measure to prevent the Scots first invading England(!), restoring the Stuart monarchy, and establishing presbyterianism by force where the Solemn League and Covenant had failed to do so by mutual agreement. Owen preached on a number of occasions, and repeatedly in Old St Giles, in Edinburgh. In Glasgow he appears to have suffered a mild set-back to his morale. According to the story (perhaps exaggerated in Scottish legend!), Hugh Binning,[4] a presbyterian minister in his early twenties, took part in a conference with Cromwell and his chaplains over the question of their presence in Scotland. Apparently young Binning was able to confound Cromwell's heavy artillery. But the General was not rendered defenceless.

---

[1] Antonia Fraser, *Cromwell Our Chief of Men*, London 1973, p. 335. Owen did not witness the massacre, Toon, *God's Statesman*, p. 39.

[2] VIII.235.   [3] VIII.235–6.

[4] Hugh Binning (1627–53) was Professor of Philosophy in Glasgow University at the age of 19. At the time of Owen's visit (1651) he was minister in Govan (now Glasgow). A prodigious intellect he died prematurely of consumption. His works were published in 1768 and in 1858.

Enquiring for the name of the young presbyterian, and discovering it to be Binning, Cromwell punned, 'He hath *bound* well, indeed', and, laying his hand on the sword at his side, added, 'But this will loose all again!'[1]

iv. *Dean and Vice-Chancellor*

Within another year, in 1651, Owen was advanced to the appointment as Dean of Christ Church, Oxford. Cromwell was now the Chancellor of the University, and clearly anxious to promote his cause by shrewd appointments. Under normal circumstances, the deanery commanded the almost princely stipend of £800 per annum, which was more than ten times the figure earned by well-established clergy in ordinary parishes.[2] This may help to explain Owen's reputation for sartorial elegance!

According to Anthony Wood's (doubtless overplayed) caricature, he

scorned formality and undervalued his office by going in quirpo like a young scholar, with powdered hair, snakebone bandstrings, lawn bands, a very large set of ribbons pointed at his knees, and Spanish leather boots with large lawn tops, and his hat mostly cocked.[3]

Owen now preached regularly in Oxford, at Christ Church where he was Dean, and also on alternate Sundays with Thomas Goodwin, at St Mary's. Those who listened to Owen would have heard, at least in embryo, his later published treatises on *Mortification*,[4] and *Temptation*.[5] It is instructive for our generation to remember that this material was preached to congregations composed of teen-aged students!

[1] I.xlv. See Orme, *op. cit.*, p. 127 and J. Howie, *Biographia Scoticana*, Edinburgh, 1823, II, p. 167. The conference is described by Sir James Balfour in *The Annals of Scotland*, Edinburgh, 1824–5, IV.298, but (unfortunately!) not in detail.

[2] Sir George Clark, *The Later Stuarts*, London, 1955, p. 26. He suggests that 'lesser clergymen' had an income of £50, and 'eminent clergymen', £72 per annum.

[3] A. Wood, *Athenae Oxonienses*, London, 1691, ed. P. Bliss, London, 1813–20, IV, col. 98. Hence Maurice Ashley's description of Owen as 'a dapper Independent minister'! *The Greatness of Oliver Cromwell*, London, 1957, p. 264.

[4] VI.3ff.   [5] VI.89ff.

In 1652, Owen was appointed Vice-Chancellor of the University 'notwithstanding his urgent request to the contrary'.[1] His opening oration in that office has a remarkably contemporary ring sounding through its latinate sentences:

In what times, what manners, what diversities of opinion (dissensions and calumnies everywhere ranging in consequence of party spirit), what bitter passions and provocations, what pride and malice, our academical authority has occurred, I both know and lament. Nor is it only the character of the age that distracts us, but another calamity to our literary establishment, which is daily becoming more conspicuous, – the contempt, namely, of the sacred authority of law, and of the reverence due to our ancestors; the watchful envy of Malignants; the despised tears and sobs of our almost dying mother, the university (with the eternal loss of the class of gownsmen, and the no small hazard of the whole institution); and the detestable audacity and licentiousness, manifestly Epicurean, beyond all the bounds of modesty and piety, in which alas! too many of the students indulge.[2]

To this perplexing situation Owen brought a measure of security and sanity by the wisdom and tolerance of his use of power. Doubtless Andrew Thomson writes as an enthusiastic admirer of Owen, but his words crystallize Owen's achievements:

By infusing that tolerant spirit into his administration which he had often commended in his days of suffering, but which so many in those times forgot when they rose to power, – by a generous impartiality in the bestowal of patronage, – by an eagerness to detect modest merit, and to help struggling poverty, – by a firm repression of disorder and licentiousness, and a steadfast encouragement of studious habits and good conduct, – he succeeded, during the few years of his vice-chancellorship, in curing the worst evils of the university, and restoring it to such a condition of prosperity as to command at length even the reluctant praise of Clarendon.[3]

In October 1653, Cromwell invited him to take part in a potentially significant conference 'to persuade them that hold

[1]Quoted Orme, *op. cit.*, p. 143, from Wood's *Fasti*, II.777.
[2]Oratio Prima, XVI.481, translated by Orme, *op. cit.*, p. 170. See Peter Toon, *Oxford Orations of John Owen*, Linkinhorne, Cornwall, 1971, p. 5.
[3]I.li.

Christ, the head, and so are the same in fundamentals, to agree in love, – that there be no such divisions among people professing godliness as hath been, nor railing or reviling each other for difference only in forms'.[1] The discussions did not bear the intended fruit, as far as union was concerned, but they were another striking instance of the ecumenical and evangelical concern of Owen and many of his contemporaries. It was probably at this time that, without his consent, (and partly contrary to his private wishes[2]) the University conferred on him the degree of Doctor of Divinity.

His life continued to be devoted to literary activity. His *Diatriba de Divina Justitia* (*Dissertation on Divine Justice*)[3] was published in Latin in 1653, and the following year, *The Doctrine of the Saints Perseverance*,[4] a remarkably extensive (666 pages!) theological review of John Goodwin's Arminian treatise, *Redemption Redeemed*.[5] The wording of the dedication to Oliver Cromwell gives some indication of the esteem in which Owen then held him:

The series and chain of eminent providences whereby you have been carried on and protected in all the hazardous work of your generation, which your God hath called you unto, is evident to all. Of your preservation by the power of God, through faith, in a course of gospel obedience, upon the account of the immutability of the love and infallibility of the promises of God, which are yea and amen in Jesus Christ, your own soul only is possessed with the experience.[6]

The dedication is simply a summary of the general argument of the whole book.

By the end of 1653, Cromwell had dissolved the Long Parliament. Within a few months he had made the necessary arrangements for the election of a new one. Owen was returned

---

[1] I.liii. [2] XIII.302. [3] X.48off. [4] XI.5ff.

[5] For John Goodwin's life, T. Jackson, *The Life of John Goodwin*, London, 1822; *Dictionary of National Biography (D.N.B.)*, ed. L. Stephen and S. Lee, London, 1885–1913, XXII.145–8.

[6] XI.5. It was to the covenant of grace that Cromwell's mind seemed to turn in his last hours, when he said, 'Faith in the covenant is my only support'; 'I am in covenant with thee through grace.' A. Fraser, *op. cit.*, pp. 675–6.

as the Member of Parliament for the University, and actually took his seat in the House, until the Committee of Privileges, realizing presumably that this J. Owen was none other than Dr John Owen, Dean of Christ Church, declared his election, as a minister of religion, to be void! It is unlikely that Owen was wanting to make capital, in any sense, out of this unusual situation.[1] He regarded himself as a servant of the University, and desired to serve it in any capacity he could.

In 1655 another work of polemical theology was published. It was entitled *Vindiciae Evangelicae*,[2] and runs to six hundred pages in the Goold edition of his works. While it was aimed at the heart of the Socinian controversy, his analysis *Of the Mortification of Sin in Believers* in 1656,[3] and his remarkable *Communion With God* in 1657,[4] went to the heart of Christian experience. In the latter work, in which he discusses the communion which the believer enjoys distinctly with each person of the Trinity, there is what Daniel Burgess called, 'the very highest of angel's food'.[5]

Oxford certainly contained a galaxy of stars in its firmament in those days, among them Thomas Goodwin and Stephen Charnock, theologians and pastors, Christopher Wren, William Penn and John Locke,[6] who held a junior studentship at Christ Church while Owen was there. Each of them was to make a permanent contribution to western culture; yet Calamy was able to write of Owen that, 'He was reckoned the brightest ornament of the university in his time'.[7]

As the political situation changed, Owen's fortunes began to change and grow dim, and his place in Oxford looked increasingly uncertain. A majority of Parliament proposed to bestow the crown on Cromwell. Owen was completely opposed to such an idea, and he joined the movement, supported by a majority of the army, to prevent such an occurrence. He was instrumental in framing the petition which constrained

---

[1]Despite the contention of Daniel Cawdrey (see XIII.284) and A. Wood, *op. cit.*, II p. 557.

[2]XII.6ff.   [3]VI.3ff.   [4]II.3ff.   [5]II.4.

[6]Orme, *op. cit.*, p. 106, contends that Locke's treatise on *Toleration* owes its origin to Owen's work.

[7]I.lxv, fn. 1.

Cromwell to decline the honour.[1]

Soon afterwards Cromwell was invested as Lord Protector at Westminster Hall. The officiating ministers were Thomas Lockyer and Thomas Manton. Owen was not even an invited guest. On July 3 Cromwell resigned from the chancellorship of the University, and his son was appointed to succeed him. Two months later, Owen's period of academic leadership came to an end, although his appointment at Christ Church continued until 1660.

In his final oration, Owen summed up some of the achievements of his period of leadership in Oxford:

Professors' salaries, lost for many years, have been recovered and paid; some offices of respectability have been maintained; the rights and privileges of the university have been defended against all the efforts of its enemies; the treasury is tenfold increased; many of every rank in the university have been promoted to various honours and benefices; new exercises have been introduced and established; old ones have been duly performed; reformation of manners has been diligently studied, in spite of the grumbling of certain profligate brawlers; labours have been numberless; besides submitting to the most enormous expense, often when brought to the brink of death on your account, I have hated these limbs, and this feeble body, which was ready to desert my mind; the reproaches of the vulgar have been disregarded, the envy of others has been overcome: in these circumstances I wish you all prosperity, and bid you farewell. I congratulate myself on a successor who can relieve me of this burden; and you on one who is able completely to repair any injury which your affairs may have suffered through our inattention. . . . But as I know not whither the thread of my discourse might lead me, I here cut it short, I seek again my old labours, my usual watchings, my interrupted studies. As for you, gentlemen of the university, may you be happy and fare you well.[2]

v. *The Congregational Leader*

In September 1658, Owen participated in a synod of congregational churches meeting at the Savoy Palace. He was appointed, with Thomas Goodwin, Philip Nye, William Bridge,

[1]Fraser, *op. cit.*, p. 612.
[2]Quoted by Thomson, I.lvii–lviii. See Toon, *Oxford Orations*, p. 45. Strictly speaking this was the penultimate oration, but in the sixth oration he is addressing Richard Cromwell.

William Greenhill and Joseph Caryl (who had all been members of the Westminster Assembly fifteen years before), to prepare the draft of *The Declaration of Faith and Order*, more commonly known as *The Savoy Declaration*. Owen himself was almost certainly responsible for the lengthy preface. In a real sense this was the climax of a process that had begun many years before when he had started reading John Cotton's *Keyes of the Kingdom of Heaven*, which Nye and Goodwin had been instrumental in bringing into England. The *Declaration*, as might be expected, is clearly and deliberately a revision of the *Confession of Faith* which these Independents had earlier helped to frame.

Earlier in that same month Cromwell had died, on the anniversary of his victories at Dunbar and Worcester. Despite the estrangement that had existed between them in the previous period, Owen seems to have taken part in his funeral, and would certainly have been glad to do so. But coupled with the Savoy Conference, it marked the end of another period of his life. From now on his contribution to the church and the nation was largely unofficial, and made from outside of positions of recognized authority.

In the political macrocosm, the protectorate, under Oliver's weak son, Richard, was on the verge of collapse. Owen again was at the heart of matters in the period leading up to Richard Cromwell's resignation, and indeed there were reports and rumours that he was largely responsible for it. Certainly Richard Baxter thought so. But Owen's conscience was clear. The accusations of Baxter were, unfortunately, somewhat prejudiced; those made by George Vernon, that Owen had been 'the ruin of his [Cromwell's] son', Owen denied: 'With whose [Cromwell's] setting up and pulling down I had no more to do than himself'. Vernon also accused him of wearing a sword, and blaspheming against the Lord's Prayer by putting his hat on when it was being said! The accusations were on equally shaky ground.[1]

In 1660 the monarchy was restored. Charles II was enthroned, and Owen removed from the Christ Church Deanery

[1] XVI.277. Orme, *op. cit.*, p. 279, suggests there was definite proof that Owen was not involved in the 'ruin' of Cromwell. Vernon's accusation, which Wood repeated, was so rife that Meric Casaubon actually wrote *A Vindication of the Lord's Prayer as a Formal Prayer*, London, 1660.

some months before. He moved to his small estate at Stadhampton, and continued his ministry to a gathered congregation. He clearly hoped for continued usefulness as a writer and pastor, but his leisure was disturbed, and his hopes for the Congregational churches thwarted by the various acts of the Clarendon Code. Within two years the presbyterian party, who had hoped (if not actually anticipated) that the Restoration of the Monarchy would involve their inclusion in the new establishment of the church, found themselves confronted with the Act of Uniformity. In the Great Ejection of 1662, almost two thousand Puritans were driven by conscience into persecution and poverty.[1]

Owen had already suffered the loss of his ministry. He added to this a willingness to lose his civic freedom by continuing to preach despite the Five Mile Act forbidding ministers to return to their pastoral and preaching duties in their own parishes and in the cities. He did not lack opportunities. He declined the offer of a bishopric, and later the invitation of the First Congregational Church in Boston (John Cotton's congregation) to minister to them.[2] Nevertheless, he probably suffered less than some of his brethren. He must have been wealthy by comparison. Furthermore, the continuing theological battles common to Anglicanism and Puritanism demanded the employment of his intellectual resources.[3] But the sacrifices involved in the Five Mile Act (1665) must have reached into his soul. As we will later see, his primary commitment in life was to the pastoring of the people of God; the ultimate sacrifice for such a pastoral spirit is prolonged separation from the flock. The spoiling of his goods he might allow, and even do so with a measure of joy that he was counted worthy to suffer for the sake of the gospel; but the spoiling of the flock was his greatest sorrow, and one beyond recompense. Owen did not regard this intolerant law as binding on his conscience, even if its effect was necessarily restrictive on his own ministry.

[1]This was Owen's own estimate, Toon, *Correspondence*, p. 130.

[2]Orme, *op. cit.*, pp. 301f., prints this letter inviting Owen. In fact Owen almost went, pp. 302f. In 1671 he was also offered the President-ship of Harvard College.

[3]It was in fact at Lord Clarendon's instigation that Owen wrote *Animadversions On Fiat Lux*, XIV.3ff.

Later, with other ministers of Puritan persuasion, Owen returned to preach in London after the Plague and the Great Fire. In an atmosphere in which these events were regarded as judgments from God for the extreme response of the establishment to nonconformity, 1667 was an opportune time to plead for liberty. This Owen did, in *Indulgence and Toleration*[1] and *A Peace Offering*.[2] Several years passed before The Declaration of Indulgence was enacted in 1672. During this period he found sufficient leisure to write up much of his earlier preached material and some of his most valuable works made their appearance. His *Indwelling Sin*,[3] *Exposition of Psalm 130*,[4] and the monumental commentary on *Hebrews*[5] all date from this period.

In 1673, Owen's own congregation in London united with the fellowship of which Joseph Caryl had been pastor. At the formal union on June 5, Owen preached on Colossians 3.14, 'And above all things put on charity, which is the bond of perfection'.[6] Here he was assisted by men of diverse talents and interests including David Clarkson, Isaac Loeffs and Robert Ferguson, known as 'The Plotter'. Owen was now, not least in the eyes of his opponents, 'The Prince, the Oracle, the Metropolitan of Independency',[7] and in that capacity he made every effort to help his brethren. Robert Asty, once a member of his Coggeshall congregation and father of the biographer; Thomas Jollie, John Bunyan, and others, were encouraged by him in spiritual or material ways. In fact it was at Owen's suggestion that Bunyan took his *Pilgrim's Progress* to his own publisher, Nathaniel Ponder.[8] He may well have been one of the very first readers to be impressed by the Baptist's unique work. Certainly he thought highly of the Bedford Tinker, and greatly appreciated his preaching, confessing to Charles II, 'Could I possess the tinker's abilities, please your majesty, I would gladly relinquish all my learning'.[9] He also seems to have had a hand in relieving the

---

[1]XIII.519ff. [2]XIII.543ff. [3]VI.155ff.

[4]VI.325ff. [5]Vols. XVIII–XXIV.

[6]IX.256ff. The united congregation had 171 members (Orme, *op. cit.*, p. 363), including some of Cromwell's relatives.

[7]George Vernon, *A Letter to a Friend*, 1670, p. 53.

[8]*The Pilgrim's Progress* sold so successfully that Nathanial Ponder became known as 'Bunyan Ponder'!

[9]John Asty, *A Complete Collection of the Sermons of John Owen* (with biographical memoir) London, 1721, p. iii.

excessive hardships Bunyan experienced in jail.

The first fruits of what is almost certainly his greatest contribution to the systematization of doctrine came in 1674, with the publication of his work on the Holy Spirit, *Pneumatologia*.[1] In the preface Owen confessed: 'I know not any who ever went before me in this design of representing the whole economy of the Holy Spirit'.[2] The completed work was not published during his life time, the *Spirit as Comforter*[3] and the *Discourse of Spiritual Gifts*[4] being published posthumously (1693).

In 1676 Owen lost his first wife. Little is known or written of their life together. It is only possible to guess its influence on him; but it must have been a painful blow to one whose entire offspring were snatched from his presence by 'the last enemy'. His sense of loss may perhaps be measured by the testimony she received: 'an excellent and comely person, very affectionate towards him, and met with suitable returns'.[5] It ought also to be measured by the fact that he married again within eighteen months, and thus filled the void Mary Rooke left behind. His second wife was Michel, the widow of Thomas D'Oyley of Chislehampton near Stadham.

vi. *Last Days*

Owen was evidently now drawing towards the end of his life. He was afflicted with severe asthma and apparently gallstone. He was frequently incapable of preaching. At such times Robert Ferguson and Alexander Shields,[6] the author of the *Hind Let Loose*, acted as assistants and amanuenses, and David Clarkson a gifted theologian, ministered to the congregation. With such help he was able to write his work on *Justification*[7] and a number of other books defending Protestantism in general, and the Puritans in particular. More positively he wrote on

[1] *Works* III–IV.   [2] III.7.   [3] IV.353ff.
[4] IV.420ff.   [5] Anon., *The Life of John Owen*, xxxiv.
[6] 1660–1700. Shields was a strong preacher. In a sermon preached in Aberdeen, he is reported to have recommended to his hearers, 'a pint of hope, three pints of faith, and nine pints of hot, hot, hot burning zeal'. He took part in the ill-fated Darien Scheme, and on its failure went to Jamaica, where he died; Orme, *op. cit.*, p. 394.
[7] V.3ff.

Union among Protestants[1] and also saw *Inquiry Into . . . Evangelical Churches*[2] through the press. In the realm of devotional and theological works came his *Christologia*,[3] *The Grace and Duty of being Spiritually Minded*[4] and finally his *Meditations and Discourses on the Glory of Christ*.[5] Soon after, when he had moved to the then 'quiet village of Ealing', he dictated a last letter to his friend Charles Fleetwood (on 23 August 1683):

I am going to Him whom my soul hath loved, or rather who hath loved me with an everlasting love; which is the whole ground of all my consolation. The passage is very irksome and wearysome through strong pains of various sorts which are all issued in an intermitting fever . . . I am leaving the ship of the church in a storm, but whilst the great Pilot is in it the loss of a poore under-rower will be inconsiderable . . . the promise stands invincible that he will never leave thee nor forsake thee . . . Remember your dying friend. . . .[6]

On the morning of 24 August, William Payne, a Puritan minister of Saffron Waldon, who was seeing *Meditations on the Glory of Christ* through the stages of publication, called to tell him that the work was already being printed. Owen's biographers record his eloquent reply:

I am glad to hear it; but O brother Payne! the long wished for day is come at last, in which I shall see that glory in another manner than I have ever done, or was capable of doing, in this world.[7]

Later in the day he took his final breath and passed from the world of faith into the world of sight. Just as Cromwell went to his rest on the anniversary of his greatest conflicts and victories, Owen died on the anniversary of 'Black' Bartholomew's Day, the day of the Great Ejection, when Puritanism and its greatest theologian had also fought their most memorable battle.

Eleven days later he was buried in Bunhill Fields, the resting place of many of his greatest Puritan companions, in the confidence that he would rise together with them on the day of resurrection. The following Sunday David Clarkson preached

---

[1]XIV.519ff.   [2]XV.189ff.   [3]I.3ff.   [4]VII.263ff.
[5]I.275ff.   [6]Thomson, *op. cit.*, cii.
[7]I.ciii. Anon., *The Life of John Owen*, p. xxxvi. records the opinion of his physicians who 'ascribed his dying hard, to the strength of his brain'.

his funeral sermon. Owen was, in Clarkson's estimation, 'a great light . . . one of eminency for holiness and learning and pastoral abilities'.[1] In another's opinion, there was in him 'much of heaven and love to Christ, and saints and all men; which came from him so seriously and spontaneously, as if grace and nature were in him reconciled, and but one thing'.[2]

There is widespread agreement that John Owen was *the* theologian of the Puritan movement. Witness to the value of his writings can be found among Christians from his own day until ours. His contribution to the life of the church is beyond dispute. But perhaps the most telling testimony to the purpose of his writings – and one which both justifies and illuminates the chapters which follow – is to be found coming from Owen's own pen:

I hope I may own in sincerity, that my heart's desire unto God, and the chief design of my life in the station wherein the good providence of God hath placed me, are, that mortification and universal holiness may be promoted in my own and in the hearts and ways of others, to the glory of God; that so the gospel of our Lord and Saviour Jesus Christ may be adorned in all things.[3]

These words lead us directly to the theme of Owen's teaching on the Christian life.

[1] D. Clarkson, *Funeral Sermon*, London, 1720, p. lxxi.
[2] *Vindication of Owen by a Friendly Scrutiny etc.*, London, 1684, p. 38 quoted Thomson, I.cv.
[3] VI.4.

— 2 —

The Plan of Salvation

The life and writings of John Owen span the period during
which Puritan theology reached its maturity. The problem of
defining the concept 'Puritan' in historical terms has been
frequently and inconclusively discussed.[1] One common aspect
of the Puritan theology was the federal, or covenant structure
within which the Christian gospel was normally understood.
This is not to say that all Puritans held the same view of divine
covenants, but covenant was coming to be recognized as a
fundamental theme of redemptive history and biblical doctrine.

1. The Doctrine of the Covenant

The origins of federal theology have recently been subjected
to considerable scholarly research. Our interest, however, lies
more narrowly in the question of exactly how the divine
covenants form the framework for all of Owen's thinking about
being a Christian.

The relevance of the development of covenant theology to
the teaching of Owen may be summarized thus: during the
sixteenth century covenant theology came to be regarded as a
key to the interpretation of *Scripture* and, during the seventeenth
century, a key to the interpretation of *Christian experience*. It
brought with it a fresh insight into the *unity* of Scripture. This
led, in time, to a doctrinal scheme in which God's dealings with
his people through these covenants formed the pattern for

[1]Cf. Basil Hall, 'Puritanism: the Problem of Definition' *Studies in Church
History* II, ed. G. J. Cuming, London, 1965, pp. 283ff.

understanding his dealings with us now as individuals.

The premise of covenant theology is that God's relationship with men is always in terms of a *covenant*. Man's responsibility to God must also, therefore, be understood in covenant terms. Owen taught that God had made a number of covenants, and each of these must be examined in turn.

But first, some consideration must be given to the way in which Owen defined the nature of a covenant, not least because the exposition of each species of covenant theology is invariably dependent upon the definition of covenant it employs.

For Owen a covenant is an arrangement into which two or more parties mutually enter. In the case of a divine covenant, it is constituted by provisions on God's part, and is attended with promises and threats related to man's faithfulness or disobedience.[1] A covenant is a 'compact', 'convention', or 'agreement'.[2]

Owen realized the difficulties involved in such a definition. While classical Greek appeared to have a ready-made word for covenant, *suntheke*, he appreciated that the Septuagint did not employ it as a translation of the Hebrew *berith*, although it was used 'in all good authors'.[3] *Berith* conveys something more than the mutual agreement of *suntheke*. That is why the New Testament uses the word *diatheke* a will, or testament. Here he recognizes that *suntheke* might imply that the covenants of God are conditional. Owen opposed this view when it appeared in John Goodwin's *Redemption Redeemed* (1651). *Berith*, Owen argued, can mean a promise that is unconditional.[4] 'It is therefore certain that where God speaks of his covenant, we cannot conclude that whatever belongs unto a perfect, complete covenant is therein intended . . . what is intended by it must be learned from the subject-matter treated of, seeing there is no precept or promise of God but may be so called.'[5]

Owen is wrestling here with a fundamental problem in interpreting the Bible. His readers knew, from everyday experience, the contemporary significance of the word 'covenant'. It was a legal contract made between two parties

---

[1] V.275.
[2] VI.470; X.168; XI.210; XIX.77, 78, 82; XXIII.55.
[3] XIX.79.   [4] XI.218.   [5] XIX.81.

when they entered into an agreement. But, he warned his contemporaries, *biblical* covenants do not always involve precisely the same elements. Biblical covenants must be interpreted in their biblical context, not their seventeenth-century context.

It should be noted that Owen did not simply state the significance Scripture attaches to divine covenants, and proceed from that point, as some later writers have sought to do.[1] Had he done so, he might more clearly have emphasized the central element in God's covenants with men – not the reaching of a mutual agreement, but commitment to fulfil his promises, at whatever cost.

Owen's exposition suggests that four covenants appear in Scripture.

i. *The Covenant of Works*[2] (Creation, Life)

'Man in his creation, with respect unto the ends of God therein, was constituted under a covenant.'[3] Such a divine covenant is always sealed in some symbolic and external way: 'There was never any covenant between God and man but it had some ordinances or arbitrary institutions of external divine worship annexed unto it.'[4] Thus, in a seminal passage, Owen writes about man:

The law of his obedience was attended with promises and threatenings, rewards and punishments, suited unto the goodness and holiness of God; for every law with rewards and recompenses annexed hath the nature of a covenant. And in this case, although the promises wherewith man was encouraged unto obedience, which was that of eternal life with God, did in strict justice exceed the worth of the obedience required, and so was a superadded effect of goodness and grace, yet was it suited unto the constitution of a covenant meet for man to serve God in unto his glory; and, on the other side, the punishment threatened unto disobedience in death and an everlasting separation from God, was such as the righteousness and holiness of God, as his supreme governor, and Lord of him and the covenant,

---

[1] *Cf.* John Murray, *The Covenant of Grace*, London 1953, pp.5–7.
[2] Owen generally refers to the first covenant as the covenant of works, but also as the covenant of creation, life or nature. XIX.388; XXIII.62.
[3] XIX.337.   [4] XXIII.185.

did require. Now, this covenant belonged unto the law of creation.[1]

A number of things should be noted here. (i) Owen stresses the justice and righteousness of this first covenant. The commands involved in it 'were all suited unto *the principles of the nature of man* created by God'.[2] (ii) Of greater significance is the suggestion that the reward of eternal life far exceeds strict justice, for the very reason that the reward is a matter of promise. The first covenant was an expression of infinite love, not merely of justice. Everything is set in the context of God's will for man's happiness.[3] In fact, it is fundamental to Owen's theology that every covenant involves the promise of God. In other words Owen teaches that there is the *grace of promise* even in the covenant of works, although it is *not* the covenant of grace. Thus he writes, 'There is infinite grace in every divine covenant, inasmuch as it is established on promises. Infinite condescension it is in God, that he will enter into covenant with dust and ashes, with poor worms of the earth'.[4] This thought he finds rooted in the very nature of the divine-human relationship. It is also the underlying assumption of Romans 4.2: even if a man were to keep the covenant of works, he would acquire no merit.

Eternal life by the covenant of works would not give a man ground for boasting, since that life would be his because of God's promise, not because of his merit.[5] This eternal life, or rest of man in God, was, for Owen, symbolized in the institution of the Sabbath.

This emphasis on grace on Owen's part is all the more significant in view of the strictures sometimes passed on federal theology. T. F. Torrance, for example, speaks of the 'clear-cut distinction between the covenant of grace and the covenant of works as the covenant made with man in his creation *apart from grace*'.[6] This brings out the distinction which many seventeenth-century theologians made between the two

[1]*Ibid.* cf. XIX.337.   [2]VI.472; cf. VI.165.   [3]VI.472.
[4]XXIII.68, cf. VI.472; VI.470–1; XXIII.116.
[5]XXIII.66.
[6]T. F. Torrance, *The School of Faith*, Edinburgh, 1959, Introduction p. IV, (emphasis mine). It should be noted that this comment fails to recognise that, following *biblical* usage, Puritan theology usually reserved the term 'grace' for the activity of God towards *fallen* man.

covenants, but not in the precise way they made it. In much Puritan theology, every divine covenant is a gracious one, as in the *Westminster Confession*: a 'voluntary condescension on God's part, which He hath been pleased to express by way of covenant'.[1]

Thus, 'Man in his creation . . . was constituted under a covenant'.[2] It was made with Adam as the head and representative of all mankind. His failure to keep the covenant conditions brings 'the guilt of condemnation upon all them in whose room he was a public person (being the head and natural fountain of them all, they all being wrapped up in the same condition with him by divine institution)'.[3] This is classic federal theology. Owen sees in the fall the breach of the covenant of works for the whole human race. Adam and Eve are turned away from Eden and all it represents. Consequently mankind, represented by these first parents, is alienated from God.

It is these circumstances that, from the viewpoint of man's salvation, make the establishing of another covenant so necessary. For this second covenant Owen adopts the classical terminology.

ii. *The Covenant of Grace*

What is the difference between this and the first Covenant?

The covenant of grace is not made with Adam, or men, in and of themselves, but with a Mediator on their behalf. It is thus *structurally* similar to the first covenant, but in terms of its *conditions* is significantly different. The great issue which federal theology raised as it developed was whether the covenant of grace had *conditions* at all;[4] but Owen had no hesitation in affirming that there are conditions in *every* covenant.

How, then, can the covenant of grace be a *gracious* arrangement? Owen's answer is that the conditions for its fulfilment devolve on the Mediator, rather than on those for

---

[1] *The Confession of Faith*, VII.i.
[2] XIX.337.   [3] X.354.
[4] See John Murray, *Collected Writings*, Edinburgh, 1982, 4, p. 229ff.

whom the covenant is made. 'God himself hath undertaken the whole'.[1] Furthermore, the conditions involved in participation in the covenant are *guaranteed*, so that 'the condition of the covenant should certainly, by free grace, be wrought and accomplished in all that are taken into covenant'.[2] In contrast to the first covenant, and in view of the guarantee of its fulfilment, the covenant of grace is described in Scripture as an 'everlasting covenant'.[3] In essence, the difference between the 'old' and the 'new' lies in the greatness and the certainty of the new covenant.[4]

The new covenant is fulfilled through Jesus Christ. To discover the implications of this we need to consider Owen's teaching on a third covenant, which lies at the foundation of the covenant of grace.

iii. *The Covenant of Redemption*

The fulfilment of the covenant of grace by Christ is viewed as the result of a 'transaction' in eternity between the Father and the Son which, according to Owen, was carried on by means of a covenant.[5] This is *possible* because within the unity of the Trinity there is the activity of distinct persons; it can be made *actual*, with a view to the intended assumption of man's nature by the second person: 'The will of God the Father, Son, and Holy Ghost, is but one . . . but in respect of their distinct personal actings, this will is appropriated to them respectively, so that the will of the Father and the will of the Son may be considered [distinctly] in this business'.[6] Thus, in order to fulfil the covenant of grace, a covenant of redemption, sometimes called 'the covenant of the Mediator or Redeemer'[7] was made with Christ for the benefit of the elect. It too falls into the overall covenant pattern, with conditions and promises, and contains

---

[1]XI.210 (in fact, in Owen's theology, this is what makes the covenant of redemption a logical and theological necessity).

[2]X.237.

[3]Owen does acknowledge this may be an allusion to the covenant of redemption, but, in view of the reference in Hebrews 13.20 to 'the blood of the everlasting covenant', prefers to think of it as the covenant of grace completed in the New Testament. Cf. XXIV.475.

[4]VI.474ff.   [5]XIX.77.   [6]XII.497.   [7]XIX.78; XXII.230.

'A prescription of personal services, with a promise of reward; and all the other conditions, also, of a complete covenant before laid down are observed therein'.[1]

Owen sees evidence for this covenant in numerous biblical passages. He argues that wherever the Father is called 'God' by the Son, a covenantal relationship is indicated, over and above the eternal relationship between the first and second persons of the Trinity.[2] These transactions are designated 'counsel' also.[3]

It is interesting to note that Owen is not satisfied with the thought that the incarnate Son's acknowledgment of his 'God' (Jn. 20.27) is an expression exclusively of the humanity of Christ. He regards such a confession from the humanity of Christ to be so fundamental as not to warrant expression. Similarly, when 'counsel' is taken between Father and Son, the reference is to this pre-incarnational covenant. For the incarnate Christ is not counsellor, but servant.[4] Thus both the will and the authority of the Father are expressed in the covenant, and the willingness and agreement of the Son in his devotion to the Father.[5]

What are the *conditions* of this covenant of redemption? They are basically threefold:[6] (i) Christ is to assume human nature and be made flesh. (ii) He is to be the servant of the Father in obedience to the general law of God, to the particular law of God for Israel, and also to the special law of God in the compact with a Mediator. (iii) He is also to make atonement for sin, and receive the just judgement of God with respect to the broken covenant of works. *All* of these conditions the Son would fulfil in and by man's nature.[7]

As in all covenants, however, there are *promises* annexed to this one – to Christ personally and in his capacity as Mediator.

[1]XIX.84.
[2]Owen cites Psalms 16.2; 22.1; 40.8; 45.7; Micah 5.4; John 20.27; Revelation 3.13. See XII.497 for the significance of this for the persons of the Trinity.
[3]He cites Zechariah 6.13.
[4]Isaiah 42.1, cf. XIX.85. Owen refers Isaiah 9.6 'Wonderful Counsellor' to Christ in the covenant of redemption rather than to the incarnation.
[5]XII.503.
[6]These are expanded to five in XII.500ff.
[7]XIX.94–5.

He is promised assistance to accomplish the work of atonement,[1] and exaltation as the result of it.[2] As the reward for his work, he is promised the deliverance and glorification of those for whom he died.[3]

It is such a covenant alone, Owen says, which gives significance to the death of Christ as atonement. Only by virtue of it can the sufferings of Christ under the sentence and curse of the law be regarded as good and glorifying to God. Only in covenant terms can the pardoning of sinners be evidence of God's righteousness. In the covenant, therefore, the wisdom, justice and grace of God can be seen, as well as the reason for the special honour and exaltation of Christ as Mediator.[4]

The covenant of grace thus *depends* upon the covenant of redemption as its foundation, and for its saving power. Inaugurated after the fall, and made known to Adam and Eve in Genesis 3.15,[5] the promise of the covenant is to be traced through Scripture to its complete fulfilment in Christ. The promise is repeated and enlarged in various ways in the Old Testament.

Owen sees yet *another* covenant, which we must now consider.

iv. *The Covenant at Sinai*

Owen has thus far outlined alternative ways to eternal life. The way of works and the way of grace are clearly antithetical. It is therefore correct to align the covenants of redemption and grace over against the covenant of works, which, 'absolutely considered', is the 'old covenant'. But when the rest of Scripture is reviewed this presents a problem of harmonization, since Sinai seems to be referred to as the 'old covenant'.[6] How are these covenants related to one another? This question is all

---

[1]Owen cites Is. 42.4, 6; Ps. 16.10–11; Ps. 22; 89.28; Is. 50.5–9.
[2]Owen cites Is. 53.12; Zech. 9.10; Ps. 110.6; Ps. 2.8–9; Ps. 72.8; Dan. 7.14; Rom. 14.11; Is. 45.23; Phil. 2.10. Cf. XIX.93.
[3]XIX.94.
[4]XIX.95.
[5]I.120; X.290; XI.305f.
[6]Cf. 2 Corinthians 3; Hebrews 8.

the more pressing in view of the legal character of the fourth covenant, forged at Sinai.

Owen was not, of course, alone in wrestling with this question. It had been raised and answered many times before, and in a number of different ways. Some had adopted the view that the covenant at Sinai was simply the covenant of works, and that its great principle was 'Do this and live'.[1] Other Puritans had adopted Calvin's view that it was the covenant of grace, since it was given during the post-Adamic administration.[2] Yet this latter view seemed hedged with difficulties in view of the sharp contrast presented in the New Testament between the 'new' and the 'old' covenants. Nevertheless, it had been adopted by Calvin, and also received mature expression in the Westminster Confession.[3]

This was a view which Owen was reluctant to adopt. He emphasized that there is basic agreement about the truth; the issue was more a matter of its harmonious interpretation.[4] In company with a number of others, he adopted a third, mediating position.[5]

In the first place, Owen is certain that, through the disorder and confusion which sin has brought into the world, men cannot please God through the broken covenant of works.[6] Yet it is the precepts of that first covenant which seem to be renewed at Sinai, in a new and objective way, whereas previously they had been written in man's heart. 'The law thus declared and written by him was the same, I say, materially, and for the substance of it, with the law of our creation, or the original rule of our covenant obedience unto God.'[7] However, this does not mean the Law *is* the covenant of works

---

[1]X.237; XXIII.78. Cf. William Pemble, *Vindiciae Fidei*, London, 1624, p. 138; John Preston, *New Covenant*, London, 1634, p. 318.

[2]John Ball, *A Treatise of the Covenant of Grace*, London, 1645, p. 93. 95. Samuel Rutherford, *The Covenant of Life Opened*, Edinburgh, 1655, p. 60. Quoted, E. F. Kevan, *The Grace of Law*, London, 1964, pp. 115–6.

[3]*Confession of Faith*, VII.5.   [4]XXIII.71.

[5]See S. Bolton, *The True Bounds of Christian Freedom* (1645), r.i. 1964, pp. 89ff. In view of this, and some of the statements quoted, Dr Kevan (*op. cit.*, pp. 113ff.) might have more accurately divided Puritan opinion on the Sinaitic Covenant into three groups.

[6]XIX.387.   [7]XIX.388; cf. VIII.293, XXIII.215.

'absolutely'[1] for, 'Notwithstanding, I say, this renovation of the first covenant materially unto them, they were so far freed from its covenant terms as that they had a relief provided against what they could not answer in it, with the consequences thereof'.[2] In one sense then, the people were under the covenant of grace, and yet in a dispensation governed by the principles of the covenant of works. To employ Owen's own expressions, there is 'renovation' and 'innovation' together:[3] the covenant of works is 'not absolutely changed or abolished, but afresh presented unto the people, only with a relief provided for the covenanters against its curse and severity'.[4] This is why the Sabbath remains the seventh day; when the covenant of works is absolutely abolished, then the symbol of that dispensation (the *seventh* day Sabbath) must by necessity be changed, (i.e. into the *first* day Sabbath). Sinai should not then be thought of as the covenant of works; but Sinai does involve a renewal of the principles which partly constituted the covenant of works.

On the other hand, the Sinaitic covenant cannot be thought of as the covenant of grace. Owen refers here to Hebrews 8 and 2 Corinthians 3, and to the sharp contrasts there drawn between the present covenant (in Christ) which is a *better* covenant than the one made at Sinai, and also between the liberty of the new and the bondage associated with the old (Gal. 4.25). For Owen this is too pronounced a contrast to be thought of in terms of different dispensations of the one covenant of grace (although he acknowledges these are recognizable).

What then is the relationship between Sinai and Calvary? Owen illustrates it by the story of the man whose eyes Christ had to touch twice in order to provide complete restoration of sight (Mk. 8.23–5). After the first touch he saw men 'as trees walking'; after the second, he saw clearly.[5] Owen argues there is a similar contrast between the Sinaitic covenant and the new covenant: (i) in the way Christ's love is declared, (ii) in the communication of grace received, (iii) in the access to God

---

[1] XIX.389.   [2] *Ibid.*
[3] VI.471; XIX.390; XXIII.91.   [4] XIX.391.
[5] XXIII.72. Cf. I.383 for another use of this illustration.

enjoyed, (iv) in the gracious rather than legal way of worship, and (v) in the universal spread of the gospel.[1] In this respect he finds himself in harmony with earlier reformers such as Calvin and Bucer, and is happy to admit it.

Owen, however, wishes to go further. He argues for a *distinction* to be made between the covenant of grace and the new covenant, in terms of salvation in Christ as a principle and a promise, and salvation in Christ established in historical redemption.[2] It was *under* the covenant of grace that Old Testament saints were justified, and not *by virtue* of the old covenant (Sinai) in which the substance of the covenant of works was renewed. Owen's position is that during the dispensation of this Sinaitic covenant believers were reconciled and justified by virtue of the promise in the covenant of grace, which finds its fulfilment in the new covenant.[3] His conclusion then is that the Sinaitic covenant revived the commands, sanctions and promises of the covenant of works, and that when the apostle Paul disputes about works or law-righteousness it is the renovation of the Edenic covenant in the Sinaitic covenant he has in mind. Sinai therefore is 'a particular, temporary covenant . . . and not a mere dispensation of the covenant of grace.'[4]

Why was such a covenant given? It was given to Israel as the posterity of Abraham, in order that the seed of salvation might be planted; it was necessary for them to have a country in which they could live apart from other nations to fulfil God's promise in a conspicuous way,[5] and for a pure testimony to God to be raised and preserved. This was precisely the purpose of the ordinances of the Law. To this people God prescribed rules for life, to subdue the pride of their spirits, and to make them long for deliverance. It was, in short, a *temporary preserving measure*, 'until the seed should come'.[6]

The structure of Owen's thought is now clear. It moves from the covenant of redemption through the covenant of works, the covenant of grace and the new covenant in Christ. Since all covenants have conditions, the eternal covenant between

[1]XXIII.71ff.   [2]XXIII.75.   [3]XXIII.79.
[4]XXIII.86.   [5]XXIII.82.   [6]Gal. 3.19.

the Father and the Son also has conditions.[1] But the problem created by the existence of conditions in the covenant of grace is resolved by the presence of conditions in the covenant of redemption.

The expression 'condition' was to prove highly problematic in reformed theology.[2] 'Response', 'responsibility', or even 'obligation' would have been safer expressions.

The difficulties involved in Owen's view become all the clearer when he discusses the differences between the covenant of works and the covenant of grace. In the latter the conditions are not only prescribed, but their fulfilment is guaranteed. It contains a conditional promise the fulfilment of which is in the hands of the Promiser. The question arises whether two such diverse arrangements can adequately be defined by the same terminology. Owen is so conscious of this difficulty that he suggests that 'this covenant [of works] being once established between God and man, there could be no new covenant made, unless the *essential form of it* were of another nature'.[3] The covenant of grace differs 'in the essence, substance, and nature of it'.[4] He would have been on more secure biblical ground if he had begun with a clear exegesis of the notion of covenant as it appears in Scripture, and refrained from employing this term except where exegesis demanded its use.[5]

This analysis of Owen's teaching naturally leads to a consideration of the consequences of his covenant theology for practical Christian experience. His teaching on the Christian life naturally and inevitably takes the shape of the objective covenantal relationship forged between God and man. But before this is explored, some comment on the implications of

[1]XII.498–9.
[2]For Owen's recognition of the problems involved in the terminology, see V.105.
[3]V.276.   [4]*Ibid.*
[5]The essence of the problem, and its resulting confusion appears in such a statement as 'if we take "covenant" in *a strict and proper sense*, it hath indeed no place between God and man. For a covenant, strictly taken, ought to proceed on equal terms. . . .' XIII.111 (emphasis mine). In mitigation of Owen, it should be said that this weakness influenced the formulation of federal theology more than it affected his exposition of the gospel.

Owen's covenant-centred theology is required. This takes us to the heart of the divine relationship with man.

2. *Union with Christ*

The heart of revelation is found in the covenant. Just as the divine decrees are, for Owen, the *principium essendi* (principle of being) of the stability of the love of God for his people, the covenant of grace (including the oath and promise annexed to it), is the *principium cognoscendi* (principle of knowing) of that love.[1] The ultimate function of the covenant is to bring men into union with Jesus Christ. Indeed it is only in this way that the covenant effectually functions: 'Now, this covenant is made with us under this formal consideration, that we are the children and seed of Abraham, which we are not but by our union with Christ, the one seed, to whom the promises of it were originally made'.[2] This union is 'the principle and measure of all spiritual enjoyments and expectations';[3] it is effected through the Spirit who is given according to the ancient covenant promise.[4]

In analysing this, Owen deals only briefly with the question of the plan of salvation (*ordo salutis* – the pattern on which believers receive the benefits of Christ's work). By and large, the order he sees in the work of grace is an order of nature rather than of chronology: 'in the *same instant* wherein anyone is united unto Christ, and by the *same act* whereby he is so united, he is *really* and *habitually purified* and *sanctified*'.[5] The *basis* of this union is the union of Christ with his people in the incarnation, in which Christ took their flesh and blood, to provide the arena of all his sufferings,[6] and experienced 'the greatest humiliation of the Son of God'.[7] Furthermore, it is in this capacity that all 'the treasures of grace' are to be found in Christ and received from him.[8]

Union with Christ is *effected* in us by the ministry of the Holy Spirit, in effectual calling. In the Westminster standards, calling

[1]XI.205, cf. VI.587. [2]XXI.151.
[3]XXI.146, cf. III.516, cf. VI.586.
[4]I.330; II.8; XI.123; XXI.147.
[5]III.517. [6]XIII.22. [7]XXI.148.
[8]I.363.

was virtually synonymous with regeneration and was over-emphatically attributed to the Holy Spirit. Little notice was taken of the biblical emphasis on the call of *God the Father*.[1] Owen does not quite put it like this. Rather he stresses that effectual calling takes place *in Christ*, and is an act of Almighty God[2] and specifically of the Father,[3] by which the believer is bound to Christ by the indwelling of the Spirit.[4] The 'first signal issue and effect' of it is a *'union . . . a spiritual union, –* the great union . . . that is the sole fountain of our blessedness, – our union with the Lord Christ'.[5]

It is interesting that, for Owen, the Holy Spirit who is the substance of the promise of the covenant, is given, as it were, from the heart of the covenant of redemption. Christ received the promised Spirit for his church in his ascension;[6] the Spirit receives from Christ, and what he receives is communicated to the believer.[7] Thus, through the agency of the Spirit, he is 'the cause of all other graces that we are made partakers of; they are all communicated unto us by virtue of our union with Christ. Hence is our adoption,[8] our justification, our fruitfulness, our perseverance, our resurrection, our glory'.[9] In this way, the image of Christ – his grace and holiness – in principle – becomes ours.[10] Effectual calling into this union thus involves regeneration[11] and produces a radical change in both (status) (justification) and (life) (sanctification). This notion lies at the very heart of Owen's teaching.[12] It indicates the fine grasp he had of the distinction and inter-relation in Scripture between justification and sanctification. Thus he says:

Indeed, in *vocation* it [sanctification] seems to be included expressly. For whereas it is *effectual vocation* that is intended, wherein a holy principle of spiritual life, or faith itself, is communicated unto us, our *sanctification* radically, and as the effect in its adequate immediate cause, is contained in it. Hence, we are said to 'be called to be saints,' Rom. 1.7; which is the same with being 'sanctified in Christ

[1] *Confession of Faith*, X. See *Shorter Catechism*, Q.31.
[2] I.486.   [3] XX.498.   [4] XXI.147.
[5] XI.336.   [6] Acts 2.33.   [7] III.516.
[8] Cf. XXIII.327.   [9] XXI.150, cf. IV.385.   [10] XXI.148.
[11] IX.291; XX.498.
[12] See below, pp. 54ff.

Jesus,' 1 Cor. 1.2. And in many other places is *sanctification* included in *vocation*.[1]

Owen also indicates the *character* of this union. Through it the believer is reckoned to have done *in* and *with* Christ whatever his Lord accomplished.[2] This implies a continuity and analogy between what Christ has done *for* men, and what the Spirit does *in* men. As Christ took flesh and blood for us, in his union with man, so by the work of the Spirit, 'in our regeneration he bestoweth on us his flesh and blood by the operation of the same Spirit'.[3] He incorporates believers mystically,[4] or spiritually, into himself, so that they become 'one Christ' 'by the effectual energy and inhabitation of the same Spirit',[5] whereby he is the head of that body of which the church is the members.[6] In turn, as we will later notice,[7] union is the foundation of all communion, and therefore the necessary prerequisite for fellowship with God.

What then of the form Owen gives to the *ordo salutis*? This is almost a determining factor in the view he ultimately expounds of the progress of the Christian life.

Calvin had taught that faith preceded repentance in the *ordo salutis*.[8] He also insisted that repentance is regeneration.[9] But repentance and regeneration for him were not the inauguration of the Christian life so much as its continuing character, namely the mortification of sin and vivification in Christ.[10]

Calvin had formulated his thought out of and over against the language of the medieval Catholicism he was combatting. Owen denotes different things when he employs the same language. Repentance for him is not penitence as a Christian grace, but, more narrowly, the initial turning from sin which is associated with conversion. Regeneration is not the new life in

---

[1]V.131; cf. III.299.   [2]V.351.   [3]XIII.22.   [4]I.365.

[5]XIII.22, cf. VIII.462ff., a sermon entitled 'The Glory and Interest of Nations Professing the Gospel', first published in 1659.

[6]XIII.340, cf. XIII.22.   [7]See below, pp. 74ff.

[8]*The Institutes of the Christian Religion*, trs. F. L Battles, ed. J. T. McNeill, London, 1960, III.iii.1. Although he defined his terms differently, Owen adopted the same position, XXII.32.

[9]*Institutes* III.iii.9.

[10]*Ibid.*, III.iii.1. For Owen's view that repentance continues throughout the Christian life, see XXII.27, 31.

general, but the new birth, divinely and therefore sovereignly bestowed. Any investigation of the development of soteriology from Calvin through the Puritans needs to take account of this development in theological language.

In his *Greater Catechism* of 1645 Owen spoke of *calling*, rather than regeneration, as the initial stage of saving grace in the heart.[1] Elsewhere[2] and particularly in his *Pneumatologia* of 1674, his emphasis is on regeneration as the fountain of all actual experience of grace.[3] Nowhere does he clearly attempt to relate these two aspects of the work of grace, nor does he identify them as being the same. The emphasis rather is that effectual calling is the *terminus a quo*, regeneration the *terminus ad quem* of the divine work of conversion. Calling is 'the first effect of our everlasting election',[4] and, since regeneration 'is given out in the pursuit of the decree of election',[5] it is also the fountain and embryo of sanctification.[6]

Since faith comes in effectual calling,[7] it follows that it is its fruit, as it is the *instrumental* cause of justification which therefore cannot precede faith.[8] Effectual calling is also accompanied by *adoption*,[9] which, in the order of nature follows the acceptance and cleansing of justification, although again it cannot be separated from it.[10] Thus, speaking of the *ordo salutis* outlined in Romans 8.30, Owen comments: 'Nor is there intimated by him [Paul] any order of *precedency* or connection between the things that he mentions, but only between justification and adoption, justification having the priority in order of nature. . . . All the things he mentions are inseparable'.[11]

For Owen, then, such order as there is in the *ordo salutis* would seem to be: Effectual Calling; Regeneration; Faith; Repentance;[12] Justification; Adoption; and Sanctification. Thus, he writes:

---

[1] I.486; cf. XI.123; XIII.327.
[2] e.g. V.133; VI. 585, 587.
[3] III.188–206.   [4] I.486.   [5] VI.585.   [6] III.299.
[7] I.486.   [8] X.449. See V.108–112.   [9] XXIII.327.
[10] II.207, 173, 197.   [11] V.133.
[12] Owen regarded faith and repentance as chronologically inseparable, IV.442. Cf. XXIII.137 where he speaks of faith 'from which *evangelical repentance* is inseparable'.

That, I confess, which the method of the gospel leads unto is, that absolution, acquitment, or the pardon of sin, is the foundation of the communication of all saving grace unto the soul, and so precedeth all grace in the sinner whatever. But because this absolution or pardon of sin is to be received by faith, whereby the soul is really made partaker of it and all the benefits belonging thereunto, and that faith is the radical grace which we receive in our regeneration, – for it is by faith that our hearts are purified, as an instrument in the hand of the great purifier, the Spirit of God – I place these two together, and shall not dispute as to their priority in nature; but in time the one doth not precede the other.[1]

Thus divine election, and the outworking of it through the *ordo salutis* find their meeting place in *union with Christ*. This union, and all aspects of the plan of salvation are, for Owen, the application and fruit of the covenant of grace.[2] To become a Christian is therefore to be taken into covenant with God in Christ, by the Holy Spirit. How this begins, continues, and finds its consummation is the question we must now further consider.

[1] VI.597, cf. VI.598; XXI.147; and Calvin, *Institutes* III.iii.20.
[2] VI.585, 587; XI.123.

3

Grace Reigns Through Righteousness

Owen's most systematic treatment of the beginning of Christian experience is to be found in his lengthy treatise on the Person and Work of the Holy Spirit.[1]

He is deeply concerned to stress the background against which *regeneration* takes place,[2] and so, following a discussion of the Spirit's work under the Old Testament dispensation[3] and in the humanity of Christ,[4] he deals with the nature of man before regeneration. Owen stresses two elements in the fallen condition of man, namely, the corruption of the mind by sin, and spiritual death.[5] He is at great pains to clarify the *extent* and the *complexity* of this condition.

Three things sum up unregenerate man: he experiences *darkness* (in the mind), *depravity* (in the will) and *death* (in the soul).[6] Drawing heavily on Pauline theology, Owen deals

---

[1] *Works* III and IV.

[2] The terms 'regeneration' and 'conversion' are not as clearly defined and differentiated in Owen as they would be in later reformed authors. Cf. Calvin, *Institutes* III.iii, title, 'Regeneration by faith' in which the same lack of differentiation is apparent. For Owen the terms are virtually synonymous, cf. III.330 'regeneration or conversion', though, by and large, *conversion* is the whole process of entering on the Christian life, with both divine and human aspects involved, and *regeneration* is the work of God exclusively.

[3] III.92–159.

[4] III.159–188.

[5] These are, suitable to the context in which Owen writes, only aspects of his teaching about the nature of man before conversion. He does not at this point deal with the defacing of the image of God, nor with the federal union of men to Adam as their representative head (cf. X.353, 'all and every one died in Adam'). He discusses the defacing of the image of God in 1.181; III.339, 580.

[6] III.244.

firstly with the nature of the darkness of mind, and its consequences in man's life. It alienates man from God (witness his unreadiness to receive instruction from God, and his preference for any life, either sinful or legal, rather than the life which God offers through the gospel).[1] The darkness of sin clouds man's view of the nature of the gospel and the necessity of faith.[2] But further, darkness in the mind produces a real aversion to God, filling it with enmity against him[3] and with desires that are antagonistic to him, as well as with prejudice against spiritual realities.[4]

For Owen the mind (*nous*) is the leading and ruling faculty in man,[5] and the channel to the will and affections. It is the fulcrum of spiritual life: 'In the Scripture the deceit of the mind is commonly laid down as the principle of all sin whatever',[6] hence the necessity for a work of renewal which is 'internal, especial, immediate, supernatural, effectual, and enlightening'.[7]

But not only is man's mind alienated; his soul is dead.[8] It is this which makes *regeneration* so necessary. That men are 'dead' to God by nature can be demonstrated in two ways from the Scriptures:[9] by the use of the expression itself and its parallels, and also by the descriptions which signify the reversal of such a 'death' – 'quickening' and 'raising'.

Following the analogy of natural death, Owen holds that spiritual death is constituted by: (i) a privation of the principle of life, (ii) a cessation of all acts of true obedience to God, and (iii) a lack of power or ability to perform such acts (even if desired).[10]

Owen is here paving the way for his view of grace as sovereignly effectual and irresistible. He has traced out aspects of man's spiritual impotence; now he must meet the objection that this denies human responsibility and impugns the justice of God. He answers both of these objections with three observations. (i) The commands that God gives are suited to the moral nature of man; (ii) exhortations are addressed to

---

[1] III.255. [2] III.257ff. [3] Romans 8.7.
[4] See III.413; V.430, where, incidentally, Owen states the *imago dei* is 'lost'.
[5] III.250–252. [6] III.281.
[7] III.282. This is a work of Christ as King, by the Spirit, cf. I.98–9.
[8] III.282. [9] *Ibid.* [10] III.283ff.

duties, not to abilities; (iii) God in fact can, and does make his commands, exhortations and promises to be means of grace, and uses them to produce in men what they are not able of themselves to perform.[1] As to the justice of God, those who perish through sin 'feed on the fruit of their own ways'.[2] Furthermore, men neglect the will of God even in the matters which they have the power to perform. They are not guiltless, nor are they sinful in a merely deterministic way. Observation demonstrates that men exercise their minds and wills in opposition to Jesus Christ. This is not merely a matter of predetermined condition, but of actual, responsible exercise.

Owen is concerned to *illustrate* this teaching as well as expound it. In a chapter entitled 'The manner of conversion explained in the instance of Augustine',[3] he makes use of the self-analysis which is contained in Augustine's *Confessions* to provide an account of the development of sin, and 'the effects of that depravation'.[4]

i. *The Effects of sin*

(i) Corruption is at work from the earliest moment of life; it is 'original' in this sense and its depravity is universally evident, preventing all the 'actings' of the grace of God. Owen sees a striking proof of this in Psalm 58.3, where infants are described as 'speaking lies' from their birth and going astray 'from the womb'. In keeping with others, Owen saw the high infant mortality rate in his time as an evidence of the imputation of Adam's sin and its outworking in the lives of even the youngest.[5]

(ii) As the capacity of a person develops, so his native corruption exercises its influences with greater frequency and

---

[1]III.289–90.   [2]III.290.   [3]III.337ff.   [4]III.338.

[5]III.339. His actual words are: 'As the dying of multitudes of infants, notwithstanding the utmost care for their preservation, whereas the young ones of other creatures all generally live, if they have whereby their nature may be sustained, argues the imputation of sin unto them – for death entered by sin, and passed upon all, inasmuch as all have sinned – so those irregular actings peculiar unto them prove sin inherent in them, or the corruption of their nature from their conceptions'.

potency. Again Owen draws on Old Testament Scripture – Ecclesiastes 11.10, 'childhood and youth are vanity', – and reminds his readers of the vagaries and follies of Augustine's youth. He knows that many in his own day, regarded these things as but 'childish innocencies',[1] part of the natural process of maturation. But, like Augustine, he takes the view that these very things 'carried over unto riper age and greater occasions, bring forth those greater sins which the life of men are filled withal in the world. . . . By this means is the heart prepared for a further obduration in sin'.[2]

(iii) Following these 'irregularities' come actual sins. Such are lying and deceit, exercised even against parents, patterned after the sin of Adam and Eve. 'They rob their father and mother and say, It is no transgression'.[3]

(iv) As men mature sin begins to develop a lodging place in their lives, both subjectively and objectively.[4] They continue to increase in their capacity for sin, as their physical and mental powers mature. Objectively they have greater occasions for sin as the opportunities to be freed from parental and pedagogic restraint increase.[5]

At this juncture an increasing consciousness of the nature of sinful behaviour may produce a measure of restraint and even repentance in some individuals, while their conscience is still tender. But unless accompanied by the work of the Holy Spirit, that consciousness of sin may give birth to a desire to cast off all restraint.[6] Again Owen finds instruction in Ecclesiastes: 'Because sentence against an evil work is not executed speedily, therefore the heart of the sons of men is fully set in them to do evil'.[7]

(v) Finally, 'A course in, and custom of, sinning with many ensues hereon'.[8] Referring to Paul's incisive description of the effects of sin in Ephesians 4.18ff., Owen writes: 'Custom of sinning takes away the *sense* of it; the course of the world takes away the *shame* of it; and love to it makes men greedy in the pursuit of it'.[9] There may be marked differences in the ways in which this tendency appears in men's lives. But Owen argues

---

[1]III.340. [2]*Ibid.* [3]Prov. 28.24.
[4]III.342. [5]*Ibid.* [6]III.343.
[7]Eccles. 8.11. [8]III.343. [9]*Ibid.*

that the only reason its full impact is restrained is the goodness of God.

Here then is the 'experimental' aspect of man's depravity and death in sin. It is delineated at length by Owen, because the magnitude of regeneration is measured by the fact that grace delivers, renews and alleviates man from all he has known by way of bondage, darkness, death and corruption under the dominion of sin.

ii. *Regeneration*

Describing man's fallen condition is considerably easier than defining the mysterious work of regeneration.

Regeneration is neither the reception of the first gospel sacrament (Baptism), nor is it the experience of a moral reformation.

Owen gives four reasons why it cannot be *Baptism*.[1] (i) In sacraments, the sign, while having a sacramental union with the reality signified, is distinguished from it; (ii) 1 Peter 3.21 explicitly denies that baptism is an internal saving work; (iii) Paul emphasizes the grace of inner reality *in opposition* to mere sign; (iv) all who are baptized, under this argument, would be regenerate, but many baptized persons live unregenerate lives. The premise, therefore ('all baptized persons are regenerate') must be false.

As for *moral reformation*, Owen gladly concedes that this is a duty for all men. It is 'infallibly'[2] produced by regeneration, more completely in some, but 'sincerely'[3] in all. But regeneration cannot be reduced to moral reformation. Regeneration consists in a spiritual renewal of our nature, whereas in the Socinian view which Owen so strongly opposes, it consists only in a moral reformation of life.[4] The Socinian view confuses effect with cause, habit with action, faculties with occasional acts, infused principles with acquired habits, spiritual with moral, grace with nature!

In contrast, Owen defines regeneration as a new creation. This cannot be regarded merely as a new course of actions, but

---

[1]XVII.484, cf. III.216.   [2]III.219.
[3]*Ibid.*   [4]*Ibid.*

involves new dispositions, powers, and abilities, which in turn *produce* such a new course. The *cause* of this error in thinking is, according to Owen, the denial of the full reality of original sin and innate corruption, a point to which he later returns.[1]

Owen's concern to 'Keep watch over . . . the flock' (Acts 20.28) involved him not only in giving warnings against moralism, but also against fanaticism. So, he also stresses that regeneration is not to be thought of as *'enthusiastical raptures, ecstasies, voices*, or any thing of the like kind'.[2] For the work of the Spirit is 'rationally to be accounted for by and unto them who believe the Scripture'.[3] Regeneration involves a *moral* operation on the mind of man: 'yea, this is ordinarily the whole external means that is made use of in this work'.[4] But the emphasis here is on the *'external'*. Owen is concerned to demonstrate and defend the view that this external work must be accompanied by 'a *physical* immediate operation of the Spirit, by his power and grace, or his powerful grace, upon the minds or souls of men in their regeneration'.[5] It is then 'a real physical efficiency of divine power';[6] 'the acting of his divine power by a real internal efficiency';[7] 'The new birth is the effect of an act of his power and grace'.[8]

This emphasis on the 'physical' nature of regeneration demands comment. Owen offers Ephesians 1.18–20, 2 Thessalonians 1.11, and 2 Peter 1.3 as supporting biblical evidence for his view. He is, of course, contending with the Arminian view of regeneration ('which one observation is sufficient to evert the whole hypothesis of Arminian grace').[9] But his language raises the question whether grace can ever be thought of in physical terms.

Even from within the tradition which Owen so powerfully influenced, reluctance to follow him is evident. Thus George Smeaton comments, 'It is better to say "analogous to what is physical" (*analoga phusicae*)'.[10] Owen, however, uses the

---

[1] In a chapter entitled 'The filth of sin purged by the Spirit and blood of Christ', III.436ff.

[2] III.224.   [3] III.225.   [4] III.316.   [5] *Ibid.*
[6] III.317.   [7] *Ibid.*   [8] *Ibid.*   [9] III.317.

[10] George Smeaton, *The Doctrine of the Holy Spirit*, Edinburgh, 1882, p. 329 fn. 1.

expression with considerable frequency[1] and it is clear that he is heavily committed to its employment.

The difficulty is not to be solved along the lines suggested by Smeaton, but rather in the common seventeenth-century use of the expression 'physical' as the antithesis of 'moral'. Richard Hooker, for example, wrote that 'Sacraments are not physicall but morall instruments of salvation'.[2] It is in this sense that Charles Hodge understands Owen to take over the distinction of the medieval scholastics for his own purposes, although he rather sanguinely remarks that this is 'too obvious to need remark!'[3] The real locus of Owen's concern then, comes into view when he writes, 'This *internal efficiency* of the Holy Spirit on the minds of men, as to the event, is *infallible*, victorious, irresistible, or always efficacious'.[4] Man's natural state (*phusis*) is transformed by irresistible grace. While recognizing the opposition that is made to it, he proceeds to clarify his teaching, and if possible, conciliate its opponents. He makes three comments:

Firstly, the power of the Holy Spirit involved in regeneration is suited to the nature of man's mind, will, and affections 'according to their natures and natural operations . . . it carries no more repugnancy unto our faculties than a prevalent persuasion doth'.[5] Efficacious grace, then, does not 'unman' men, and make them less than fully human. Indeed, from Owen's standpoint, only efficacious grace can make men truly human.

Secondly, in regeneration, God 'works on the minds of men in and by their own natural actings, through an immediate influence and impression of his power'.[6] In other words, in the process of regeneration, God addresses the mind and its abilities;[7] regeneration is not a mindless process.

Thirdly, God 'therefore offers no violence or compulsion unto the will'.[8]

[1] e.g. IV.166; X.459; XI.443; 448; 567.
[2] Richard Hooker, *Of the Laws of Ecclesiastical Polity*, Oxford, 1592–97, V.lvii.4.
[3] Charles Hodge, *Systematic Theology*, London, 1871–73, II, p. 687.
[4] III.317, i.e. grace affects man's *phusis* (nature).
[5] III.318.   [6] III.319.
[7] Cf. I Peter 1.23; James 1.18.   [8] III.319.

Indeed, if the will is compelled, 'it is destroyed', and the purpose of this gracious work, after all, is not to destroy the will, but to set it free, and to destroy that by which the will is dominated in the unregenerate man. Owen admits that there is a certain opposition, or better 'reaction' between grace and the will, but denies that there is any real conflict, since 'the opposition is not *ad idem*', but against grace 'as *objectively proposed*'. As far as Owen is concerned grace 'is not proposed unto it [the will] as that which it may accept or refuse, but worketh effectually in it'. Furthermore, 'in the first *act* of conversion' the will '*acts* not, but as it is *acted*'. It is therefore *passive*, but, in the moment of being acted upon, it acts itself, freely.

The conclusion of the matter for Owen is: 'There is, therefore, herein an inward almighty *secret act* of the power of the Holy Ghost, producing or effecting in us the will of conversion unto God, so acting our wills as that they also act themselves, and that freely'.[1] He goes on to 'confirm the truth proposed with evident testimonies of Scripture.'[2] It might have been better had he done this first, but he was, no doubt, anxious to defend his propositions against the current criticism of them.

His defence from Scripture follows customary lines: *First*, Scripture attests that conversion is '*wrought in us*' by God: not just made possible for us (Phil. 2.13; John 6.65; Eph. 2.8–10); and that repentance is something God *gives*, (2 Tim. 2.25; Acts 11.18). *Second*, the manner in which God works shows that he does so by an '*infallibly efficacious power*'.[3] He circumcises the heart (Deut. 30.6; 29.4; Ezek. 36.26–7; Jer. 24.7; Is. 44. 3–5; Jer. 31.33). All this is fulfilled in Christ (Col. 2.11).

The nature of the work of regeneration will become clearer, maintains Owen, 'if we consider the faculties of the soul distinctly, and what is the especial work of the Holy Spirit upon them'.[4] The mind is granted understanding and renewal, the will receives vivification, being set free for God, and the affections have a new and prevalent love implanted in them. In place of the lust and affection for sin, God fills the regenerated

[1]III.320. [2]*Ibid.* [3]III.324. [4]III.330.

man with '*holy spiritual love, joy, fear and delight*, not changing the being of our affections, but sanctifying and guiding them by the principle of saving light and knowledge'.[1]

Just as Owen was able to delineate the 'vital' aspect of man's depravity through sin from Augustine's *Confessions*, so too he delineates the doctrinal aspect of regeneration from the same source.[2] The result is an outline of the Puritan view of conversion. Owen maps this out for his readers.

First of all he brings forward the consideration that many (in his own day) had a remnant of a ministry of grace in their memories, for example from the days of their minority, when they were perhaps under godly parental care. There may remain 'certain sparks of *celestial fire*',[3] which can be fanned into life. Furthermore, God works in men's lives to produce an awareness of himself, to make them conscious of their separation from him, and their 'obnoxiousness unto his righteousness on the account of sin'.[4] He may do this by a great variety of circumstances: (i) by sudden judgments, such as overtook the prophet Jonah; (ii) by personal afflictions: 'I find, by long observation,' he writes in another connection, 'that common light, in conjunction with afflictions, do begin the conversion of many, without this or that special word';[5] (iii) by remarkable deliverances, such as that of Naaman; (iv) by the witness of other Christians' lives, and, (v) pre-eminently by the ministry of God's word, either read or preached. It is ultimately by the law that the knowledge of sin comes.[6]

---

[1]III.335.

[2]Like most Puritan writers, Owen cites Augustine far more frequently than he cites Calvin or any of the magisterial Reformers.

[3]III.345. Owen does not mean that men naturally possess 'sparks' of spiritual life, but that some have already received 'sparks' of gospel teaching in earlier years, as Augustine had from his mother Monnica.

[4]III.346.

[5]IX.460. A sermon on the duty of a pastor from Jer. 3.15. Owen would not have meant by this that God works in contradiction to the Scriptures; nor did he believe that such an experience could be a final authority or guide. He recognizes that *circumstances* may draw people to the message of the gospel, in the providence of God.

[6]Owen is expressing the accepted view of the relationship of law and gospel. Thus, 'The *order*, *relation*, and *use* of the law and the gospel do un-controllably evince the necessity of this conviction previous unto believing.

But again, this work may be hindered and may not be given the opportunity to reach fruition. There are many reasons for this: (i) man's natural darkness; (ii) a facile presumption that the present condition of an awakened conscience is all that God requires; (iii) the fear of being teased and mocked by the ungodly; (iv) a failure to 'improve' the work that God has already performed in the heart; (v) the 'wiles of the devil,' or as Owen picturesquely describes them, his 'engines' of war; or simply (vi) 'mere love of lusts and pleasures, or the unconquered adherence of a corrupted heart unto sensual and sinful objects, that offer present satisfaction unto its carnal desires'.[1] Clearly a further, effectual work of the Spirit is required.

Consequently, Owen focuses attention on the work of the Spirit in convicting men of sin, and discusses the nature, causes, refusal, and completion of this work. As to its *nature*, the conviction of sin involves 'a fixing the vain mind of a sinner upon a due consideration of his sin' and also 'a fixing of a due sense of sin'.[2] The first has reference to the false *vanity* of the mind, in that it does not feel any compunction to consider sin at all. The second has reference to the false *security* of the mind, in that it fails to grasp the enormity of the blasphemy which sin entails. This producing of a sense of sin's sinfulness constitutes the Spirit's convicting work.

The cause of such conviction is also two-fold. The *efficient* cause is the Spirit of God; the *instrumental* cause is the word of God, and specially the law:[3]

But this is the second work of the law: when it hath by its convictions brought the sinner into a condition of a sense of guilt which he cannot avoid, – nor will anything tender him relief, which way soever he

---

For that which any man hath first to deal withal, with respect unto his eternal condition, both naturally, and by God's institution, is the law. This is first presented unto the soul with its *terms* of righteousness and life, and with its *curse* in case of failure. Without this the gospel cannot be understood, nor the grace of it duly valued. For it is the revelation of God's way for the relieving the souls of men from the sentence and curse of the law, Romans 1.17.' V.75.

[1]III.348.   [2]III.350.   [3]III.351, cf. Romans 7.7.

looks, for he is in a desert, – it represents unto him the holiness and severity of God, with his indignation and wrath against sin; which have a resemblance of a consuming fire. This fills his heart with dread and terror and makes him see his miserable, undone condition.[1]

Even at this stage, the Spirit's ministry may be *resisted*. Conviction of sin is not conversion. Consequently Owen emphasizes that there can be no rest from 'conversion work' until it has been consummated, and the new work of sanctification and mortification begins.[2] Such a consummation is often preceded by a violent conflict between the corruptions of the soul and the newly impressed convictions of the mind. This was the experience of Paul in Romans 7.7–9. The initial reaction may be a vow to live a different life.[3] The voice of the law and of conscience may thus be silenced temporarily, but frequently these ungrounded resolves last only until the next onslaught of temptation. This is really a confusion of the work of mortification (the proper work of the *believer*) with that of conversion (the proper concern of the *unbeliever*). Owen returns to this in his treatise on *Mortification*:

When the Jews, upon the conviction of their sin, were cut to the heart, Acts ii.37, and cried out, 'What shall we do?' what doth Peter direct them to do? Does he bid them go and mortify their pride, wrath, malice, cruelty and the like? No; he knew that was not their present work, but he calls them to conversion and faith in Christ in general.[4]

Thereafter, as the Spirit's work continues, the individual may be torn between 'the power of corruption and the terror of conviction'.[5] His sense of conviction may be heightened, and the principle of grace, at work secretly and internally, will begin to overcome in the war with the flesh, until the dominion of sin is overthrown (though the presence of sin remains). So Augustine speaks of a 'new will which began to be in me'.[6]

Sometimes God speaks a calming word to silence the tumult

[1]XXIV.315.   [2]III.353.
[3]III.354.   [4]VI.35.
[5]III.355.   [6]*Confessions*, VIII.v, quoted III.356.

of the soul, as in Augustine's case.[1] While under conviction of sin, Augustine heard a child's voice in a garden, calling 'Tolle, lege' – Take up [the book] and read it. He began to read Paul's words in Romans 13.14: 'Clothe yourselves with the Lord Jesus Christ, and do not think about how to gratify the flesh'. It was precisely the word he needed to hear. Others may have to walk further, increasing in their sense of dread with respect to their eternal condition. Thus conviction of sin leads to a sense of shame on the one hand, and fear of wrath on the other, giving rise to 'perplexing *unsatisfactory enquiries* after means and ways for deliverance out of this present distress and from future misery'.[2] But, even at this stage, insists Owen, it is possible for a man to draw back.

Owen suggests that there are two things in general which precede the consummation of conversion work: the first is a conviction of sin that makes the individual conscious that he is by nature under the curse of the law; the second is a realization that there is no other way of salvation than that which is offered in the gospel of Christ.

iii. *The Use of the law*

We have already seen that, for Owen, subjective saving experience is moulded by the objective provision of salvation by God in the covenant. The theological question which Owen saw as 'Why the Sinaitic covenant?' is intimately related to the apostolic, experimental question, 'Why then the law?'[3] It is in the context of the experiences involved in regeneration and conversion that this question was answered for him. Here too, many of Owen's contemporaries gave attention to Paul's question about the law,[4] believing that it was this question which the preaching of God's grace in the gospel always

[1]III.357.
[2]III.360.
[3]Gal. 3.19.
[4]The standard work on the Puritan doctrine of law is E. F. Kevan's *The Grace of Law*. His bibliography of primary sources extends to some twelve pages (pp. 269–280), and this gives some indication of the interest in the theme during the seventeenth century.

evoked.[1]

Owen draws together the three traditional uses of the law in reformed theology, giving each his own distinctive emphasis.

Firstly, the law reveals the character of God in his goodness, holiness, and wisdom.[2] It makes known his sovereign will and authority. Thus, 'Sin, with respect unto his authority, is attended with guilt; and this, in the conscience of the sinner produceth fear: as it respects the holiness of God, it is attended with filth or uncleanness; and this produceth shame'.[3]

Secondly, the law reveals the duty of man, whether as man, sinner, or saint.[4] Materially God's commands remain the same for all men, 'But there is a great difference in the manner and ends of these commands'.[5] In the life of the Christian, a universal sincerity, and not a perfect obedience is in view. In this sense the law is *always* the restrainer of sin.[6]

Thirdly, the law brings men to Jesus Christ. It would be an exaggeration to say that Owen sees this as the law's primary use, but there is a greater elucidation of this use than either of the others, precisely because it is so vitally significant from the point of view of Christian experience. While the application of the other uses is relatively straightforward, here we are in an area of fine doctrinal and pastoral issues.

The law, according to Owen, brings a man to Jesus Christ by three stages.

(i) It reveals sin as sin, 'by one means or other'.[7] More accurately, this is the work of the Holy Spirit, who uses the law as an instrument. He alone is the principal and efficient cause of conviction of sin, for 'Without his especial and immediate

---

[1]Cf. Luther's comments 'When we teach that a man is justified without the law and works, then doth this question *necessarily* follow: If the law do not justify, why then was it given? Also: why doth God charge us and burden us with the law, if it do not quicken and give life?' *Commentary on Galatians*, Middleton edition, revised P. S. Watson, London, 1953, p. 294. Also, Calvin, 'When we hear that the law is powerless to give justification, various thoughts immediately arise, that it is either useless, or opposed to God's covenant, or something of that sort.' *Commentary on Galatians to Colossians.* trs., T. H. L. Parker, ed. D. W. & T. F. Torrance, Edinburgh, 1965, p. 60.

[2]III.616.   [3]III.428.   [4]I.476.
[5]III.606.   [6]III.351; II.95.   [7]III.351.

actings on us to this end, we may hear the law preached all the days of our lives and not be once affected with it'.[1]

(ii) It reveals the 'sinfulness of sin', its 'ugliness and deformity'[2] since it is a mirror in which a man's true nature will be seen. When a man thus sees 'a *distinct sight of this indwelling sin*'[3] he will discover how *dangerous* it is, and that the language of the law is 'Abide in this state and perish'.[4] His soul will become like 'a poor beast that hath a deadly arrow sticking in its sides, that makes it restless wherever it is and whatever it doth'.[5] Indeed, it will slay his soul.[6] These two stages are frequently concurrent and lead to a third.

(iii) The law brings men 'under bondage to sin, death, Satan and hell, – so making us long and seek for a Saviour'.[7] This stage marked a definite transition in experience for Owen so significant that it must be given more careful attention. It is *the* work of the Spirit through the law,[8] to bring men into this 'spirit of bondage',[9] before, through the grace of the gospel, he is experienced as a Spirit of adoption. This is a distinctively Puritan understanding of the text of Romans 8.15.[10]

Many of Owen's contemporaries interpreted the words of Romans 8.15 as follows: 'You have not again received the Spirit who brings you into bondage to the law and so breeds fear of judgment, but now you have received the Spirit of God through grace and by faith in Christ, and have been adopted into God's family, so that you cry "Abba" and have a spirit of filial affection'. This view was adopted by Owen, although he hesitated to speak of the Spirit of God as the Spirit 'of bondage', and preferred to think of this bondage as a *result* of his work. The effect is essentially the same: Romans 8.15 summarizes the experience Paul describes in Romans 7.7–13, and describes the

---

[1]III.352. [2]II.95. [3]VI.314. [4]VI.315.
[5]*Ibid.* [6]Rom. 7.9. [7]I.476. [8]IV.267.

[9]Romans 8.15. See XXIII.91–2 for the nature of this bondage under the law.

[10]Cf. John Cotton's particularly relevant words, 'God doth not call any into fellowship with himself in a Covenant of Grace, but ordinarily he first bringeth them into a Covenant of Works, and casteth them out of doors by a spirit of bondage and burning, and then bringeth them in by the true door, and Jesus Christ is that door, Jno. 10.9', *The New Covenant*, London, 1654, pp. 49–50.

definite transitional experience when 'the commandment
came' (Rom. 7.9). Owen notes that while this is the fruit of the
Mosaic dispensation the 'again' of Romans 8.15 indicates that
even Christians may experience it.

This pattern of experience, <u>bondage through the law followed by freedom in the gospel</u>, was normative for conversion
experience according to the Puritan teaching; but it raised
profound questions about the degree of this bondage-experi-
ence which preceded a genuine conversion,[1] and these issues
were also handled with discrimination. Owen himself is quick
to point out that there is no question of a standard or level to
be reached. Scripture teaches that such experiences are 'no
part of what is required of us, but of what is inflicted on us'.[2]
Some may 'walk or wander long in darkness; in the souls of
others Christ is formed in the first gracious visitation'.[3] All
aspects of Augustine's 'classic' conversion will not be found in
every Christian. Elsewhere Owen answers the question, '*What
conviction of a state of sin, and of the guilt of sin, is necessary to cause a
soul sincerely to look after Christ?*' He draws on three texts to
answer: *Mark 2.7*, a man must realize he is not righteous in
and of himself; *Matthew 9.12*, he must have a sense of dis-ease
with sin, and some consciousness that it leads to spiritual
death. *Matthew 11.28*, he must be weary of his own efforts for
acceptance with God, and see that it can be found in Christ
alone.[4]

While this may remind us of the agonies of a Bunyan or
others whose experience exemplifies this pattern in a vivid way,
Owen is not setting the law against the gospel. Since sin
essentially involves separation from God, the knowledge of sin
will come through the knowledge of God in both law *and* gospel.
Owen is aware of this, and insists that the gospel as well as the
law reveals the nature of sin. The Spirit of God interprets
Calvary as well as Sinai, to show the desert of sin and man's
impotence to deal with it.[5]

---

[1]See Thomas Manton, *Works*, ed. T. Smith, London, 1870–71, XII.107;
John Preston, *The Saint's Qualification*, London, 1637, pp. 20, 101; *The New
Covenant*. London, 1634, pp. 394–396, 407, 410; *A Treatise of Effectual Faith*,
London, 1631, p. 46.
[2]III.360.   [3]III.361.
[4]IX.359–61; cf. IX.292–3.   [5]II.95.

This question, *why* the law is an instrument of bondage in the hands of the Spirit, brings together the objective pattern of Owen's theology, and the subjective spiritual experience of grace.

Why then is the law an instrument of bondage?[1] Because the law renews the terms of the covenant of works (although not itself that covenant)[2] and does so in a covenant form.[3] The result, both for those of the old dispensation, and for those who have not been brought into the grace of the new covenant, is that the law brings a 'servile and bondage frame of spirit upon them in all wherein they had to do with God'.[4] Added to this, the manner of the delivery of the law itself promotes dread and fear; the severity of the law's penalties brings anxiety and insecurity; the emphasis of the law is on the sentence of judgment and death upon sinners; the darkness of mind, characteristic of the unregenerate knows no way of escape from such bondage, nor from the increased yoke of duties which accompany both the law and the legal spirit.[5] Owen believed that this work alone brings men to see the urgency of their need of Christ. The law is their pedagogue, not only restraining them in the infancy of their spiritual development, but finally driving them to the freedom of Christ and the gospel.[6]

We have seen that, for Owen, man's salvation involved the Son of God undertaking to fulfil in and for man the covenant of works, and to sustain on his own shoulders the penalty incurred by man in his breach of it. Having accomplished this through the whole of his incarnation, Christ became 'the end of the law for righteousness to every one that believeth'.[7] Those who have been driven to him by the law find in him the end of all efforts to self-justification by the deeds of the law. He fulfilled its ceremonies, revealed its true spiritual nature,[8] representatively obeyed its precepts and bore its penalty.[9] The believer is thus free from the law in each of these respects.[10]

[1] XXIII.91.   [2] I.476, note 2: cf. above, p. 27ff.
[3] XIX.389; XXIII.91.   [4] XIX.389.
[5] XXIII.92.   [6] *Ibid.*   [7] Romans 10.4.
[8] *i.e.* in the Sermon on the Mount.
[9] V.338f.   [10] II.212; XXIII.91.

This does not mean that when a man enters into the liberty of the gospel the law becomes irrelevant to him. Owen argues that the New Covenant, rather than abolish the law, restores it to its true place in man's life. Here his use of the scholastic distinction between 'form' and 'substance' allows him to clarify his thought. The *substance* of the covenant of works was renewed in the Sinaitic covenant, but the *form* of that renewal was changed. It was now given to a people who were under the covenant of grace (though not yet in the new covenant). The substance of the covenant of works is God's will for man *as man*, and in that sense unalterable.

The law is *connatural* to him; his domestic, his old acquaintance. It came into the world with him, and hath grown up with him from his infancy. It was implanted in his heart by nature, – is his own reason; he can never shake it off or part with it. It is his familiar, his friend that cleaves to him as the flesh to the bone; so that they who have not the law written cannot but show forth the work of the law, Rom. ii. 14, 15, and that because the law itself is inbred to them.[1]

The law as a 'rule of life' is therefore a constant factor in the earlier covenants, and remains so under the new covenant, and consequently in the personal experience of the Christian, who is being restored to the image of God through Christ and by the Spirit.

The law of God, which was never given as a means of justification in the Sinaitic covenant is thus restored to its true function in the gospel: the righteousness that law requires is fulfilled in the believer through faith in Christ and by the inward work of the Spirit (*cf*. Rom. 8.3–4). The law is written in his heart in regeneration, and for Owen this means he receives a new principle of obedience.

This raises a further issue: What distinguishes a preparatory work of the Spirit from a consummated work? Owen's answer is that the preparatory work affects mind, conscience, affection and conversation – *but not the will*.[2] But regeneration involves the renewal of the will. The preparatory work does not advance to the point where the *mind* enjoys '*delight, complacency* and

---

[1] VI.389–90; XX.400.
[2] III.238.

satisfaction[1] in what is revealed to it, nor does it *fully* affect the *conscience* to 'purge from dead works'.[2]

The *affections* are neither fixed on Christ nor filled with Christ. While a preparatory work may produce a *reformation* of life, this can co-exist with the continued reign of sin, a lack of universal reformation and a merely temporal change in lifestyle. Eventually the convictions that produced the reformation dissolve, and men become, in Owen's vivid expressions, 'walking and talking skeletons in religion' and 'dry, sapless, useless, worldlings' instead of growing spiritually 'fat and flourishing in old age'.[3]

What must a man do, then, to be saved? How is an enquirer to be directed? His responsibility, according to Owen, is to look to Christ,[4] not accepting the remedies that may be first offered to his awakened and tender conscience, such as human superstitions, or even the dictates of the law itself. He is also to beware of the 'entangling temptations'[5] which are peculiar to his condition, such as believing he does not feel sufficient sorrow for sin, or, that those who are helping him do not understand that he is beyond redemption.

In this way, through response to the preaching of the gospel, the moment will come when, secretly and sovereignly, faith will be wrought in the heart – provided Christ crucified and exalted is presented as the Saviour through whom convicted sinners may be pardoned. When this response is truly made, it will be accompanied by '*a universal engagement of heart unto all holy obedience to God in Christ, with a relinquishment of all known sin*'.[6] Those who have experienced this will then be admitted to the fellowship of the church, since they have, indeed, been converted.[7]

iv. *The Structure of sanctification*

Whereas Regeneration is an *act* of God the Spirit, for Owen the *work* of sanctification[8] has both a divine and a human aspect.

---

[1]*Ibid.*   [2]Hebrews 9.14.   [3]III.241.   [4]III.364.
[5]III.362.   [6]III.364.   [7]III.365.
[8]The stress on sanctification as a 'work' or process is reflected in *The Confession of Faith*, XIII, and *Longer Catechism* Q.75, *Shorter Catechism* Q.35.

God is the *author* of sanctification[1] in his character as the 'God of peace'.[2] The work of sanctification is essentially the outworking of the peace of God in the whole of life. The *agent* of this sanctification is the Holy Spirit, but the *sphere* of it is the life of man, and in this operation he actively responds to the grace of God. This is consistent with the whole pattern of the divine working, as far as Owen is concerned. As in the inauguration of the new life, there is the *act* of regeneration, producing the *exercise* of God-given faith, so in sanctification, there is the *work* of grace, producing the *exercise* of duty, and the response of obedience.

We may look, first of all, at Owen's description of the nature of sanctification. The work of the Spirit is a self-consistent unity. Having created a natural body for the Son of God, suitable for his incarnation,[3] he now creates a spiritual or mystical body, suited to his resurrected and exalted condition as the God-Man and Mediator.

This work, which involves the sanctification of the church, is done individually on the 'whole nature'[4] of man, not merely (as in the Roman view) on part of him:

This subject of sanctification is the entire nature or the whole person of a believer. It is not any one faculty of the soul or affection of the mind or part of the body that is sanctified, but the whole soul and body, or the entire nature, of every believing person . . . true holiness, consists in the renovation of our whole persons; which must be demonstrated.[5]

This is in keeping with Owen's definition of sanctification[6] which implies that the restoration of the *image of God* is of the very essence of the process. Just as 'total depravity' for him does not mean that man is as bad as he could be, but that there is no part of him that remains unaffected by sin, correspondingly sanctification will touch and heal man's whole being, substantially, though imperfectly in this life.

Owen offers as his first definition of sanctification:

[1]III.372.
[2]1 Thess. 5.23–4.
[3]III.159ff.   [4]III.369.   [5]III.417.
[6]III.386; cf. III.330 for the same idea in connection with regeneration.

Sanctification, as here described, *is the immediate work of God by his Spirit upon our whole nature, proceeding from the peace made for us by Jesus Christ, whereby, being changed into his likeness, we are kept entirely in peace with God, and are preserved unblamable, or in a state of gracious acceptation with him according to the terms of the covenant, unto the end* . . . real and internal, by the communicating of a principle of holiness unto our natures, attended with its exercise in acts and duties of holy obedience unto God.[1]

By this a man is consecrated to God, since such holiness is 'nothing but the implanting, writing, and realizing of the gospel in our souls'.[2] This flows from Christ and is communicated *to* our souls by the Spirit. It is *granted* to us, but it is also *required* of us.[3] Later, Owen brings forward five great motives for meeting these duties: the nature of God, our eternal election, the commandments, the mission of Christ, and our condition in the world.[4]

v. *The Progress of sanctification*

Having earlier suggested that 'regeneration is the head, fountain, or beginning of our sanctification, virtually comprising the whole in itself',[5] Owen draws out some of the implications of the development of this principle, and offers a further definition:

Sanctification is an immediate work of the Spirit of God on the souls of believers, purifying and cleansing of their natures from the pollution and uncleanness of sin, renewing in them the image of God, and thereby enabling them, from a spiritual and habitual principle of grace, to yield obedience unto God, according unto the tenor and terms of the new covenant, by virtue of the life and death of Jesus Christ.[6] Or *more briefly: It is the universal renovation of our natures by the Holy Spirit into the image of God, through Jesus Christ.*[7]

---

[1]III.369–70.
[2]III.370–1. This would seem to cover that aspect of New Testament teaching which sees sanctification as an act rather than a work: *e.g.* Acts 20.32.
[3]III.376, 'this is that which God indispensably requireth of us'. *Cf.* Hebrews 12.14.
[4]III.566ff.
[5]III.299; what is given in regeneration is holiness in potential form.
[6]Cf. II.171.
[7]III.386.

Like conversion, sanctification is, *mutatis mutandis*, 'a real, internal, powerful, physical work'.[1] Owen is anxious again to safeguard these points against all forms of deviation whether they be Arminian, Socinian or Pelagian 'old and new'.[2] But, of course, this work differs from conversion-regeneration in certain important aspects; regeneration is *instantaneous*. It is *complete* and not capable of degrees; whereas sanctification by its very nature is progressive and capable of varying degrees.

Increase and growth in holiness are *commanded* in Scripture.[3] Owen uses the analogy of holiness as a seed,[4] planted in the soil and growing to fruition. In the case of sanctification this increase comes through the *exercise of granted grace*, encouraged by the continuing work of the Spirit in a number of ways. He works, 'exciting them unto frequent actings'.[5] The graces of faith and love are stimulated to development *morally*, by the presentation of spiritual truth to the mind, and through the encouragement of the preaching of the word, in which the ministry of the Spirit to lead and guide into the truth is fulfilled. At times Christians themselves may not be aware of the effects, but this hearing-with-faith draws out and augments the graces of holiness. These same graces are also stimulated by the secret work of the Spirit, really and internally.[6] Further, the Spirit brings an increase of grace by providing the Christian with *personal experiences* of the truth and power of the teaching presented verbally to him in the preaching of the word. There is also a providential aspect to sanctification; so that 'Experience is the food of all grace, which it grows and thrives upon'.[7]

But there are graces of the Christian life which cannot, by their nature, be in constant exercise in the same way as faith and love. What then of the development of this 'nature bestowed on us' which is 'capable of growth and increase'?[8] Owen stresses that Scripture teaches a growth in *universal*

---

[1]III.387.   [2]*Ibid.*   [3]XXIII.286ff.
[4]The analogy is a biblical one, 1 Jn. 3.9, where 'nature' (R.S.V.) is *sperma*. Owen's actual words are: 'The work of holiness, in its beginning, is but like seed cast into the earth, – namely, the *seed of God*, whereby we are born again. . . . It is small at first, but being received in good and honest hearts, made so by the Spirit of God, and there nourished and cherished, it takes root and brings forth fruit'. III.388.
[5]III.389.   [6]III.391.   [7]III.390.   [8]III.393.

holiness as well as a progress in its common graces, and so, with respect to graces not in constant exercise, 'holiness is increased by the addition of one to another, until we are brought on several occasions to the practice and exercise of them all'.[1]

This is the key lesson, for Owen, of a passage such as 2 Peter 1.5–7 ('Make every effort to *supplement* your *faith* with virtue. . . .'). Here in particular is where the providence of God and his purposes in sanctification meet, as he brings his children into situations requiring the exercise of these graces: 'All our relations, all our afflictions, all our temptations, all our mercies, all our enjoyments, all occurrences, are suited to a continual adding of the exercise of one grace to another, wherein holiness is increased'.[2] Alongside his government of life's circumstances, God works inwardly to secure the development and exercise of graces. Holiness requires the continual effort of the believer, and also the continuing nourishment of the Spirit's aid.[3] 'The Lord Christ is the head, fountain, and treasure of all actual supplies; and the Spirit is the *efficient cause*, communicating them unto us from him'.[4]

But how can there be any place for '*diligence, duty or obedience*'?[5] when sanctification is apparently a sovereign work of God? Owen recognizes the objection that had been constantly brought against the Augustinian doctrine of grace, and not infrequently against his own.[6] He answers briefly: both are taught in Scripture, and therefore are obligatory for the Christian to believe. Only carnal reason and logic will cavil at the grandeur of the logic and spiritual reasoning of Holy Scripture. The question is answered by the apostle Peter in a previously cited text, 2 Peter 1.3ff., where the two truths of divine sovereignty and human responsibility are brought together in the case of progress in holiness. It is God's divine power which provides the basis and motive for the believer's giving diligence in the exercise of graces. He must therefore

---

[1]III.391.

[2]*Ibid.* Owen believed that there is a special reason for the order in which Peter enjoins Christians to add these graces, but he seems nowhere to discuss it in published writings.

[3]Owen seems to be thinking of such passages as Philippians 1.19.

[4]III.393.   [5]III.394.

[6]*Ibid.*, 'This objection we must expect to meet withal at every turn'.

with patience and trust wait for the supply of the Spirit of God, who alone is the author of any good done in him or by him. Thus, for Owen, in keeping with the tradition of reformed teaching to which he belongs, the sovereignty of God is not a *discouragement*, but rather a most effectual *encouragement* to true holiness.[1]

Owen now proceeds to draw out some of the implications of his use of the horticultural metaphor of the seed for sanctification. He notes that trees and plants have the principle of their growth in themselves, and so, with sanctification, 'It hath a *root*, a *seed*, a principle of growth and increase, in the soul of him that is sanctified.'[2] Yet sanctification is no more really spontaneous than the growth of a tree. 'The tree must be *watered* from above' or 'it will not thrive and grow by virtue of its own *seminal* power'.[3] So it is with the believer. Again, the growth of trees and plants may be imperceptible and discerned only in the effects; similarly the believer's progress in holiness may be variable, at times erratic and irregular, 'not by a constant insensible progress, but . . . by sudden gusts and motions . . . so the growth of believers consists principally in some intense, vigorous actings of grace on great occasions'.[4] Clearly it is the same Spirit but with diversities of operations (1 Cor.12.4).

But the Spirit's work is known not only from the illustrations and plain teaching of Scripture. The Christian also discovers the pattern of his work in his *personal experience*. This is particularly so of the help given by the Spirit in prayer, which is 'an extract and copy of the work of the Holy Spirit in us, given us by himself'.[5] Spiritual *insight* is given, to direct the minds of believers in the right and godly path of life; spiritual *conviction* is given, to make them conscious of their needs, and to give a desire for their relief; and spiritual *desires* for true growth in grace are created by his secret operations.[6]

Progress is one of the evidences of a genuine conversion and a real beginning in the Christian life. Within this context certain cases of conscience arise for resolution. A major one is that many Christians look back to earlier days in their experience

---

[1]See the same point and discussion of it in Calvin, *Institutes* III.xxii.12–13.
[2]III.396.   [3]*Ibid.*   [4]III.397.
[5]III.399.   [6]III.398–9.

when they made steady and significant progress which they no longer see and therefore question whether the work of holiness is still thriving in them. In answer Owen lays down certain broad principles which further illuminate his approach to the progress of religion in the individual.

(i) Holiness in principle is one thing, but the actual manner of its working is another. There is, by the nature of things, a certain regularity in the regeneration of the Spirit, but an irregularity in spiritual growth. 'When we are regenerated, we are as new born babes, and ordinarily, if we have the sincere milk of the word, we shall grow thereby.'[1] But this may be thwarted, as in natural life, by indisposition, or by disobedience, or by the bruises and sicknesses of unresisted temptation, which lead to underdeveloped and even stunted growth.

(ii) It is one thing for holiness to be *present*, and another for the believer to be *conscious* of it in his own life. This Owen has hinted at before[2] but here he seeks to establish the scriptural nature of his contention from 2 Corinthians 4.16. The inner man is renewed, as the outer man decays – imperceptibly. Using the illustration of a storm, he points out that even the most able of mariners may not be sure of his location in a storm, but the storm may contribute to the fruit-bearing of trees![3] Continuing in the naturalist vein, he emphasizes that the rivers of grace may be directed in different ways, *now* towards peace, joy, and hope, and *then* towards humility, convictions and the development of graces in spiritual conflict: 'God will, therefore, so order his dispensations towards them, by afflictions, temptations, occasions of life in the world, as that they shall have *new work to do*, and all the grace they have be turned into a new exercise'.[4]

(iii) Alluding to the conditions of contemporary society,[5] Owen further points out the necessity of recognizing possible decay in holiness, even though the reality of an essential holiness remains. The believer who discovers himself in this condition needs to recognize that sanctification is a *duty* as well as a *work of grace*. If *he* does not attend to it, the work will be obstructed; if corruption is not dealt with, grace will be

---

[1]III.400.   [2]See above, pp. 57ff.
[3]III.403.   [4]*Ibid.*   [5]III.404.

weakened. 'If we slack or give over as to our *duty*, the work of sanctification will not be carried on in a way of *grace*'.[1]

(1). *Sanctification negatively considered*

Having thus cleared some of the ground for further exposition, Owen now turns to certain aspects of the work of sanctification which form the basis for the whole of his doctrine.

Sanctification has two sides to it, negative and positive, as it has two dimensions, divine and human. 'The first part of it is the *purifying and cleansing of our nature from the pollution of sin*'.[2] In Scripture this work is attributed to 'all the causes and means of sanctification':[3] the work of the Spirit ('I will sprinkle clean water upon you, and you shall be clean,' Ezek. 36.35); the death and blood of Christ ('Christ loved the church, and gave himself for it; that he might sanctify and cleanse it . . .' Eph. 5.25), which deals not only with the guilt, but also with the defilement of sin.[4] As to duty, sanctification is similarly described 'under this notion of *cleansing ourselves* from sin'[5] (e.g. 1 Jn 3.3, 'every man that hath this hope . . . purifieth himself'). The means of grace for sanctification, in baptism, is described as a 'washing of regeneration', and expresses the 'putting away of the body of the sins of the flesh'.[6] This notion is central in the New Testament teaching.

The *pollution of sin*, Owen argues, is more than sin's guilt. Rather it is 'that property of it whereby it is directly opposed unto the holiness of God, and which God expresseth his holiness to be contrary unto'.[7] It is 'that *pravity, disorder, and shameful crookedness that is in it, with respect unto the holiness of God as expressed in the law*'.[8] This is both *habitual* and *actual*;[9] it is inimical to true holiness and keeps men from the enjoyment of God. It is enslaving, so that they cannot set themselves free from it, and it cannot be cleansed by external rites.

How then is this pollution to be purged? Scripture delineates four agencies for this purpose: the *blood of Christ*, the agency of the *Holy Spirit, faith*, and *afflictions*. It is particularly the blood of Christ that Owen discusses, as the '*meritorious* procuring, and so

---

[1]III.405.   [2]III.423.   [3]*Ibid.*   [4]III.424.
[5]*Ibid.*   [6]III.424. Cf. Tit. 3.5; 1 Pet. 3.21.   [7]III.427.
[8]*Ibid.*   [9]III.431.

the effective cause'[1] of this cleansing. He alludes to several passages in Scripture[2] to show that by the blood of Christ is meant 'his *sacrifice*, with the power, virtue, and efficacy thereof'.[3] It was *offered* to make atonement for sin, it was *sprinkled* for purging of sin and for sanctification.[4] This sacrifice of Christ having been once offered for justification, is perpetually available for sanctification, since his blood is 'as newly slain'.[5]

But how does the blood of Christ cleanse men? Owen has two answers. It does so by removing 'all loathsomeness in the sight of God',[6] not from sin in the abstract, but from the sinner; and by taking 'shame out of the conscience'.[7] This comes about through the conviction of sin which the Spirit gives, and the testimony he offers that Christ is the remedy. The Spirit then unites men to Christ in his sanctifying power so that just as 'He is our propitiation through faith in his blood as offered', so 'he is our sanctification through faith in his blood as sprinkled'.[8] This is to enjoy a 'spiritual view'[9] of Christ's death, relying on him for the purpose for which he was sent into the world. So the Spirit '*actually communicates* the cleansing, purifying virtue of the blood of Christ unto our souls and consciences, whereby we are freed from shame, and have boldness towards God'.[10]

Owen's emphasis on Christ's blood is directed against those who 'frame us a holiness to consist only in the practice of moral virtue'.[11] Of this he will have none, though he is not averse to the notion of the imitation of Christ.[12] His concern is not, of course, centred on the blood of Christ as *blood*, but on that blood as the *sacrifice of Christ*. At this juncture, what he is saying is that faith in Christ's shed blood is necessary for the enjoyment of the twin benefits of justification, namely, a sense of peace with God and a blameless conscience.

[1]III.438ff.
[2]1 Jn. 1.7; Rev. 1.5; Heb. 9.14; Eph. 5.25–6; Tit. 2.14.
[3]III.440.
[4]See Heb. 9.12–14. Owen sees this as the point of 1 Pet. 1.2.
[5]This Owen draws from the Greek text of Heb. 10.20, 'it *admits of no decays*, but is always new, as unto its efficacy and use, as in the day of its first preparation'. XXIII.505, cf. III.440.
[6]III.442.   [7]*Ibid.*   [8]III.444.   [9]III.445.
[10]*Ibid.*   [11]III.448–9.   [12]I.169.

Owen subsumes this discussion under the thought of sanctification, and as part of its definition. It is indicative of the stress he places upon the unity of the *Spirit's work* in regeneration and sanctification, the relation of the *new nature* to both, and particularly of the central place given in his theology to Jesus Christ.

(2). *Sanctification positively considered*

We turn now in Owen's teaching on sanctification from the negative aspect to the positive. Such distinctions in his thought are not to be considered as in any sense *chronological*; the order is *theological* and *didactic*. Both negative and positive sides to sanctification are concurrent, by necessity, where sanctification is real. Thus, '*in the sanctification of believers, the Holy Ghost doth work in them, in their whole souls, their minds, wills, and affections, a gracious, supernatural habit, principle,* and *disposition of living unto God; wherein the substance or essence, the life and being, of holiness doth consist*'.[1] Here Owen states that a *new nature* is a different thing from *new habits*. This nature comes from God, and breeds a life which is taught by God alone. This is in keeping with his doctrine of conversion. It is the preserving and developing of this, the *image of God* in embryonic form, which is the process of sanctification.[2] The outworking of this in the human dimension involves the believer's obedience to God in the acts and duties of holiness. But in the divine dimension, Owen maintains,

There is an immediate work or effectual operation of the Holy Spirit by his grace required unto every act of holy obedience, whether internal only in faith and love, or external also; that is, unto all the holy actings of our understandings, wills, and affections, and unto all duties of obedience in our walking before God.[3]

The 'habit' of which Owen speaks has the character of an *instinct*. But it is not self-preserving – since it is 'an emanation of virtue and power from him unto us'[4] – it is preserved by the Spirit. This habit cannot be *acquired* by fulfilling duties to God, but it is *preserved* by them.

Owen seeks to establish that such a spiritual habit or

[1]III.469.　　[2]III.330.　　[3]III.472.　　[4]III.475.

principle *is* worked in believers; he quotes a substantial array of
Scriptures to verify the point.[1] 'This the Scripture plentifully
testifieth unto; but withal I must add, that as to the proper
nature or essence of it, no mind can apprehend it, no tongue can
express it, none can perfectly understand its glory'.[2]

Concerning this spiritual habit or nature Owen has three
comments to make.[3] (i) It is by this nature that we have union
with Christ. This union is effected by the indwelling of the Holy
Spirit, but its *formal* cause is the new principle of grace. (ii) This
nature is the root of our likeness and conformity to God, since it
is 'the reparation of his image in us'.[4] (iii) This nature is our
spiritual life by which we are enabled to live for God.

This gracious principle has both the nature and the properties of a *habit*, in that it disposes the subject to acts of its own
kind.[5] By it the law of God is written in men's hearts so that it is
fulfilled by an inner desire, rather than by an external
compulsion. It is expressed, in accordance with its nature, in
the spiritual mindedness of the believer.[6] Owen maintains that
this principle, despite the many variables in the Christian's
experience, is one which remains universal, constant, and
permanent; 'it is immortal, everlasting, and which shall never
absolutely die'.[7]

Such teaching sheds light on Owen's view of progress in
holiness. He is anxious to preserve the permanence of the
change wrought by regeneration, even in the face of sin in the
Christian. He acknowledges that there are 'contrary inclinations and dispositions also',[8] but these proceed from the
'*remainders* of a contrary habitual principle'[9] described in
Scripture as the flesh or indwelling sin. Hence conflict arises:
This is not between the 'distinct faculties of the soul itself'[10] as
in the natural man, but between contrary habits and in-

[1]These are: Deut. 30.6; Jer. 31.33; Ezek. 36.26–7; Jno. 3.6; Gal. 5.17; 2.
Cor. 5.17; Col. 3.10; Eph. 4.23–4; 2 Pet. 1.4.
[2]III.477.   [3]III.478, cf. his application, pp. 478–482.
[4]III.478. He refers here to Eph. 4.23ff.; Col. 3.10.   [5]III.482.
[6]III.484. Further discussion of this is reserved to vol. VII *On Spiritual
Mindedness*; see pp. 254ff.
[7]III.487. Owen's teaching on the nature of regenerating and sanctifying
grace necessitates his view of the perseverance of the saints.
[8]III.488.   [9]*Ibid.*   [10]*Ibid.*

clinations in the *same* mind, will and affections in the believer. That is, the conflict lies, not between the faculties, but 'in the same faculties'.[1] To this the apostle Paul refers in Galatians 5.17. Strictly speaking, 'Sin and grace cannot *bear rule* in the same heart at the same time'.[2] Yet, while sin is dethroned it has never been 'wholly and absolutely dispossessed and cast out of the soul in this life'.[3]

Owen now demonstrates that this new *propensity* in the believer is accompanied by a new *power* of performance.[4] This power is in the mind, where it 'consists in a *spiritual light* and *ability* to discern *spiritual* things in a *spiritual* manner'.[5] It is also in the will, providing an ability to *choose* spiritual things, and in the affections enabling him to *desire* the same. Thus, negatively, the believer is cleansed from the influences of the defilement of sin, and positively he is the recipient of a nature or principle which motivates and energizes him in the ways of the new life.

But this is only one dimension of the aspects of sanctification which Owen discusses. He had maintained with some constancy that the divine element does not empty the human of significance. Now he attempts to vindicate this by dealing in various places with the human *sphere* and activity in the work of sanctification. Owen discusses this theme in the context of man as made in the image of God.

vi. *Restoration of the image of God*

For Owen, the essence of sanctification consists in the restoration of the broken image of God.[6] It is a work of re-creation; and it is by the image being restored that we discover what that image originally was.[7] The restoration 'consists in the communication of the effects and likeness of the same image unto us which was essentially in himself'.[8] Thus we discover what man lost in the fall by learning what is *restored* to him in sanctification.[9]

---

[1] III.488.   [2] III.489.   [3] III.490.   [4] III.492.
[5] III.493; cf. 1 Cor. 2.13 for the thought.
[6] See III.330, 470, 510, 523, 578.
[7] I.63, 74, 294; XII.322, cf. Col. 1.15.
[8] I.219.
[9] Owen, following Calvin, leans on Eph. 4.22–4, Col. 3.9–10 here as elsewhere.

The creation of man was a work of 'signal eminency',[1] because it is the one part of creation preceded by a consultation among the persons of the Trinity in order to display their wisdom. Man was made 'in such a rectitude of nature as represented his [God's] righteousness and holiness – in such a state and condition as had a reflection in it of his *power* and *rule*'.[2] Man's relationship to the world does not itself *constitute* the image of God, but is a *result* of it.

The purpose of God's communicating the *image* to man was threefold: (i) to represent his holiness and righteousness to his creatures;[3] (ii) as a means of rendering glory to his person, in that man alone of all creatures could apprehend and appreciate the glory of God in such a way as to offer intelligent worship;[4] and (iii) to bring man to an eternal *enjoyment* of God through his knowledge of him.[5]

It is this threefold purpose that is frustrated and destroyed by the fall. Its effect was to bring confusion and disorder into the creation.[6] Through the gospel, in the act of regeneration and the work of sanctification, the *image of God* is restored *to us* and is also restored *in us* by our union with Christ through the Spirit. It is restored through *faith* and is characterized by *love*.[7] The restoration of the *image of God* leads to obedience, which while real, is not yet perfect.[8] The *image* is both embryonic and progressive. It is expressed, in accordance with its nature, in the spiritual mindedness of the believer. Owen maintains that this principle, despite the opposition to it from within and without, remains in the believer for ever.

Certain conditions were necessary for the image to be restored through Christ and these have been fulfilled.[9] The

[1]I.181.   [2]*Ibid.*   [3]I.182.   [4]I.183.
[5]*Ibid.*   [6]I.188.   [7]I.149, 154, 168.   [8]I.183; III.482.
[9]Owen deals with these conditions I.195–205. In addition to a return to obedience in man, satisfaction and reparation for past sin needed to be made. For such a restoration, certain conditions would further require fulfilment:
1. An obedience to God bringing more glory to him than Adam's sin brought shame. Owen seems to indicate that there is a kind of moral/aesthetic necessity for Christ to keep the law, to show how suited it really is to man's nature *qua* man.
2. The *disorder* wrought through sin would need to be rectified by punishment.
3. Satan would need to be justly despoiled of his advantage, not by sheer power, but by justice and lawful judgment.

image has been restored *to* man through Christ, and it is, for Owen, by the implanting of the 'seed' of grace previously alluded to, that it is restored *in* man. This is why that 'seed' has the nature and propensities he had outlined. It is this which provides the unity of structure in the Christian life, for the diverse responsibilities of obedience to the commandments, likeness to Christ, restoration to true humanity, and the fulfilling of all duties objectively to God, and internally in personal experience. This will appear as we consider in general the 'acts and duties of holiness'[1] and in particular, the believer's duties to Christ and to his own life.

vii. *The Christian's duty*

The regularity with which Owen uses the term 'duty' indicates its importance in his theology, although nowhere in his writings does he give the idea an extended treatment. The expression covers the whole range of biblical imperatives that are rooted and grounded in the great objective facts of God's grace. The grace of God turns moral duties into evangelical obedience, since it gives men a new disposition:

It reveals its *own mysteries*, to lay them as the foundation . . . it then

---

In order that these might be accomplished:

(i) This should be accomplished *in our nature*, since it was therein that despite was done to divine glory.

(ii) This nature must be derived from the common root of humanity; it could not justly be done by a new creation of God.

(iii) This nature must yet be free from the taint of sin and liability to guilt. For this, more than a man was required:

1. An obedience that would bring more glory to God than had been lost could not be achieved by any man; that obedience needed to have an infinite value, and therefore be rendered by an infinite person.

2. The obedience of a man would affect only himself and not the whole church of God. One who is beyond the requirements of the law is necessary.

3. Since the persons, and the sins involved were innumerable, the value of the obedience and reparation must be infinite too.

4. The person undertaking this work required a special office to perform it.

5. The restoration must bring man to his former condition *and* beyond. It was therefore necessary that it be accomplished by a divine person, lest man be found to owe a special duty, and special worship to any fellow man, and thus detract from the glory of God.

[1]III.527.

grafts all duties of moral obedience on this stock of faith in Christ Jesus. This is the method of the gospel, which the apostle Paul observeth in all his epistles: first, he declares the mysteries of faith that are peculiar to the gospel, and then descends unto those *moral duties* which are regulated thereby.[1]

'Duty' is the whole of man's responsibility to God, originally as a *creature* made in his image, and for the Christian, as a new creature recreated in his image. *Mutatis mutandis*, the duties of man and Christian man are the same, but it is only in the experience of the Christian that these duties come to an obedient fruition. Owen suggests four reasons why this should be so.

(i) Duties are *consistent* with the new 'nature'. 'There is *no duty of holiness whatever*, but there is a *disposition* in a sanctified heart unto it'.[2] It may be that such duties are contrary to natural inclinations or personal advantage, but for Owen it is a fixed principle that 'every nature hath an equal propensity unto all, its natural operations, in their times and seasons'.[3] The individual may be taken by surprise and omit this duty, by sin or the indulgence of the flesh, but this cannot happen habitually where the principle of grace has been imparted.[4] Thus the new 'nature' *tends* 'to make the whole course of obedience and all the duties of it easy unto us, and to give us a facility in their performance'.[5] Since the law is written in the heart by the Spirit, there is a correspondence between our desires and the external law of God that governs our duty.

(ii) Duties cannot be performed without the Spirit's help. Owen has stressed that the seed of grace needs to be watered from above by the Spirit. This is nowhere more necessary than in duties: 'Whatever, therefore, God worketh in us in a way of grace, he prescribeth unto us in a way of duty'.[6] But what duties? Those that are 'appointed by God',[7] that is, in Scripture.

(iii) Duties are defined in Scripture. Since 'The *will of God* is the rule of men's obedience',[8] the conscience of the Christian will be regulated by the revelation of that will in the Scriptures. So 'all our graces and duties must be tried, as unto any

[1]III.279. [2]III.485. [3]*Ibid.* [4]III.497.
[5]III.498. [6]III.433. [7]III.544. [8]III.294.

acceptation with God. Whatever pretends to exceed the direction of the word may safely be rejected – cannot safely be admitted'.[1] Since it is by the hearing of the word that faith comes,[2] it follows:

(iv) Duties must be performed by faith. This is emphasized by Owen in an important passage: the gospel '*grafts all duties* of moral obedience on this stock of faith in Christ Jesus'.[3] Indeed, without faith, no duty performed by man is acceptable to God, since, 'without faith it is impossible to please God'.[4] This is the whole point of the difference between the manner in which Cain and Abel brought their sacrifices to God. Cain's was rejected because it was brought without faith.[5]

In brief, Owen is able to say: 'in every duty two things are principally considered, – first. The *life* and *spring* of it, as it is wrought in us by grace; secondly, The *principal reason* for it and motive unto it, as it is to be performed in ourselves by way of *duty*'.[6]

So much in general concerning duties, but what in particular are the duties which men are to fulfil? These belong to two areas:

(1). *Duty to honour Christ*

The acts and duties, the privileges and benefits of the Christian faith 'have all of them their formal nature and reason from their respect and relation unto the Person of Christ'.[7] Owen outlines the honour that is due to Christ under a number of heads.[8] Our *first* duty is to believe in him and worship him as the Divine Mediator, thus paying respect to both his *person* and his office. John 5.23 confirms that such honour is the will of the Father, and that Christ is to be honoured as (*kathōs*) the Father is – with the same honour, 'divine, sacred, religious, and supreme';[9] and in the same manner, – 'with the same faith, love, reverence, and obedience, always, in all things, in all acts and duties of religion

---

[1]1.143. [2]Rom. 10.17. [3]III.279. [4]Heb. 11.6.
[5]III.294. [6]III.550; V.189. [7]I.104.
[8]I. 103ff. For further elucidation of the honour the believer gives to Christ see II.173, on communion with Christ in purchased grace. Cf. II.195 for the way Christ receives this honour by men regarding him as the Saviour he is.
[9]I.106.

whatever'.[1] It is this kind of honour which is characteristic of true faith. It involves the *adoration* of Christ in his incarnation and humiliation, and now in his exaltation to the right hand of God, as both the lamb slain and the lion of the tribe of Judah (Rev. 5.5–6).[2] This worship will also be expressed in *invocation* at various seasons of the Christian's experience.[3] Such honour, which is characteristic of faith, is also a fruit of faith. Owen draws on Galatians 2.20 and emphasizes the fact that since all spiritual blessings are to be found in Jesus Christ, it is only through *faith in him* that they may be appropriated into men's lives.[4]

Obedience to Christ is an aspect of the honour due to him – not simply in the performance of his requirements, but in the submission of heart to him as God and Mediator. For Owen, it is the mediation of *Jesus* that transforms the Christian's attitude to the law of God:

This renders all our moral obedience evangelical. For there is no duty of it, but we are obliged to perform it in faith through Christ, on the motives of the love of God in him, of the benefits of his mediation, and the grace we receive by him: whatever is otherwise done by us is not acceptable unto God.[5]

It is in this sense that the apostle John speaks of an old and new commandment.[6] Faith in Christ as Mediator renders obedience which is evangelical and no longer legal.

This obedience is animated by *love*, which is its foundation. Owen asserts this from John 14.15 and indicates that already in the Old Testament love was the sum of all obedience. For obedience, '*there is and ought to be, in all believers, a divine, gracious love unto the person of Christ, immediately fixed on him, whereby they are excited unto, and acted in all their obedience unto his authority*'.[7] Owen is at great pains in this context to describe the nature and motives of the believer's love for Christ.[8]

The third way in which this honour-duty is expressed is in conformity to Christ. That conformity is two-fold: it involves the internal grace and holiness of Christ, but also following his example in duties of obedience. Internal conformity is 'the fundamental design of a Christian life'.[9] Fallen human nature

[1]*Ibid.*   [2]I.108.   [3]I.110ff.   [4]I.131.   [5]I.137.
[6]I.136, 1 Jn. 2.7–8.   [7]I.140.   [8]I.139–178.   [9]I.170.

was perfectly restored in Christ and was further granted 'many glorious endowments which Adam was not made partaker of'.[1] Christ then constitutes an example of what God plans to do in the believer. He is 'the pattern and example of the renovation of the image of God in us, and of the glory that doth ensue thereon'.[2] This image is represented to men in the gospel[3] and they are thereby transformed into its likeness, into conformity to Christ, in which the divine life in them consists.

But men are to purpose conformity to Christ by following his example: 'The following the *example* of Christ in all duties towards God and men, in his whole conversation on the earth, is the second part of the instance now given concerning the use of the person of Christ in religion'.[4] This implies an opposition to all sin (since Christ was free from all sin), and an improvement of and growth in every grace, and especially in meekness and self-denial, which Owen aptly describes as 'readiness for the cross'.[5]

(2). *Duty to mortify sin*

The Christian has a duty, secondly, to deal with sin. Owen gave repeated consideration to the problem of sin in the Christian life.[6] The purging of sin, he maintains, is frequently represented in Scripture as a duty.[7]

If sanctification, in Owen's thought, is fundamentally grace received, mortification is grace improved and applied. Owen deals first of all with the *nature* of this duty and then with the *manner* of it. The work of mortification is aimed at the *root* of sin. Owen makes a distinction between 'carnal affections' and their 'fruits'.[8] In Scripture carnal affections are called members, as sin, or the sin-principle, is called the 'body of sin',[9] and because the old man uses these as the body does its own members.[10]

---

[1]*Ibid.*

[2]*Ibid.*, cf. Rom. 8.29; 1 Cor. 15.49; 1 Jno. 3.2; Phil. 3.21; Eph. 4.13, which Owen quotes.

[3]2 Cor. 3.18.   [4]I.175.

[5]I.176, cf. Calvin, *Institutes* III.viii.

[6]See *Works* VI and VII.

[7]III.433, 539.   [8]III.539.   [9]Rom. 6.6; Col. 2.11.

[10]Owen speaks thus of the 'old man': 'These affections and lusts, the old man, – that is, our depraved nature, – useth naturally and readily, as the body doth its members.'

In Scripture mortification is expressed by the verbs *nekroun* and *thanatoun*. *Nekroun* 'signifies a continued act, in taking away the power and force of any thing until it come to be . . . "dead", unto some certain ends or purposes'.[1] Similarly *thanatoun* in Romans 8.13 is 'a work which must be always doing'.[2]

In the biblical teaching, mortification is an ever-present duty, because the presence of indwelling sin is a constant principle in men's lives. This principle is to be considered in a three-fold light: its root, its operation, and its effects. In all three it is opposed to evangelical holiness. Mortification consists of '*taking part* with grace, in its principle, actings, and fruits, against the principle, actings, and fruits of sin'.[3] It therefore consists of three things: a cherishing and improving of the principle of grace by the God-appointed means; frequent exercise in all God-given duties; and application of the principle, power and actings of grace in opposition to sin.[4] The whole process is called 'mortification' because it is opposed to the life of indwelling sin; because it is by nature a violent work, and because the end aimed at is the *destruction* of the principle of sin.[5]

Mortification takes place gradually by guarding against the inclinations and operations of sin.[6] Its end is that we should no longer serve sin.[7] If this work is to be successful it must be universally directed against sin. This is the difference between legal and evangelical mortification. Legal mortification is concerned with particular sins only when the guilt of them reflects upon the conscience; evangelical mortification is concerned to deal with sin in any of its manifestations, because it is opposed to the renovation of the image of God.[8]

In keeping with the tenor of his treatment of sanctification in general, Owen teaches that the duty of mortification can be performed only by the grace of the Holy Spirit (cf. Rom. 8.13). The presence of the Spirit in the believer is the foundation of mortification, since he inhabits men as a temple, and fits them to be his dwelling place. The great motivation to mortification lies in this – to keep the temple of the Spirit undefiled.

Owen taught that mortification by the Spirit is directed

[1]III.540.
[2]*Ibid*. Owen quotes Rom. 6; Gal. 2.20; 5.24; 6.14.
[3]III.543.   [4]III.543–4.   [5]III.544–5.   [6]III.545.
[7]Rom. 6.6.   [8]III.547.

against the old man. This is achieved by the implanting of a contrary principle of spiritual life.[1] The cherishing of this principle encourages the mortification of sin: 'The course I intend is that of labouring universally to improve a principle of holiness, not in this or that way, but in all instances of holy obedience. This is that which will ruin sin, and without it nothing else will contribute thereto'.[2] To this the Spirit enables men 'by those *actual supplies* and *assistances* of *grace* which he continually communicates unto us'.[3]

The Spirit also directs us in the *duties* of mortification, which must first be ascertained, and then rightly performed to the glory of God.

It is by a special application of the death of Christ that the Spirit carries on this work. The death of Christ, by the Spirit, has a special mortifying influence on sin[4] – since it is an oblation for expiating guilt, a power for subduing sin, and, by the Spirit, a union in which the old man is crucified with Christ. This work of the Spirit is carried on through faith and love.[5] Faith in the death of Christ receives that death as an instrument and vehicle of the sin-destroying power of God.[6] Further, when Christ is an object of love to the Christian, mortification is effected by the Christian's commitment to him and to growth in his image.

The Spirit of God further carries on this work by showing the '*true nature* and *certain end* of sin' and 'the *beauty, excellency, usefulness*, and *necessity* of holiness'.[7]

This, then, is the ground-plan of Owen's teaching on Christian living. The embryo of regeneration develops in accordance with its own nature in the vivification of spiritual life, and the mortification of sin. The course of this development is the theme of the exposition which follows.

[1]Gal. 5.16–25. [2]III.553. [3]*Ibid.* [4]III.561.
[5]III.562–5.
[6]Owen in no wise means to degrade the death of Christ; but he wants to clarify its purposiveness, that it is, among other things, a means to an end. It is more than a mere instrument, because it is the death of *Christ*; but it is an instrument in that it is the death ordained by God for dealing with the sin of man. [7]III.565.

❧ 4 ❧

Fellowship with God

We have already seen that union with Jesus Christ is, for Owen, the key to understanding the biblical doctrine of sanctification. Owen nowhere expounds in full this germinal thought. But in the context of the positive features of the Christian life, this theme is given more explicit attention.

The Christian is the object of a great work of God the Spirit. He has experienced in regeneration, however unconsciously, a transition paralleled only by the creation of the world[1] and the resurrection of Christ.[2] In terms of both *status* and *experience*, he has been brought from a condition of alienation from God to communion with him. The Christian life is nothing less than fellowship with God the Trinity, leading to the full assurance of faith.

Old Testament believers enjoyed fellowship with God, but not with the degree of *boldness* of which the New Testament speaks,[3] or in the freedom and liberty of the children of God. But now this is the enjoyment of the Christian.[4] His fellowship, or communion with God 'consisteth in his *communication of himself unto us, with our returnal unto him* of that which he requireth and accepteth, flowing from that *union* which in Jesus Christ we have with him'.[5] It is alternatively described as 'the mutual

---

[1] 2 Cor. 4.6.   [2] Eph. 2.1.   [3] XXI.429; XXIII.500–2.

[4] Owen further explains this transition from Old Testament experience to that of the New Testament. Through the gospel two things are removed: (i) a bondage frame of spirit, Rom. 8.15; 2 Cor. 3.12–18, the 'legal diffidence and distrust in our approaches unto God, which shuts up the heart, straitens the spirit and takes away the liberty of treating with him as a father', and, (ii) a disbelief of acceptation (XXI.429).

[5] II.8.

communication of such good things as wherein the persons holding that communion are delighted, bottomed upon some union between them'.[1] Both the union with Christ which gives the Christian his *status* before God, and the communion with God which is the fruit of that status, are thus subsumed under the notion of communion, and this is the sense in which Owen generally employs the expression.[2]

Owen's exposition is distinguished by the thought that the Christian enjoys a *distinct* communion with each person of the Trinity. As in the (spurious) text of 1 John 5.7 the three persons are said to bear *testimony*, so the Christian has *communion* with each.[3] More convincingly, in 1 Corinthians 12.4–6, according to Owen's exegesis, emphasis is laid upon each person, and *communion* with each in the *communication* of each.[4] Similarly in Ephesians 2.18, the approach to God in fellowship is distinctly related to each person of the Godhead.

Further support for this view is drawn from the ways in which the persons of the Trinity are combined in various passages: the Father and the Son,[5] sometimes the Son only,[6] and sometimes the Spirit only.[7] To this proof, Owen further adds the axiom that all the activity of faith has reference to one distinct person of the Trinity, as do all receptions of grace.[8] This is what he means by fellowship or communion. Thus the

---

[1] *Ibid.*

[2] See also V.34 where Owen enlarges on the foundation of this communion in terms of the Old Testament sacrificial system and its fulfilment in the New Testament.

[3] Calvin's discussion of the authenticity of the text, *The Gospel according to John 11–21 and The First Epistle of John*, trans. T. H. L. Parker, ed. D. W. & T. F. Torrance, Edinburgh, 1961, p. 303, suggests that Owen would also have been familiar with the textual problem. But he rarely employs the passage (V.406 only), and his argument is not dependent upon it for its validity.

[4] 1 Cor. 12.4 is taken as a reference to the Holy Spirit; v.5 as a reference to the Son, and v.6 as a reference to the Father. This is the accepted interpretation in the reformed tradition. Calvin says 'I have no objection to this interpretation of the verses', although he feels it did not really enhance the case of the Fathers against the Arians, *The First Epistle of Paul to the Corinthians*, trans. J. W. Fraser, ed. D. W. & T. F. Torrance, Edinburgh, 1960, pp. 259–261. Cf. C. Hodge, *An Exposition of the First Epistle to the Corinthians*, r.i. London, 1958, pp. 242–3.

[5] 1 Jn. 1.3; Jn. 14.23.   [6] 1 Cor. 1.9; Rev. 3.20.
[7] 2 Cor. 3.14.   [8] II.15.

Father communicates by original authority, the Son from a purchased treasury and the Spirit in immediate efficacy.[1] The reader of Owen might naturally remind him at this juncture of Augustine's theological axiom that the external works of the Trinity cannot be divided (*opera ad extra Trinitatis indivisa sunt*), only to discover Owen himself quoting the same maxim to balance what he has just said![2] He clarifies his position by stressing that he refers to the *eminence* of each person in respect of communion. This is the classical doctrine of *Appropriations*.

i. *Communion with the Father*

Communion with God the Father is pre-eminently in *love*, the manifestation of which is the 'peculiar work of the gospel'.[3] Numerous passages substantiate this. When God is described as love in 1 John 4.8, it is the Father who is in view;[4] in the benediction of 2 Corinthians 13.14, the love in view is that of the Father. In John 16.27, Jesus emphasizes the love of the Father as the source of salvation; in Romans 5.5 the effusion of love in the Christian's heart is the knowledge of the Father's love.[5]

By definition, however, this love must be received and reciprocated for communion to take place,[6] and so the Christian must have made a suitable response to the overtures of divine grace. How is this to be done? Owen's answer is that the love of the Father must be *contemplated* if it is to be received. He is concerned that Christians tend to look at the Father 'with anxious, doubtful thoughts,'[7] with harmful consequences to their understanding and experience of his love: 'What fears, what questionings are there, of his good-will and kindness! At the best, many think there is no sweetness at all in him towards us, but what is purchased at the high price of the blood of Jesus'.[8]

To this recurring pastoral problem we must return later in the present chapter.[9] For the moment it is sufficient to indicate that, for Owen, the death of Christ did not purchase the

---

[1]II.17.   [2]II.18.   [3]II.19.
[4]Interestingly, in IV.370 he refers these words to the whole Trinity.
[5]II.20–21.   [6]II.22ff.   [7]II.32.   [8]*Ibid.*
[9]See pp. 86ff. Cf. VI.570ff.

Father's love, but is the way in which that love is communicated. The death of Christ is not the cause of the Father's love, but is its effect.

The Christian should therefore meditate on the eternal quality of God's love, the freeness and unchangeableness of its nature, and marvel at its characteristic of distinguishing among men.[1] Here he quotes Augustine approvingly: 'God loves all things he has made; and among them he loves his rational creatures more, and, from them, he loves those who are members of his only begotten. And much more he loves his only begotten.'[2]

Given a Christian who shares Owen's Calvinistic theology and enjoys a measure of assurance of his gracious standing before God, it is not difficult to see how these last meditations will lead him to wonder at such discriminating love. But it nonetheless raises the question: 'How can I know God loves *me*?'. In fact Owen proceeds to answer a question framed in these very words, although he is more concerned to discuss the manner of knowing rather than the *assurance of love*.[3] Although this assurance 'be carried on by spiritual sense and experience, yet it is received purely by believing'.[4] But we do not need to look elsewhere for an explanation of how, in the face of distinguishing and electing love, a man may be assured of God's love for *him*: 'Never any one from the foundation of the world, who believed such love in the Father, and made returns of love to him again, was deceived. . . . If thou believest and receivest the Father as love, he will infallibly be so to thee'.[5]

ii. *Communion with the Son*

While communion with the Father is in love, communion with the Son is in *grace*.[6] He is full of grace,[7] which, Paul prays, may be shared with the Christian.

The notion of grace is a very wide-ranging one,[8] and Owen

[1]II.33.   [2]*Ibid.*
[3]II.36. We *know* by *believing* what is revealed.
[4]*Ibid.*   [5]II.36–7.   [6]II.47; cf. I.363–5.
[7]III.414, 521.   [8]II.47–8; VII.545; IX.482.

uses it in a comprehensive sense. The Christian's communion in the grace of Christ indicates his enjoyment of Christ's personal presence and graciousness.[1] This is, as Owen expresses it, 'personal grace'. But further, Christ's free favour and acceptance is enjoyed, and the characteristics of grace are produced in the Christian's life as the fruit of the Spirit. These Owen thinks of as constituting 'purchased grace'.[2]

(1). *Personal grace* is two-sided. It is seen in the mediation of Christ: in his fitness to save, from the grace of union; his fulness to save from the grace of communion, and his power to capture men's love, from his complete suitability to meet all the needs and desires of men.[3] It is also seen in the conjugal relation between Christ and his people. 'He is married unto us, and we unto him',[4] so that the true response to the offer of Christ is 'The *liking* of Christ for his *excellency*, grace and suitableness' and 'The *accepting* of Christ by the *will*, as its only husband, Lord and Saviour'.[5] Communion is then a matter for the will as much as for the spiritual senses.

This communion in the personal grace of Christ may best be summarized by considering Owen's interpretation of the Song of Solomon, which vividly illustrates his axiom that the Christian life is one of 'spiritual sense and experience'.[6]

This fact must itself be set in context. Owen was not inclined to mysticism in the narrow sense. There is therefore no suggestion that he *develops* his Christology from Canticles.[7] Rather Owen *illustrates* this doctrine in terms of the Christian's experience, by the poetry of the Song of Solomon. He does not subjectivize Christ to the point of mysticism, but rather tries to describe the subjective experience of the objective Christ to whom the rest of Scripture bears witness. The Song of Solomon is for him a transcript of the affections of Christian experience.

It should also be said in this context, that our interest in the Song of Solomon lies in Owen's use of its theme rather than the principles of his Biblical exegesis. No doubt, since this is one of only two books of the Bible (Hebrews being the other) on which he committed to print a fairly detailed exposition, it has a kind

[1]II.47. [2]II.48. [3]II.51. [4]II.54.
[5]II.58. [6]II.36. [7]See volume I, 1–272.

of antiquarian interest for the history of interpretation. But that
is of marginal significance for establishing the doctrinal and
practical use to which Owen put it.

Owen summarizes the significance of Canticles thus: 'This
sense of the love of Christ, and the effect of it in communion
with him, by prayer and praises, is divinely set forth in the Book
of Canticles. The church therein is represented as the spouse of
Christ; and, as a faithful spouse, she is always either solicitous
about his love, or rejoicing in it'.[1] 'In brief, this whole book is
taken up in the description of the communion that is between
the Lord Christ and his saints'.[2]

We are not given a full interpretation of the Song, although the main lines are made plain: Christ and the Christian (sometimes corporately one church) are the two main
characters. Owen's interpretation is largely individualistic.
The daughters of Jerusalem represent 'all sorts of
professors';[3] the watchmen represent office-bearers; and the
city represents the visible church. There is a hint here that
the interpretation is controlled by Owen's own thought on
spiritual experience, to the point that this becomes the ex-
egetical principle itself.

In *Canticles 2.1–7* we have a central passage. Here Christ is
seen as describing his own character and his significance to the
Christian: he is the rose of Sharon and the lily of the valley. He
is pre-eminent in personal graces, as the rose abounds in
perfume and the lily in beauty. The rose is from Sharon, the
fertile plain in which the choicest herds are reared. Christ can
'allure'[4] the Christian by the excellence of his character. As
God has the savour of Christ's blood[5] so Christians enjoy the
savour of him as the rose. Owen obviously found it a little
difficult to keep the allegorical method of interpretation under
control!

Now Christ describes what the church means to him. She is a
lily among thorns – the same description is given to the church
as to Christ, from which Owen draws the lesson that this can
only be through the bond that unites them as one. The church is

[1]I.116. [2]II.46. [3]II.55. [4]II.42.
[5]*Ibid.* Cf. Eph. 5.2. Owen understands this in the sense of its moral and
spiritual character as atonement.

thus described in terms of her significance to Christ (a lily) and her trials in the world (among thorns).[1]

This conversation and communion is continued by the thoughts of the spouse about her divine lover. He is compared to the apple tree,[2] since he provides fruit for food and shade for refreshment. All others are as fruitless leaves to a hungry soul. He alone provides shelter, 'from wrath without, and refreshment because of weariness from within . . . from the power of *corruptions*, trouble of temptations, distress of persecutions, there is in him quiet, rest, and repose, Matthew 11.27, 28'.[3] So, in the verses following, the communion enjoyed with Christ is further delineated, and is characterized by several features.

(i) *Sweetness*. 'He brought me to his banqueting house . . .' that is, the supplies of grace revealed in the gospel. Indeed, his love is better than wine,[4] since it is not meat and drink, but righteousness, joy and peace in the Holy Spirit.[5] Wine, says Owen, cheers the heart and makes us forget our misery; it gives us a glad countenance. This is what we receive spiritually in the ordinances of the gospel.

(ii) *Delight*. The maiden is overcome with this (Song 2.5) and wants to know more of his love. She is 'sick of love', 'not (as some suppose) fainting for want of a sense of love,' but, according to Owen, 'made sick and faint, even overcome, with the mighty actings of that divine affection, after she had once tasted of the sweetness of Christ in the banqueting house'.[6]

(iii) *Safety* (Song 2.4). His banner over her was love. Here is the symbol of safety and protection and a token of success and victory. Any experience that comes upon the Christian must first press through the banner of Christ's love. This assures him and the church of their great safety.[7]

(iv) *Support and Consolation* (Song 2.6). His left hand is under her head and his right hand embraces her.[8] Here we have the picture of Christ supporting the church and also nourishing and cherishing her. So their fellowship is sustained and

---

[1]II.42. [2]I.43. [3]II.43–44. [4]Song of Sol. 1.2; II. 44.
[5]Rom. 14.17. [6]II.44.
[7]II.45. [8]*Ibid.*

continued (Song 2.7).

The response of the Christian to this is an increased desire for the continuing presence of Christ. Thus on Song 2.7, Owen says, 'A believer that hath gotten Christ in his arms, is like one that hath found great spoils, or a pearl of price. He looks about him every way, and fears everything that may deprive him of it'.[1]

In Song 2.9 Christ reappears. The lover shows himself through the lattice, and this is interpreted as follows: 'our sight of him here is as it were by glances, – liable to be clouded by many interpositions. . . . There is . . . instability and imperfection in our view and apprehension of him. . . . In the meantime he looketh through the *windows* of the ordinances of the Gospel'.[2] When the Christian has turned away in heart, Christ comes, searching and longing for loving service. If he does not receive it, he will withdraw. It would be impossible within the general framework of Owen's theology to suppose that this involves severed relationships; rather it seems to imply disjointed experience and broken fellowship. Christ is still the Christian's possession and vice-versa, but the *sense* of this has gone from his heart.

In chapter 3 the spouse discovers that her lover has withdrawn. She is perplexed. Owen is not clear whether this is the cause or the effect of the 'night' in which she discovers herself, but points to the application: 'in the greatest peace and opportunity of ease and rest, a believer finds none in the absence of Christ: though he be on his bed, having nothing to disquiet him, he rests not, if Christ his rest, be not there'.[3] So the soul searches for Christ, first of all in the ordinary duties of faith,[4] but 'this is not a way to recover a sense of lost love'[5] – rather there must be 'Resolutions for new, extraordinary, vigorous, constant applications unto God as the first general step and degree of a sin-entangled soul acting towards a recovery'.[6]

It is evident that here the soul has lost its sense of forgiveness. The quest for its restoration involves two things: *first*, a search of the believer's soul to discover the cause of Christ's absence,

[1]II.126. [2]I.377. [3]II.128.
[4]VI.613. [5]VI.353. [6]*Ibid.*

and, *second*, a search of the promises of God to discover the means of his return.[1] Self-examination must be followed by a reapplication to the covenant of grace. If this yields no success, the solution is to be found in extraordinary duties as Owen has already hinted. So the spouse goes about the city (the visible church) looking for her lover.[2] If Christ is not found in private, it is the Christian's duty to make a special search for him in public, through worship, the preaching of the word, and the sacraments. In her search the maiden is found by the watchmen, (office-bearers in the visible church): 'it is of sad consideration, that the Holy Ghost doth sometimes in this book take notice of them on no good account. Plainly, chap. v.7, they turn persecutors'.[3] Owen finds support for this view in Luther's sentiment that 'Religion was never in danger except among the "most reverend",' a reason he elsewhere[4] gives for his dislike of the title 'reverend'! But in fact in this instance the watchmen take notice of the plight of the spouse. This is the duty of faithful office-bearers.[5] Exactly how Christ is discovered is not indicated in the passage, but Owen detects some significance in this too. When Christ is sought he comes in his own mysterious way by the Spirit.

By chapter 5 the spouse has sunk again into sloth and indolence. The shepherd-lover comes to meet with her, but she excuses herself by the inconvenience of the time and her lack of preparation.[6] Christ, thus rebuffed, leaves the believer disconsolate in the dark, and 'long it is before she obtains any recovery'.[7] He returns later in the chapter, and the description given in Song 5.10–16 provides Owen with a further opportunity to expound what the Christian finds in his Saviour.

Christ is described as being 'white and ruddy'. 'He is *white* in the glory of his *Deity*, and *ruddy* in the preciousness of his *humanity*'.[8] White is the colour of glory; red is the colour of man made from the dust of the earth, yet in the image of God, man being originally called Adam because of the redness of the earth from which he was made. So the expression here 'points him [Christ] out as the second Adam, partaker of flesh and blood,

---

[1]II.128ff.   [2]II.130.   [3]II.130–1.   [4]XIII.302.
[5]II.131.   [6]VI.520.   [7]VI.396.   [8]II.49.

because the children partook of the same, Heb. ii.14'. He is also white in his innocence, and ruddy 'in the *blood* of his oblation'; 'by his whiteness he fulfilled the law; by his redness he satisfied justice'. Further his perfect administration of the kingdom of God is expressed – he is white with love and mercy to his own people, and red with justice and revenge on his enemies. It is this perfect *union* of the 'white and ruddy', that fits him to be the Saviour, and brings salvation through our union and communion with him.[1] This is exegesis in the allegorical tradition; Owen has gathered the doctrines of the two natures of Christ, his one person, his work as second Adam, his active and passive obedience, and his life as the source of man's salvation, out of this one phrase. Nevertheless, his stress on Christ's humanity is worthy of note.

In the following verses in chapter 5 the maiden goes on to describe Christ more fully. His *head* is as fine gold, conveying the splendour and durability of Christ as the head of the government of the kingdom of God.[2] His *locks* are said to be 'bushy' or curled, 'black as a raven'. At first sight the hair seems tangled, but in fact it is well ordered, thus representing the wisdom of Christ in his mediatorial administration. The *hair* is black to indicate that his ways are past finding out, and, in a natural sense, to emphasize his comeliness and vigour.

The lover's *eyes* are like those of the dove (not a bird of prey), indicating the wealth of his knowledge and discernment. They are tender and pure as he discerns the thoughts and intentions of men.[3] His *cheeks* are like beds of spices, sweet of savour, beautiful in their orderliness;[4] so the graces of Christ, in his human nature, are gathered by Christians in prayer, from the covenant promises of God which are well ordered.[5] These graces are eminent indeed, like 'a tower of perfumes'.[6] His *lips* are like lilies dropping myrrh, a description of the riches of Christ's word.[7] His *hands*, refers to the work he has accomp-

[1]II.50–1. [2]II.70–1.
[3]II.72–3. [4]II.75.
[5]2 Sam. 23.5.
[6]II.76. Owen adopts the marginal reading for Song 5.13 (A.V.).
[7]*Ibid.*

lished, as the fruit of his love.[1] His *belly*[2] reminds us of his tenderness and affection. His *legs, countenance* and *mouth* remind the Christian of the stability of his kingdom, and the grace and faithfulness of his promises. He is completely worthy of the desires and affections of his followers[3] in his birth, life and death, in the whole course of his work; in the glory of his coronation and the supply he grants of the Spirit of God, in the ordinances of worship, the tenderness of his care, and the justice of his vengeance upon his enemies as in the pardon he dispenses to his people.[4]

It is this Christ who often draws near to the Christian, quite often by surprise, when he is engaged in his ordinary thoughts and finds them involuntarily filled with Christ. Such experiences should always be balanced, says Owen, against worldly thoughts invading the believer's devotions, lest the latter cause him to despair.[5]

Thus the Christian will be led to the prayer of Song 8.6 ('Set me as a seal upon your heart . . .') in which the worst thought 'they have of hell, is, that they shall not enjoy Jesus Christ'.[6] In this context[7] Owen stresses the importance of distinguishing between *unbelief* and *spiritual jealousy*, which are readily confused. In jealousy for Christ it is the individual's own sense of unworthiness that is the cause of his trouble;[8] he must learn not only the maiden's view of the beloved (the Christian's admiration for Christ) but also the beloved's love for the maiden (the loving justification granted by Christ to his people).

Owen's exposition is, admittedly, fragmentary and occasional. Nevertheless it is sufficient to give a lasting impression of what he believed was involved in experimental Christianity. He describes a communion between Christ and the Christian which is one of mutual affection, touching the Christian's spiritual sensitivity and moulding his affections. Thus the believer's affections, as well as his mind and will, are devoted to Christ, and increasingly restored to their

---

[1]II.77.
[2]Owen takes the expression in the A.V. sense of 'bowels'.
[3]II.77.   [4]II.78.   [5]VII.304.   [6]II.140.
[7]Cf. VI.558f.   [8]VI.559.

proper function by him. But Owen does not fall into the mistake
of teaching that a man may be *justified* by love. Yet he does
recognize that the faith that receives justification works by love,
which is the fruit of faith in the context of a true relationship to
Christ.

We noted above the emphasis that is placed by Owen on
the humanity of Jesus. This should be a principal object of
the Christian's meditations; it is the theological key which
opens the way for the development of the emotional aspect of
man's being in Christian experience. It is no surprise to
rediscover this emphasis reappearing in Owen's teaching on
the Lord's Supper.[1] Here Owen seeks to penetrate beyond
the doctrine of the humanity of Christ as a theological
formulation, to the spiritual reality of Christ's presence
clothed in that humanity, assumed and restored, in which
the believer shares by faith. For him the fact that Christ was
made like men, sin apart, is the source for the true healing of
our emotions.

This leads to the conclusion that in fact this dimension of
Owen's thought is all of a piece with his total picture of
sanctification. It is the restoring of the *imago dei* in the whole of
man, wherever it has been marred. This involves the re-
integration of all the dimensions of man's existence, so that
faith, reason, and emotion are not only cleansed and healed,
but reunited in an original harmony.

Perhaps these facts help to guard the student of Owen from
a failure to appreciate his theology. In the mass of strong and
rigorous teaching he gives, it would be possible to lose sight of
the tenderness of spiritual experience that is well brought out when
he discusses the Song of Solomon. It would be impossible to
think of some of Owen's theological discussions as tender in
any ordinary sense! But it would be unfair to his vision of
Jesus Christ and the Christian life to fail to see that tenderness
was something he trusted would be produced by it. He comes
nearest to portraying a tender Christ with a merciful heart
when he uses this love allegory. He also comes nearest here to
showing the *enjoyment of faith* which the Christian may know.
This, after all, is the goal of all his negative emphasis on sin

[1]Below, p. 220ff.

and mortification. None of that is obscured, but rather illustrated in the vagaries of the maiden in the Song. But Owen here makes plainer and simpler the fact that repentance and obedience lead to enjoyment of Christ and communion with him.

(2). Communion with Christ is also in what Owen calls *'purchased grace'*. We have already hinted that, for Owen, the picture conveyed by this expression could not be, and is *not* that of a reluctant Father being persuaded by the high bidding of the Son to pardon sinners.[1] The love of the Father 'in itself, is antecedent to the purchase of Christ'.[2] While the work of Christ is 'the way of communication', 'the free fountain and spring of all is in the bosom of the Father'.[3] It is the Father's love which provides the ransom[4] and his justice which accepts its saving merit.[5] Even when Owen is working strictly within the legal aspects of the atonement he does not for a moment lose sight of the fact that the work of redemption is the loving plan of the Father. His emphasis is rather on the fact that Christ's work *justly* provides for sinners. It is not that salvation is wrung from a reluctant Father, but rather that it is provided for undeserving sinners. In Owen's terminology, purchased grace refers to the *actual application* of the plan of redemption.

Communion with Christ in purchased grace is many-sided, because there is 'almost nothing that Christ hath done, which is a spring of that grace whereof we speak, but we are said to do it with him'.[6]

Its foundation is to be found in three aspects of Christ's mediation: the obedience of his life, the sufferings of his death, and the continuance of his intercession. These correspond to the graces of justification, sanctification, and privilege. The obedience of his life has precedence in the order of the procuring of salvation, though preceded *in application* by the benefits of his death, because of 'the state and condition

---

[1]See above pp. 76ff.   [2]II.20.   [3]II.32.
[4]X.231, 259; cf. XX.379; XXIII.283.
[5]XII.522. Cf. also XXII.508 for how Christ 'purchased' grace, and what 'grace' he purchased.
[6]II.155.

[86]

wherein we are'.[1] He became obedient to the law of creation by his incarnation, but he also became obedient to the law of Moses by way of substitution. Owen regards this as a necessity for the accomplishing of salvation. This is Christ's *active obedience*.

As man's substitute, Christ became liable to the law's penalties as well as bound to its duties: 'He lived for us, he died for us; he was ours in all he did, in all he suffered'.[2] His death, briefly expounded, is regarded as *price, sacrifice* and *penalty*. But Christ also rose 'for our justification'.[3] and this is taken to include his intercession as High Priest.[4] He now appears before God for men, having procured the Holy Spirit 'effectually to collate and bestow all this purchased grace upon us'.[5]

The grace thus purchased brings with it acceptance with God, sanctification by him, and spiritual privileges from him.[6] It *restores* fellowship because it removes the ground of enmity (that for which men are condemned) and gives in its place that righteousness for which men are accepted. The two aspects are important both doctrinally and practically for the Christian, for he is not brought by grace into a state of neutrality with God. Rather, whereas he was *an enemy* he becomes a *friend*. Guilt is indeed removed, but:

The old quarrel may be laid aside, and yet no new friendship begun; we may be not sinners, and yet not be so far righteous as to have a right to the kingdom of heaven. Adam had no right to life because he was innocent; he must, moreover, 'do this' and then he shall 'live'. He must not only have a *negative* righteousness, – he was not guilty of anything; but also a *positive* righteousness, – he must do all things.[7]

Therefore Christ's righteousness in his active obedience is imputed to men, because it was accomplished 'for us'.[8]

---

[1]*Ibid.*
[2]II.165. While using the classical reformed terminology of 'active obedience', Owen regarded the expression 'passive obedience' for this aspect of Christ's work as grammatically improper (obedience, by its very nature could never be *merely* passive) II.163; cf. II.159.
[3]Rom. 4.25. [4]II.168. [5]*Ibid.*
[6]II.169
[7]II.170. [8]*Ibid.*

Those thus accepted are progressively sanctified: 'He makes us not only *accepted*, but also *acceptable*'.[1] Christ came not only by blood (i.e. for pardon) but by water and blood (1 Jn. 5.6 i.e. for cleansing and pardon). These cannot be separated in Christian experience because they are united in the Christ from whom we receive salvation. In this way, communion with Christ involves the removal of inner defilement through the progressive cleansing of man's *nature*, by removing the pollution of actual transgressions, and also by cleansing the defilement of his best duties.[2] Thus, 'the saints' good works shall meet them one day with a changed countenance, that they shall scarce know them: that which seemed to them to be black, deformed, defiled, shall appear beautiful and glorious; they shall not be afraid of them, but rejoice to see and follow them'.[3]

Here the stress is on the negative aspects of sanctification, but of emphasizing these Owen never seems to tire. More positively, the Christian receives through Christ inner holiness by virtue of the Holy Spirit, 'the prime and principal gift of sanctification'.[4] He is the principle of all habitual grace, in the exercise of which Christ thus provides a continuing influence.

There is also the privilege of a new standing before God, of sonship in his family, and of adoption, which Owen recognizes as a primary gospel privilege from which other '*favours* of the gospel'[5] proceed.

How then is this communion enjoyed? What is required of believers if they are to see their *union* with Christ becoming a *communion* with him?

Christians must learn first of all to approve the divine way of salvation: 'they consider, approve of, and rejoice in, the way, means, and thing itself'.[6] They see the necessity for righteousness in Christ because they realize the poverty of their own righteousness. They see that Christ is full of wisdom and grace, and that the way of salvation in him brings peace and security to themselves. They rejoice in it because it brings honour to Christ from his Father, from the angels, and from the

[1]*Ibid.* [2]I.177. [3]II.171.
[4]II.172. [5]II.173, cf. below, pp. 123–4. [6]II.193.

reconciled universe.[1] This leads men to 'an *actual commutation* with the Lord Jesus as to their sins and his righteousness'.[2]

The Christian, according to Owen, maintains a sense of his continuing sinfulness; he gathers together his thoughts about individual sins, and, deliberately remembering that Christ died for these, and hearing his summons to come to him, makes an exchange, laying down his sins at the cross of Christ, and taking from him the righteousness, in all its dimensions, that he procured.[3] Here we meet again the recurring theme in Owen's teaching, that the pattern of inauguration into Christian experience is the foundation on which the whole of it is to be built. If becoming a Christian involves faith and repentance,[4] then the whole of the Christian life will also bear that character. Sanctification is the flower from the seed of regeneration.

The Christian also enjoys communion with Christ in his holiness. Christ's part in such fellowship lies in his intercession and sending of the Spirit who binds his people in union to him.[5] The Christian's experience then is of '*a new, gracious . . . principle, created, and bestowed on the soul, whereby it is changed in all its faculties and affections, fitted and enabled to go forth in the way of obedience unto every divine object that is proposed unto it, according to the mind of God*'.[6] Holiness is therefore developed in the character of the Christian because he receives grace from 'the Lord Jesus as the great Joseph, that hath the disposal of all the granaries of the kingdom of heaven committed unto him; as one in whom it hath pleased the Father to gather all things unto a head'.[7]

The Christian finally enjoys communion with Christ in the privileges of grace. The highest of these is *adoption*. Christians are the sons of God: '*adoption is the authoritative translation of a believer, by Jesus Christ, from the family of the world and Satan into the family of God, with his investiture in all the privileges and advantages of that family*'.[8] It might be thought that any treatment of *adoption* should really be reserved under the heading of communion with the Father. But Owen is concerned to emphasize that the grace of adoption is only possible *through Christ*.

Five things are required for adoption: (i) that the person first belongs to another family; (ii) that there is a family to which he has no right to belong; (iii) that there is an authoritative legal

[1]II.191–2.   [2]II.193.   [3]II.193–4.   [4]II.196.
[5]II.202.   [6]II.200.   [7]II.203.   [8]II.207; cf. II.173.

translation from one family to another; (iv) that the adopted person is freed from all the legal obligations of the family from which he came; (v) and that by virtue of his translation he is invested with all the rights, privileges, and advantages of the new family.[1] All of this is exemplified in the divine adoption. Thus, John 1.12 describes the legal aspect of spiritual adoption ('the right [= authority] to become children of God'), Colossians 1.12 the public proclamation of it: to angels, who are also sons of God;[2] to Satan, to whom it is 'denounced';[3] and *to the person adopted*, through whose conscience the Spirit of God bears witness to his sonship.[4]

Furthermore, the Christian is invested with the rights of sonship, and receives a new name,[5] the guarantee of his admission to the house of God. His own name is written in the Lamb's Book of Life.

The primary privilege of union to Christ,[6] that of being adopted sons, brings with it subsidiary blessings. In particular, spiritual freedom is enjoyed, coming from the Spirit of adoption; freedom from the condemnation of the law and its penalty; and freedom from the dominion of sin. But freedom *for* God and his service is also enjoyed in the household of faith. The only freedom a slave could enjoy would be *from* his duty, says Owen, but God's child may enjoy a freedom *in* his duty, since it is grounded in love, reciprocally manifested between Father and son. The child can therefore experience largeness of heart and a 'son-like freedom of the Spirit in obedience'.[7] He is not without law to God, but under the law of Christ.[8] The maintenance of liberty for the main-stream Puritans was always dependent upon this paradox.[9]

It is worth noting how Owen develops this theme of son-like obedience. It is seen in the *principle* of spiritual service, which is life and love;[10] life gives power for obedience, love gives joy and pleasure in it. The way of new obedience is now a pleasure, since God is a Father, whereas before it was a burden because God was regarded as an enemy. Love has become the *motive*: 'What a freedom is this! what a largeness of spirit is in them

[1]II.207–8.   [2]Job 1.6; Lk. 15.10.   [3]II.210.
[4]Rom. 8.14–15; Gal. 4.6.   [5]Rev. 2.17.   [6]I.469.   [7]II.213.
[8]1 Cor. 9.21, which Owen nowhere seems to have treated.
[9]See Kevan, *op. cit.*, pp. 185–6.   [10]II.213.

who walk according to this rule!'[1] The *manner* of obedience is willingness, since his sons give themselves with a whole heart to God. The *rule* of it is the law of liberty, since the law is stripped of all its terrifying power to condemn 'and rendered, in the blood of Jesus, sweet, tender, useful, directing, – helpful as a rule of walking in the life they have received'.[2]

As well as liberty, sonship brings *title*: the Christian is an heir of grace and of the promises of God. This respects *spiritual* wealth primarily, and a place in the kingdom of heaven now, followed by a future entrance into the kingdom of glory. But since Christ, with whom the believer is a fellow heir[3] is himself the heir of all things[4] the believer also has a share in this world, and a right to possess its goods. The title deeds to the world, forfeited by Adam, were regained by Christ, and through grace are shared with his disciples.[5] He has the rights of the Lord of the house; Christians have the rights of servants.[6] Owen has already conveyed the wonder of the privilege of adoption. Now he balances it with the paradox that the Christian never ceases to be a servant in relation to his Lord.

Sonship also brings *boldness*, which Owen has already treated briefly. It also involves the *discipline* which is described in Hebrews 12.3–6. The child of God sees his sufferings as 'for our education and instruction in his family'.[7] The Christian is enjoined not to despise these,[8] but to use them for personal benefit, and to seek for the will and purpose of God through such chastisements. Indeed this is the evidence of God's love for us and of the genuineness of sonship, since the motive behind chastisement is love: 'there is nothing properly penal in the chastisements of believers'.[9] Chastisement therefore is 'a companion of them that *are in the way*, and of them only'.[10] Thus, 'There is no chastisement in heaven, nor in hell. Not in heaven, because there is no sin; not in hell, because there is no amendment'.[11] This puts the Christian's suffering in its true context of spiritual and moral growth to such an extent that Owen can insist that 'Divine love and chastening are inseparable',[12] so that when Hebrews speaks of God 'scourging every

[1]II.215. [2]*Ibid.* [3]Rom. 8.17. [4]Heb. 1.2.
[5]II.219. [6]*Ibid.* [7]XXIV.257. [8]*Ibid.*
[9]XXIV.260. [10]*Ibid.* [11]*Ibid.* [12]XXIV.261.

son . . .',[1] Owen takes this as referring to the special severity of chastening which the most outstanding Christians have known.[2]

What then is the Christian's attitude to be when he suffers as a child of God? He is not simply to steel himself against suffering, but rather to 'take in a deep sense of his rebukes and chastisements'.[3] This is something only faith can do.

The *benefits* of such chastisement and discipline are simple but important. It yields spiritual fruit, through faith;[4] the pruning of sin brings an increase in the growth and progress of holiness.[5] It produces righteousness in the life, and especially submission to the will of God and a weaning from the world.[6] It brings forth peace. This of course is *through* and *after* chastisements, since 'They first tend to subdue the flesh, to root up weeds, thorns and briers, to break up the stubborn fallow ground, and then to cherish the seeds of righteousness'.[7]

iii. *Communion with the Holy Spirit*

The Holy Spirit proceeds from the Father and the Son[8] and that in two ways: with respect to his substance (*phusikē*) and his 'dispensatory proceeding' (*oikonomikē*).[9] Owen focuses his attention on the latter in this context. The coming of the Holy Spirit (Jn. 15.26–16.5) is not his eternal procession, but his economic function, to testify to Christ. He comes willingly and freely, but he is also given authoritatively by the Father and the Son. But distinction in office does not deny equality in nature.[10] For the *authority* of the Spirit is one with that of the Father and the Son. For Owen this explains why the sin against the Spirit should be alone without pardon, since he comes *in the name of* the Trinity.[11]

If believers are to know the Father through the Son, they must first experience the Spirit and know his influences on their lives leading them to the fountain of grace. So prayer is made to the Father for the gift the Spirit, who, in the New Testament

---

[1]Heb. 12.6. [2]XXIV.262. [3]XXIV.273. [4]XXIV.279.
[5]XXIV.274. [6]XXIV.275. [7]XXIV.276. [8]II.226.
[9]II.227. [10]II.229. [11]*Ibid.*

dispensation is poured out with a fulness that is without precedent in the Old Testament dispensation.

The initial *reception* of the Spirit is passive. There is, says Owen, 'an active power to be put forth in his reception for consolation, though not in his reception for regeneration and sanctification'.[1] He is thinking here of regeneration and sanctification as two dimensions of the one entity. In this respect, the coming of the Spirit and his work is sovereign. The Spirit is a *gift* freely bestowed. He is received by us, but not *because of* human response. Owen's interest here is on the *active* reception of the Spirit as the Comforter or Paraclete, which he sees as central to communion with the Spirit.

This distinction between passive and active reception is an unusual one to draw (although based on John 14.17, Galatians 3.2, and John 7.39).[2] But Owen's main emphasis is that men must possess the Spirit before they can receive the benefits of his presence through faith. The Spirit must first indwell them if he is to comfort them (although he may abide in them without exercising that ministry of comfort).[3] In contrast to his work as the Spirit of *holiness*, his operations as Comforter depend not only on his presence, but on his sovereign purpose. While the former is his constant employment, the latter may be experienced irregularly. Nevertheless the Spirit never leaves the Christian utterly without consolation.

Owen makes it plain in this context and elsewhere[4] that while not forgetting his ministry as Advocate,[5] he prefers to translate *paraklētos* as *Comforter*. In this he follows the Greek Fathers against the view of modern exegesis that the notion is that of advocacy rather than of comfort.

(i) Indwelling

The Christian's first knowledge of the Spirit is by *inhabitation*.

---

[1]II.231. Owen here means by 'sanctification' the maturation of the new birth which inaugurates Christian experience.

[2]'Unusual' not in the sense that commentators do not note the distinction made, e.g. in John 14.17, between the world and the church, but rather do not discuss the significance of this in terms of the Christian's ongoing experience.

[3]II.233.   [4]IV.361.

[5]*Ibid.*, cf. IV.368 and especially II.225.

This is 'among those things which we ought, as to the nature or being of it, firmly to believe, but as to the manner of it cannot fully conceive'.[1] This indwelling is real and personal.[2] Rather than detract from the mystery and glory of the Spirit, Owen argues that his indwelling the believer increases and enhances both, for Christians 'are not able to form any conception in their minds of the manner of his presence and residence in them'.[3]

In what, then, do Christians have fellowship and communion with the Spirit? They receive his teaching ministry. The Spirit came as the great Reminder to the disciples (Jn. 14.26), bringing the teaching of Christ to their memories and leading them into its meaning and significance. This is primarily a promise of inspiration to the apostles according to Owen,[4] but through this he also brings personal comfort, and not simply official aid. In particular the Spirit glorifies Christ and reveals the blessings of the covenant of grace which Christ has purchased for his people.[5]

The Spirit is also the Spirit of adoption, bearing witness to our sonship and producing the enjoyment of it. In this sense, Owen sees him as an Advocate, overpowering the accusations of law, conscience and Satan, and giving an immediate assurance to the Christian.[6] He sheds abroad in the heart the love of God (Rom. 5.5), which is essentially the enjoyment of this assurance of acceptance by him.[7] He is also the Spirit of supplication, through whom the Christian maintains in prayer his communion with the Father.[8]

Owen concentrates attention on several different aspects of the Spirit's ministry. These are, his work in anointing, as an earnest, and as a Comforter. He also stresses that there is a special work of the Spirit in *sealing*, but his views on this were so

---

[1] IV.383, cf. 384, 385.
[2] IV.384; XI.329–365. Cf. Thomas Goodwin, *The Work of the Holy Ghost in our Salvation*, London, 1696, *The Works of Thomas Goodwin*, ed. J.C. Miller, Edinburgh, 1861–65, VI.63–7; John Preston, *Sinnes Overthrow*, London, 1635, p. 39. The view that the indwelling of the Spirit is not personal was taught by R. Hollinworth, *The Holy Ghost on the Bench*, London, 1656, pp. 8, 10.

[3] IV.386.   [4] II.236.   [5] II.230.   [6] II.241, cf. XI.335.
[7] II.240.   [8] II.249.

germane to his teaching on assurance that they are best considered in that context.[1]

Anointing

The Spirit of God gives believers an anointing, or unction.[2] But what is this unction? Owen refutes, as alien to the biblical context, the view of Episcopius[3] that it is the doctrine of the gospel.[4]

It is the doctrine of the gospel that is at issue (in 1 John 2.20), whereas the *unction* abides and teaches the doctrine. Others have interpreted 'anointing' as the testimony the Spirit gives to the truth, for example by miraculous operations. Cornelius à Lapide as representative of Roman Catholic exegesis regarded it as the chrism of baptism.[5] But Owen sees the clue in the anointing of the Mosaic ordinances, types which are fulfilled in Christ, and shares Augustine's view that it is his anointing with the Holy Spirit, in which the Christian shares.

In the case of Jesus, the anointing was 'carried on by several degrees and distinctions of time':[6] in the womb, at the baptism, on the cross, and finally at his ascension, when he was anointed with the oil of gladness above his fellows.[7] Thus believers receive their anointing immediately from Christ: 'It is therefore manifest that the anointing of believers consisteth in the communication of the Holy Spirit unto them from and by Jesus Christ. It is not the Spirit that doth anoint us, but he is the unction wherewith we are anointed by the Holy One'.[8]

---

[1]See below, pp. 116ff.   [2]2 Cor. 1.21; 1 Jn. 2.20.

[3]Simon Episcopius, Biscop, Bischop or Bisschop (1583–1643) the Dutch theologian who systematized the theology of Arminius.

[4]IV.390.   [5]IV.391.   [6]IV.392.

[7]This post-ascension anointing which Owen regards as so significant has received little attention. The consummation of incarnation, in soteriological terms, begins, for Owen, with the reception of the Spirit by Christ for the church, John 14.16; 15.26. Owen refers to Luke 1.35; Luke 2.40, 52; Matthew 3.16; John 1.32 to support this interpretation of the anointing. He contends that it refers not simply to the ascension of Christ, but peculiarly to his exaltation in heaven, when he entered into the possession of all his offices: 'the joyful, glorious unction of his exaltation, when he was signally made Lord and Christ, and declared to be the anointed one of God' (XX.196).

[8]IV.393.

The effects of this unction are twofold. (i) The teaching of the gospel is impressed on the mind. Just as the Spirit had a teaching office in the experience of Christ[1], so too in the disciple he will teach by illumination and conviction. (ii) This anointing brings stability to life. In 1 John 2.20–7, for example, it strengthens the recipient against the seductions of false teachers.[2]

Earnest[3]

Owen regards the 'earnest' of the Spirit not as an act, but as an aspect of his indwelling.[4] *He* is the *earnest*. The enjoyment of him in the present is part of that 'fulness of the Spirit in the enjoyment of God'[5] to be known in the future. In particular he is the earnest of the inheritance.[6] Owen takes this to refer to the inheritance lost by Adam, regained by Christ and invested in him.[7] Through our union to Christ, by the Spirit, he becomes the guarantee of glory.[8] He thus brings a knowledge of the love of God, of acceptance with him, and adoption into his family. This produces a further measure of stability in the Christian life. The presence of the Spirit as earnest reminds the Christian that he lives in the interim between salvation inaugurated in Christ and consummated at the end of time. The Christian life is presently characterized by the perspective of hope that will not be disappointed. The Christian meanwhile realizes that there is a certain incompleteness in his experience of salvation, and finds assurance in the presence of the Spirit as *arrabōn*, guarantee, pledge and 'down-payment' on the future.

These aspects of the Spirit's work clarify the reason why Owen thinks of him in the further capacity of Comforter.

Comforter.

The Spirit works from the motive of *love*.[9] This, Owen claims 'is principally to be considered in this office and the discharge of it'.[10] If this is not recognized, the Spirit's work will be of minimal

[1]Isaiah 11.1ff.   [2]II.248.   [3]2 Cor. 1.22; Eph. 1.14.
[4]IV.407.   [5]II.245.   [6]Eph. 1.14.   [7]IV.409–410.
[8]IV.410.   [9]2 Cor. 13.11; Rom. 5.5; 15.30.   [10]IV.371.

blessing. If it is, 'this is of great use unto us, as that which ought to have, and which will have, if duly apprehended, a great influence on our faith and obedience, and is, moreover, the spring of all the consolations we receive by and from him'.[1]

Consolation is one effect of the Spirit's ministry in the people of God.[2] He encourages them to see that God has a greater purpose in view than the evil which they presently experience. This is the constant emphasis in the New Testament's approach to suffering and affliction, and Owen sees the Spirit bearing witness to this in experience.[3] Consequently, *peace* arises from his work, as well as hope.[4] Indeed the Christian may be brought to the point of rejoicing in his tribulation, because through hope he knows that God will give him the oil of joy for mourning.[5]

In this way Owen balances his stress on fellowship with each person of the Trinity with his conviction of their unity in the work of grace. Through fellowship *with Christ* comes adoption *by God the Father* and the gift of *the Spirit of adoption*.[6] Yet as part of that same fellowship the believer suffers as Christ did in the world, under the discipline and chastising love of the Father. But we are not left comfortless, since the Spirit comforts us in our afflictions. In this way the Spirit of God safeguards the Christian from falling to the twin temptations of chastisement: to despise it, and be deaf to God's voice, or to faint and sink under it by failing to recognize his presence.[7]

In his communion with the Spirit, the believer has certain duties and responsibilities.

(i) With respect to his *personal indwelling*, he is not to be grieved.[8] If he is grieved there is a shortfall in universal sanctification, which leads to a loss of both '*the power and pleasure* of our obedience'.[9]

(ii) With respect to his *activity*, his influence is not to be *quenched*; he is like a fire to be kept alive.[10] Owen indicates the aptness of Paul's expression to Timothy (2 Tim. 1.6) to 'stir up

[1]IV.370–1. [2]Acts 9.31. [3]III.409.
[4]II.251; cf. Rom. 15.13. [5]II.252; cf. Is. 61.3. [6]II.249.
[7]II.259; XXIV.256, cf. Heb. 12.5.
[8]Cf. also with respect to the Father, IV.373.
[9]II.266. [10]*Ibid.*

with a new fire' the gift of the Spirit he had received by the laying on of his hands.

(iii) With respect to Christ's *ordinances* the Spirit is not to be *resisted*, which Owen interprets in terms of Acts 6.10 and 7.51–2, as a resistance to the servants of God and their service of Christ.[1]

The apex of the Christian's fellowship with the Spirit, as with the Father and the Son, is *worship*. But true worship of the Spirit always takes place according to the rule of Scripture. Such worship is encouraged by the knowledge that the Spirit is *the Comforter*, just as the worship of Christ is encouraged by the knowledge that he is *the Saviour*. But Owen cautions that the Spirit cannot be worshipped without worshipping the Trinity, and comments by way of polemic: 'Hence is that way of praying to the Trinity, by the repetition of the same petition to the several persons (as in the Litany), groundless, if not impious'.[2] The proper object of worship is the essence of God.[3]

Owen finds Ephesians 2.18 a 'heavenly directory' in this matter.[4] It indicates the nature of the fellowship of which he has been speaking, which is an access to the Father, by the Son and through the Spirit.[5]

This, then, is the high calling and privilege of the Christian. But Owen has hinted in the course of his exposition that not every believer experiences the full enjoyment of his communion with God. Many lack assurance, and what Owen elsewhere calls 'an assured expectation of the promised inheritance'.[6] We must therefore examine how Owen builds on this foundation to lead the believer to a fuller enjoyment of faith and sonship.

---

[1]II.267.   [2]II.268.

[3]Calvin's comment that 'Only fools, therefore, seek to know the essence of God' would seem to reflect Owen's thought that this is the proper object of worship in a poor light! *The Epistle of Paul the Apostle to the Romans and the Thessalonians*, trans. R. Mackenzie, ed. D. W. & T. F. Torrance, Edinburgh, 1961, p. 31. Owen and Calvin are, however, addressing rather different circumstances. Owen's stress is that it is God as Trinity, in essence and economy, who is worshipped. Calvin is counteracting a false mysticism which *hides* God's essence *behind* the revelation of his attributes, and rationalism which usurps the place of adoration.

[4]II.269.   [5]IX.57. See below p. 275.   [6]I.489.

∾ 5 ∾

The Assurance of Salvation

John Owen's teaching on Christian assurance can be understood only against the backcloth of the historical development of the doctrine.

It is often stressed that the Reformers, in their reaction to Rome's wholesale denial of the possibility of assurance, taught that assurance belongs to the very essence of faith. Calvin's definition of faith is well known: 'A firm and certain knowledge of God's benevolence toward us, founded upon the truth of the freely given promise in Christ, both revealed to our minds and sealed upon our hearts through the Holy Spirit'.[1] But Calvin consciously makes room for weak and faltering faith, and for a lack of assurance. The contrast should not be drawn too sharply.[2]

In Puritan teaching, the doctrines of limited atonement and predestination often raised the question of personal assurance. The necessity of treating the subject was *theological*. But it was even more vitally *pastoral*. For it was not simply the doctrinal

[1] *Institutes* III.ii.7, In the light of the wedge that is often driven between Calvin and later writers, this should be compared with Owen's similar definition of faith as 'a firm persuasion of heart', I.486.

[2] See, for example, Calvin's comments in the rest of *Institutes* III.ii. Owen's definitions of faith and assurance, which *contrast* with Calvin's are to be found in V.419.

An interesting catena of quotations from 17th-century writers indicating their agreement at this point will be found in the appendix to an address given on the subject of Assurance by the 19th-century evangelical leader, J. C. Ryle *(Holiness*, r.i., London, 1956, pp. 126–133). He quotes from the Puritans Greenham, Sibbes, Adams, Rogers, Ball, Ward, Greenhill, Perkins, Brooks, S. Bolton, Watson, Charnock and Flavel, as well as others. But not from Owen!

system that gave rise to the need to discuss assurance, but the Puritans' analytical and applicatory *preaching* on the nature of Christian experience. The *pulpit* was the creator of anxious hearts, and therefore the *pulpit* had to bring them comfort and assurance. It is significant, therefore, that when Owen turns to deal with this theme, his work is a result of personal experience. Indeed, his treatment of assurance is partly a transcript of how he himself came to enjoy assurance of faith.[1]

i. *Assurance of Forgiveness*

Owen's treatment of assurance is an expository, rather than a systematic one, and occurs in the course of a lengthy study of Psalm 130 in which he devotes some two hundred closely argued pages to explaining the statement 'There is forgiveness with thee that thou mayest be feared' (Ps. 130.4).[2]

Owen describes the practical importance of assurance in the following way: 'Faith's discovery of forgiveness in God, though it have no present sense of its own peculiar interest therein, is the great supportment of a sin-perplexed soul'.[3] The assurance of forgiveness safeguards the believer from the tyranny of his own emotions, and is essential to his spiritual stability.

Owen recognized how common was the assumption that

[1]The life of Richard Davis, minister in Rothwell, Northamptonshire, provides a rare insight into the autobiographical nature of Owen's exposition. Davis had sought out Owen for spiritual counsel and arranged an interview with him. In the course of conversation, Owen asked him, 'Young man, pray in what manner do you think to go to God?' 'Through the Mediator, sir,' answered Davis. 'That is easily said' replied Owen, 'but I assure you it is another thing to go to God through the Mediator than many who make use of the expression are aware of. I myself preached Christ some years, when I had but very little, if any, experimental acquaintance with access to God through Christ; until the Lord was pleased to visit me with sore affliction, whereby I was brought to the mouth of the grave, and under which my soul was oppressed with horror and darkness; but God graciously relieved my spirit by a powerful application of Ps. 130.4 "But there is forgiveness with thee that thou mayest be feared", from whence I received special instruction, peace, and comfort, in drawing near to God through the Mediator, and preached thereupon immediately after my recovery'. See Goold's comments in VI.324. Cf. also VI.400, 407.

[2]VI.379–606.   [3]VI.384.

God is a God who forgives men's sins. But these common thoughts of men are superficial, confessing the '*old doctrine*' of forgiveness, but knowing nothing of its '*fresh power*'.[1]

Three things militate against a real knowledge of forgiveness in such men's lives. (i) *Conscience* speaks against it, for it 'knows nothing of forgiveness; yea, it is against its very trust, work, and office to hear anything of it'.[2] (ii) *The law of God* is also against it, since it knows neither mercy nor forgiveness.[3] Law agrees with conscience, or rather, conscience agrees with law, speaking against the soul of man, with divine authority. (iii) *The sense men have of the justice of God* breeds doubts about forgiveness.[4]

So the heart of the natural man presents a kind of paradox. On the one hand, he doubts the reality of forgiveness and lacks genuine assurance, and on the other, he unwarrantably presumes upon the forbearance of God.[5] Men think that God is not really just and holy in the way Scripture teaches, but, recreating him in their own image, imagine him to be like themselves.[6] This error is reinforced by their vague sense that God is willing to forgive, without taking account of *the way* in which God forgives. It is a cardinal principle in Owen's thought that genuine acceptance of the gospel and all its benefits requires an *approval* of the gospel method of justification.[7] The method of grace is that a *righteous* and *holy* God forgives. This is the heart of the gospel. It is also the paradox at the heart of the gospel, resolved only in Christ.[8] It is one thing, therefore, to have a vague hope of forgiveness, another to discover that there is forgiveness with the true and living God.

This common, but false assurance of forgiveness can be distinguished from the true. It does not produce a real love for God, but a contempt and indifference in spirit when dealing with him, so that 'There are none in the world that deal worse with God than those who have an ungrounded persuasion of forgiveness'. By contrast, '*Great love will spring out of great forgiveness*'.[9] Again, 'This *notional apprehension of the pardon of sin*

---

[1]VI.387.   [2]*Ibid.*   [3]VI.389.
[4]VI.391.   [5]VI.393.   [6]VI.394; cf. Ps. 50.21.
[7]V.100, 411.   [8]VI.395.   [9]VI.396.

begets no serious, thorough hatred and detestation of sin, nor is prevalent to a relinquishment of it; nay, it rather secretly insinuates into the soul encouragements unto a continuance in it'.[1] Nor, claims Owen, does this general notion bring any blessing to life and character. The corollary of which is that among the accompanying marks of a genuine assurance will be found love for God, hatred of sin and graciousness of character. Those, then, who rest content with false assurance can only be thought of as making use of it for false ends, and 'Self righteousness is their bottom'.[2]

What is the nature of this forgiveness of which men may be assured? It comes from '*the gracious heart of the Father*',[3] that is, from his sovereign and gracious purpose. Only when the greatness of this is realized do men truly know forgiveness. Some are concerned only with immunity from punishment, and not the full forgiveness of the gospel, in which Christ is at the centre and forgiveness is brought through him from the love of the Father. Ephesians 1 gives Owen the clue to the grandeur of this: 'The rise is his eternal predestination; the end, the glory of his grace; the means, redemption in the blood of Christ; the thing itself, forgiveness of sins'.[4] It is the fruit of his death and of his resurrection: 'It flows from the cross, and springs out of the grave of Christ'.[5] He *purchased* forgiveness by his death[6] and sealed the promise of it;[7] as the head of the body of believers, he received justification for all the members by his rising from the grave, and to him has been committed the management of forgiveness. Thus, Owen concludes, 'to hold communion with God, in the blood of his Son, is a thing of another nature than is once dreamed of by many who think they know well enough what it is to be pardoned'.[8] This represents again Owen's personal experience.[9]

How, then, may forgiveness be discovered? It is brought into personal experience through faith.[10] Since there are various

---

[1]VI.397; cf. Jude 4.   [2]VI.398.   [3]VI.399.   [4]VI.404.
[5]VI.405.

[6]The notion of atonement as redemption involving a ransom is discussed in a number of places by Owen: X.225, 233, 259. He discusses the question to whom the ransom is paid in XII.521ff. In terms of the ransom price being paid, Owen takes it to have been paid to God, i.e. within the godhead.

[7]2 Cor. 1.20.   [8]VI.407.   [9]Cf. V.72; XIII.134.
[10]V.108; VI.910.

elements in the divine provision of forgiveness, faith may grasp one or more of them according to the individual's present sense of need. But no element can be experienced except through faith. Divine forgiveness is too great a mystery to be experienced by anything except faith. Hence the emphasis of Hebrews 11.1 where faith is the *hupostasis* (substance) of things not seen, giving to them a reality and substance in the soul.[1] This fact itself, is a great help to anyone who is not yet persuaded of his own state of forgiveness. He must believe that 'there is forgiveness with thee' before appropriating it for himself. This will encourage him to a personal assurance of Christ's forgiveness, which is, in general, the fruit of a more plentiful supply of the Spirit of God.[2]

In ordinary circumstances only negligence and sloth can prevent anyone from attaining assurance.[3] This is an important, if brief, comment from Owen, showing that for him assurance is the natural fruit of faith and is to be *expected* in normal Christian experience. His position is far removed from the frequent caricature of Puritan teaching.

Nevertheless there may be a saving relationship without assurance of it. Owen takes this to be the significance of Isaiah 50.10: 'Who among you fears the Lord and obeys the voice of his servant, who walks in darkness and has no light, yet trusts in the name of the Lord and relies upon his God?'[4] This is clearly consistent with the classical Puritan preaching of the gospel; it is not preached with an individual's name on it, but with the offer of pardon to all who receive Christ. Where he is received and trusted there is certainly salvation, but not necessarily assurance of it. This Owen sees as one of the primary lessons of Psalm 130. The psalmist *discovers* that there is forgiveness with God and consequently *waits* upon God and hopes in his promise with a view to receiving it.[5] He notes the same lesson in Lamentations 3.21ff. where the anxious man discovers the covenant love and faithfulness of God, and learns that 'It is

---

[1]VI.412; cf. XXIV.8.
[2]VI.413–4; cf. Romans 5.1–5.   [3]VI.414.
[4]VI.415; cf. *The Confession of Faith*, XVIII.iv, and especially T. Goodwin, *Works*, III.235ff.
[5]Ps. 130.4–5.

good that one should wait quietly for the salvation of the Lord'.[1]

Owen's preliminary investigation therefore leads him to stress the central themes in the Puritan doctrine of assurance: false assurance is a dangerous possibility. On the other hand, true assurance 'founded upon the divine truth of the promises of salvation' is not only desirable: it is actually possible through ordinary means. But this does not imply that assurance is always easily obtained.[2]

Forgiveness can be known only by biblical revelation. God's eternal power and deity may be known by the light of nature inbred *in* man, and from the works of God shown *to* man (Rom. 1.18ff.); but forgiveness as a free act of God's will cannot be known in this way.

In fact, says Owen, 'it *is a great and rare thing to have forgiveness in God discovered unto a sinful soul*'. It is therefore '*a thing precious and excellent, as being the foundation of all our communion with God here, and of all undeceiving expectation of our enjoyment of him hereafter*'. It is therefore incumbent on the Christian '*to consider what sure evidences faith hath of it, such as will not, as cannot fail us*'.[3]

Owen discovers this 'infallible assurance' in the testimony of Scripture. It is 'founded upon the divine truth of the promises of salvation'.[4] Owen shows this from a lengthy historical and theological review of the idea of forgiveness.[5] While important in its own right, Owen's exposition also provides an insight into his appreciation of the ideas, other than divine inspiration, which provide Scripture with a fundamental unity.[6] The evidence that there is forgiveness with God is summarized as follows:

The first promise of forgiveness appears in the *Protevangelium* in Genesis 3.15, where it forms a ray of light and hope against the dark backcloth of man's sin and God's righteous judgment

---

[1]Lamentations 3.16: cf. VI.417.
[2]*The Confession of Faith*, XVIII.ii, iii.
[3]VI.431.
[4]*The Confession of Faith*, XVIII.ii.
[5]His embryonic history of salvation was later enlarged in the reformed tradition by Jonathan Edwards, *Works*, London 1840, I.532–614.
[6]VI.427–498.

on it.[1] Precisely where sin abounds grace has much more abounded. This promise was followed by the institution and the development of the sacrificial system.[2] While the Old Testament sacrifices could not make perfect (Heb. 10.1),[3] they did nevertheless indicate and typify the taking away of sin, and the possibility of forgiveness. Repentance, the sinner's turning back to God, *depends* on this, because he realises that God has provided a way of forgiveness: 'the great call to saving repentance is by the revelation of forgiveness'.[4] The possibility of real repentance is created by the promise of assured forgiveness. Conversely, those like Judas, who seek to repent without a knowledge of forgiveness, will perish.[5]

A further evidence that God grants forgiveness may be seen in his patience. The delaying of his judgment indicates his faithfulness to his promise of forgiveness rather than betrays his promise to judge the world.[6] The experience of the saints provides practical evidence, since they have lived in the blessing of such forgiveness.[7] Forgiveness is also the anchor of the institution of worship;[8] without it sinful man's honouring and blessing would be impossible. The ordinances of worship are given as specific confirmation of the divine forgiveness: baptism; the Lord's supper; the fellowship of the church; and the words of the Lord's Prayer ('forgive us our debts').[9]

Forgiveness is also a fundamental element of the covenant of grace. The purpose of this new covenant is 'that man might serve [God] aright, be blessed by him, and be brought unto the everlasting enjoyment of him; all unto his glory.'[10] In the old covenant, its glory notwithstanding,[11] there was no promise of forgiveness and no provision made for it. This appears only in this new covenant, through the blood of Christ, and shows us its greatness and certainty.[12]

---

[1]I.120; VI.434; XVIII.170.   [2]VI.435.   [3]XXIII.425.
[4]VI.430, 437.   [5]VI.438.   [6]VI.448–9.   [7]VI.452.
[8]VI.461.   [9]VI.465–7.   [10]VI.471.
[11]Owen is thinking here of 2 Cor. 3.7 in the context of his own distinctive understanding of the relationships of the divine covenants. See above, pp. 20–32.
[12]VI.470–5 yields important material for the understanding of Owen's view of the relationship of the covenants.

To the covenant, God has added his oath, in which he has sworn by his own name and being. He thus gives his assurance that his covenant will be kept. His oath shows the immutability of his counsel[1] so that the Christian, assaulted by the temptations of the devil, may find support. Further, God has sworn that he has no pleasure in the death of the wicked.[2]

This is again reinforced by the name of God: he is 'a God of pardons'.[3] Owen here stresses a basic maxim of reformed and biblical theology: 'Whatever, therefore, any name of God expresseth him to be, that he is, that we may expect to find him'. He 'will not deceive us by giving himself a wrong or a false name'.[4] It is surely symbolic, remarks Owen, that, having rejected the full revelation of the covenant God in Christ, no Jew is now certain how to pronounce his covenant name.

The covenant finds its highest expression and fulfilment in the person of Jesus Christ; he is the centre and fountain of all these other streams in which the believer may find encouragement for faith.[5] The God who did not spare his own Son will not withhold any necessary comfort from those who trust in him. Christ's death is the demonstration of this, since he died to make atonement for sin, to receive the penalty and curse of a broken law, and to destroy the work of the devil.[6] He lives after death for this same purpose, since the resurrection indicates the success of his work and points further to his ministry of intercession.[7] Then, 'What ground is left of questioning the truth in hand? What link of this chain can unbelief break in or upon?'[8]

The final evidence is this: God requires men to forgive.[9] How can this be unless he himself forgives? There is, therefore, forgiveness with him. 'Our forgiving of others will not procure forgiveness for ourselves; but our not forgiving of others proves that we ourselves are not forgiven.'[10]

This exposition of Owen's has not been above criticism even by his admirers, for the complexity it seems to introduce to the experience of assurance.[11] But the purpose of his lengthy review of salvation, from promise to fulfilment, is clear. For Owen the

---

[1]Heb. 6.17. [2]Ezek. 32.11. [3]Neh. 9.17; cf. Mic. 7.18.
[4]VI.478. [5]VI.487. [6]VI.489–492. [7]VI.492.
[8]VI.494. [9]Ibid. [10] VI.497 [11]Orme, *op. cit.*, pp. 316ff.

assurance of faith arises through the ministry of the Holy Spirit. But faith depends for its character, stability and assurance upon that on which it rests. Faith never points to itself but to the testimony upon which it is founded. By expounding the assurance of forgiveness from the divine testimony, Owen argues that infallible faith, or assurance of faith, will result.

The vital point that Owen makes is that while assurance is experienced subjectively by the believer, it is grounded in the promises of God which find their 'yes' and 'amen' in Christ.[1]

Concerning this assurance, Owen was convinced that such experience was all too rare. 'Many, I say, the most of men who live under the dispensation of the gospel, do wofully deceive their own souls in this matter.'[2] They do not appreciate that this is a gospel truth and 'the turning-point of the two covenants, as God himself declares, Heb. viii.7–13'.[3] If a man believes and receives the assurance of forgiveness there is nothing he prizes more highly. But Owen saw little evidence that the mass of men do so value it. Not only so, but this truth is not revealed by flesh and blood, and those who make of it a light and easy matter face the reproach:

I would but desire them to go to some real believers that are or may be known unto them. Let them be asked whether they came so easily by their faith and apprehensions of forgiveness or no. 'Alas!' saith one, 'these twenty years have I been following after God, and yet I have not arrived unto an abiding cheering persuasion of it.' 'I know what it cost me, what trials, difficulties, temptations I wrestled with, and went through withal, before I obtained it,' saith another. 'What I have attained unto hath been of unspeakable mercy; and it is my daily prayer that I may be preserved in it by the exceeding greatness of the power of God, for I continually wrestle with storms that are ready to drive me from my anchor.' A little of this discourse may be sufficient to convince poor, dark, carnal creatures of the folly and vanity of their confidence.[4]

Too few know what it is to receive forgiveness by bowing before God's sovereign love and drinking from the infinite ocean of grace. In this respect Adam is the prototype: 'convinced of sin, afraid of punishment, he lay trembling at the

[1]2 Cor. 1.20. [2]VI.505. [3]VI.506. [4]VI.508–9.

foot of God: then was forgiveness revealed unto him'.[1] All of
which Owen applies with the repeated question, 'Have you . . .
have you then . . . have you. . . ?'[2] If Scripture teaches that the
fruit of forgiveness is the renunciation of sin, how can anyone
believe that most men have received forgiveness? If it is to be
received it must be for the end for which it is intended, namely,
'a new foundation of obedience, of love, and thankfulness'.[3]

There are, however, encouragements to believe that there is
forgiveness with God. The picture of the writer of Psalm 130 is
of one of those 'who have received it [forgiveness], but being
again *entangled by sin,* or *clouded by darkness* and temptations, or
weakened by unbelief, know not how to improve it to their peace
and comfort'.[4] To help such Owen provides practical rules
which should lead to a fuller daily experience of assurance. It is
on these that Owen's pastoral teaching on assurance is really to
be judged.

ii. *Practical Rules for Assurance*

(i) As Christians, we must allow Christ to be the judge of our
spiritual condition. Scripture abounds with examples of faulty
self-judgment. Christ alone discerns and judges infallibly, by
his word in Scripture, and by his Spirit.[5] By the same Spirit he
bears witness with the believer's spirit to his true condition.
Therefore the rule is, 'Self-determinations concerning men's
spiritual state and condition, because their minds are usually
influenced by their distempers, are seldom right and according
to rule . . . let Christ, then, be the judge in this case by his word
and Spirit, as hath been directed'.[6]

(ii) Christians need to learn that *'Self-condemnation and
abhorrency do very well consist with gospel justification and peace'.*[7] It is
faith only that can bring these two dimensions of experience
together into the soul, since it 'will carry heaven in one hand and
hell in the other; showing the one deserved, the other purchased . . . David was never more humbled for sin than when
Nathan told him it was forgiven'.[8] Owen would go further.
Such a sense of sin is *necessary* to true assurance,[9] since it will be

[1]VI.511.   [2]VI.510, 512.   [3]VI.514.
[4]VI.515.   [5]VI.542–6.   [6]VI.546–7.
[7]VI.547.   [8]*Ibid.*   [9]VI.548.

accompanied by clear conviction, bringing us to see that the grounds of assured acceptance with God do not lie in ourselves.[1] Sorrow without faith in forgiveness is legal bondage; assurance without sorrow is presumption. So, 'gospel sorrow and gospel assurance may dwell in the same breast at the same time'.[2]

Indwelling sin is a feature of every Christian's inner warfare. It is not inconsistent with the cry of assured deliverance with which Paul concludes his soliloquy in Romans 7. Even doubts and fears may be held to be consistent with this, for, 'We may have peace with God when we have none from the assaults of Satan'.[3] Unless the Christian is aware of this he may well sink in a mire of despair, and live in bondage to fear all his life, no matter how genuine is his profession. This teaching will bring stability and discernment to his spiritual condition.

Here Owen is simply reiterating the reformed teaching that assurance is capable of variation and degrees.[4] But for the most part it will be evidenced by true joy in obedience to God, and freedom from fear,[5] leading to an expectation of the glory which is to be revealed. Owen is aiming here for a balance between the great blessing of full assurance and the many factors which militate against it in the Christian life. He finds this balance in Scripture in terms of two extremes, conflict and victory, sorrow and joy, depth and height, rather than in any mean between the two. To be in Christ means to have the horizons of experience extended as well as stabilized. Owen does not mistakenly minimize the joy of assurance because of sorrow for sin. He finds the biblical pattern not in the emphasis on one or other, but both together.

(iii) A third practical rule insists on the importance of patient waiting for a fuller experience of forgiveness. Here again he is able to return directly to Psalm 130 to show that 'Waiting is the only way to establishment and assurance'.[6]

(iv) Next comes self-examination: '*make thorough work in the search of sin, even to the sins of youth*', for, 'If there be much rubbish left in the foundation of the building, no wonder if it always

---

[1]IX.359–60.　　[2]VI.549.　　[3]VI.550.
[4]*The Confession of Faith*, XVIII.4.
[5]Rom. 8.15; Heb. 2.14–15; 1 Jn. 4.18.　　[6]VI.554.

shake and totter'.[1]

Owen gives directions for this work: Reduce your sins to general principles. Note those which tend to produce depths of despair or confusion in your mind. If either of these is present, then allow your mind to dwell on God's patience with you; this will speed recovery.[2] Consider whether anything you have done may have provoked God, either in your Christian or pre-Christian life, especially in the way you have responded to the prosperity or affliction which God has brought your way. This will form the basis of a renewal of forgiveness.[3]

(v) Owen's fifth rule is that Christians should learn to distinguish between unbelief and jealousy; that is, 'the solicitousness of the mind of a believer, who hath a sincere love for Christ, about the heart, affection, and good will of Christ towards it, arising from a consciousness of its own unworthiness to be beloved by him or accepted with him'.[4] This is really the classic case of lack of assurance illustrated in Psalm 130.[5] The cause of this jealousy Owen sees, in a strikingly modern insight, is *insecurity*. Unless it is controlled and disciplined by a faith that grasps the superabundance of grace over sin in Christ, such anxiety will almost inevitably be mistaken for complete unbelief.

How can we distinguish between them? Owen gives two indications. First, unbelief is 'a *weakening, disheartening, dispiriting* thing'. On the other hand, jealousy produces a quite different effect: 'It cheers, enlivens, and enlargeth the soul'.[6] In other words it motivates the heart toward Christ rather than toward self. This dovetails with the second difference, for unbelief is '*universally selfish; it begins and ends in self*', whereas 'The jealousy we speak of hath the person of Christ and his excellency for its constant object'.[7]

(vi) The next important lesson is learning to distinguish

---

[1]VI.555.   [2]VI.557.   [3]VI.557–8.
[4]VI.559; cf. above p. 84.

[5]Cf. A. Weiser, 'The psalm is the confession of a God-fearing man who was able to rise from the uttermost depth of anguish by sin to the assurance of the divine grace and forgiveness. . . . The worshipper sees his personal assurance of forgiveness in connection with the presence of God (v. 4) . . .'. *Commentary on Psalms*, trans. H. Hartwell, London, 1962, p. 773.

[6]VI.560.   [7]VI.561.

between faith and spiritual sense. These *are* to be distinguished because faith can exist where the sense of it is absent. Owen supports this view with a number of Scriptures, notably Habakkuk 3.17, Psalm 73.26 and Romans 4.18. He believes that there is a spiritual sense-experience in both justification and sanctification. In Romans 5.1 the peace of justification brings rest and satisfaction, with its fruit in joy. But, 'He, then, that would place believing in these things, and will not be persuaded that he doth believe until he is possessed of them, he doth lose the benefit, advantage, and comfort of what he hath, and, neglecting the due acting of faith, puts himself out of the way of attaining what he aimeth at'.[1]

(vii) Owen's seventh rule is simple and practical. '*Mix not too much foundation and building work together.*'[2] The foundation is Christ alone, the building is holiness and obedience. The Christian should be clear that mortification is no part of justification.[3]

(viii) Owen's eighth rule shows a striking insight into the kind of personality with which he must often have found himself dealing in his pastoral ministry: '*Take heed of spending time in complaints when vigorous actings of grace are your duty*'.[4] The temptation of some is to be always discussing their problem and constantly looking for advice, instead of pressing on with the routine activities of their Christian life. This is not the scriptural way, which is to take the kingdom of God by force and to press into it:

Get up, watch, pray, fast, meditate, offer violence to your lusts and corruptions; fear not, startle not at their crying or importunities to be spared; press unto the throne of grace by prayers, supplications, importunities, restless requests. This is the way to take the kingdom of heaven. These things are not peace, they are not assurance; but they are part of the means that God hath appointed for the attainment of them.[5]

Spiritual peace and sloth cannot dwell together in the same life.[6]

(ix) Rule nine issues a warning against harsh thoughts of

[1]VI.563.   [2]VI.564.   [3]VI.564–5.   [4]VI.566.
[5]VI.567–8.   [6]VI.570.

God, when we are in deep perplexity or undergoing long temptation, or disappointment in our efforts to subdue sin.[1]

(x) Rule ten enjoins the Christian to make use of every manifestation of the rich grace of God in his life. Those who are in danger will make use of the slightest opportunity to receive help. So too should the child of God.[2]

(xi) Finally, it is the duty of the child of God to consider carefully where the hindrances to peace in his life are located: 'Search out your wound, that it may be tried whether it be curable or no'.[3]

iii. *Hindrances to assurance*

According to Owen, there are four main obstacles to assurance.[4]

(i) The first is the experience of affliction, which may lead the Christian to feel that he is under the displeasure of God, and so his sense of assurance weakens. 'The complaints of David are familiar to all who attend unto any communion with God in these things'.[5] God seems to be hiding his face! This is precisely what is described in Psalm 130. There are certain things which seem particularly to promote this experience: the memory of past sins often does this in Scripture,[6] so that 'The deep of afflictions calleth up the deep of the guilt of sin, and both in conjunction become as billows and waves passing over the soul.'[7] A new experience in affliction may accentuate this. God himself 'will put an edge upon it, in matter, or manner, or circumstances, that shall make the soul feel its sharpness'.[8] This may be particularly distressing if the Christian's affections have been set upon *lawful* things. If, on the other hand, severe affliction combines with our corruption, 'It is not conceivable what a combustion they will make in the soul'.[9] At such a time the devil will try to use these sufferings to his own end, just as in the passion of Christ he attacked him to turn his experience into the hour of 'the power of darkness'.[10]

How is the Christian to cope with himself and with this kind of situation? Once again we see Owen's stress on the primacy of

---

[1]VI.570–2.   [2]VI.573–4.   [3]VI.574.   [4]VI.575.
[5]VI.576.   [6]Job 13.23–7; I Kings 17.18.   [7]VI.578.   [8]*Ibid.*
[9]VI.579.   [10]VI.580, cf. Lk. 23.53.

the understanding for stable Christian living; there are certain truths which must be known in order to produce a measure of peace.[1] The Christian needs to learn that great afflictions can be consistent with the pardon of sin. In the light of Christian biography Owen sees it almost as a fixed principle that 'those who have had most of afflictions have had most of grace'.[2] He interprets the smoking furnace in Genesis 15.17 accordingly. When God sealed his covenant with Abraham, 'It was to let him know that there was a furnace of affliction attending the covenant of grace and peace'.[3] In that covenant a man may also experience affliction because of his sin, and yet be persuaded of his forgiveness.[4] Faith will discover this, as Owen indicates in a sermon entitled 'God the Saints' Rock', in which he demonstrates that faith distinguishes between the *covenant itself* and the *outward administration* of it.[5] The former is for ever constant, while the latter is variable. The clouds may hide the sun, but they cannot make it cease to exist.[6]

Length of affliction is no reflection on the weakness of grace; Christ himself endured suffering from the cradle to the grave. Our lives are patterned on his because we are united to him. But what of affliction caused by past sin? Owen's counsel is, '*separate them in your minds and deal distinctly about them*'.[7] This was the practice of David.[8] He first considered his sin and guilt, and when he had received forgiveness he then dealt with the 'troubles' which they had brought upon him. Sin is the disease, trouble the symptom. The disease needs to be cured before the symptoms can be effectively treated.[9] In this context discernment is needed, and the ability to distinguish natural from spiritual, between what is an inherited trait and may have a biological origin and what is a sinful propensity originating in the soul.

The fact that there are afflictions in the life of the Christian may catch him off guard in two ways, and a warning is sounded about both. He may forget that a time of affliction may also be a time of temptation. Satan, like Pharaoh of Egypt, attacks those he discovers in the wilderness: 'Watch, therefore, and pray,

---

[1]VI.580–3; cf. II.259–61. [2]VI.580. [3]VI.581.
[4]VI.338–9. [5]IX.242. [6]IX.244. [7]VI.581; cf. II.145.
[8]Ps. 32.3–5. [9]VI.582.

that you enter not into temptation, that Satan do not represent God falsely unto you.'[1] Conversely, in times of ease and freedom, it is possible to live in such a way that any future affliction will be greatly aggravated through the memory of squandered opportunity and abused grace.

The supreme aspiration of the afflicted believer should be to grow better through affliction. That is God's purpose, for he 'will not cease to thresh and break the bread-corn until it be meet for his use.'[2] What should be done to bring relief? 'Hath he a cup of affliction in one hand? – lift up your eyes, and you will see a cup of consolation in another.'[3]

(ii) Another cause of despondency Christians experience in a time of perplexity is confusion and concern about their regeneration.[4] How in the midst of these sufferings can a man know that he is regenerate? Owen suggests that the following principles will be found helpful:

He should be seeking for a *regular* assurance, rather than one that is free from trial and fear, or doubts and questions. 'Regeneration induceth a new principle into the soul, but it doth not utterly expel the old'.[5] It is wrong for the Christian to seek an *extraordinary* experience of assurance if he is in a state of anxiety. True, the Spirit sometimes gives this, by his internal witness; but when he does it is a sovereign act on his own part, and is not to be expected solely by the use of means.[6] If, however, such a benefit has been received in the past, an effort should be made to recover the sense of it. Owen believed that most Christians have had some such experience. But they often do not appreciate that the significance of these testimonies is not as passing experiences of the moment, but as helps and treasures that will bring blessing in the future if used for the proper ends.[7]

It is also vital to return to first principles, and give consideration to the causes and effects of regeneration; this is the ordinary way for the child of God to be reassured of his true

---

[1]*Ibid.*   [2]VI.583.   [3]*Ibid.*
[4]VI.554.   [5]VI.593.

[6]For Owen the Spirit is Christ's witness; but that witness is given in different ways – here to provide assurance of faith and forgiveness; elsewhere to convince of the divine origin of Scripture, IV.7ff.

[7]VI.594–5.

condition.[1]

Some Christians will not know the time of their new birth, and that itself may cause further anxiety. But this is a groundless fear: the trial of faith does not depend upon only one piece of evidence. To have such evidence is undoubtedly of some benefit, but even without it, 'He that is alive may know that he was born, though he know neither the place where nor the time when he was so'.[2] When the groundwork of regeneration has been done, the way is prepared for full assurance.

(iii) A third common difficulty is the consciousness of believers that there are so few evidences of grace in their lives and those that are present seem so slight. What is the Christian to do? He is to continue in all his spiritual duties, for his great temptation is to turn in upon himself and his own degree of sanctification.[3]

Self-examination is an important facet of spiritual growth for Owen, but he recognizes that there are times in Christian experience when to embark upon the wrong duty may prove fatal. Holiness never has itself in view, but Christ and others; and while the Christian is concentrating on Christ's righteousness he will be little preoccupied with his own holiness. This is a perceptive comment, and Owen adds: 'To *be holy* is necessary; to *know it*, sometimes a temptation.'[4] In fact holiness can only be measured by the opposition overcome, and not merely by the external evidences seen, for 'He may have more grace than another who brings not forth so much fruit as the other, because he hath more opposition, more temptation, Isa. xli.17.'[5]

(iv) A final obstacle is the doubt caused by the power of indwelling sin and its effects.[6] The teaching of Scripture is that 'they that are Christ's have crucified the flesh with the lusts thereof.'[7] How then can one who discovers sin's corrupting influence in the heart really be sure he is a Christian at all?

Owen gives two answers. The first is the biblical teaching that the presence of indwelling sin is not inconsistent with the presence of renewing grace.[8] These two principles, the flesh and the Spirit, war within every believing heart. This is really a sign of faith and grace rather than of unbelief. Secondly, Owen stresses that the state of grace '*is not at all to be measured by the*

---

[1]VI.595.   [2]VI.599.   [3]VI.600.   [4]VI.601.
[5]*Ibid.*   [6]VI.603.   [7]Gal. 5.24.   [8]Gal. 5.17.

opposition that sin makes to you, but by the opposition you make to it.[1] The *nature* of sin does not change when a man becomes a Christian, though its *status* in him is fundamentally altered.[2] Assurance therefore will not be enjoyed while indwelling sin and its accompaniments are the focus of concentration; indeed *concentration* on what the Christian is in himself can only lead to despair. The eyes must be raised to God, and what he has done for, and continues to do in, his children.

This will bear fruit in love for God and joy in obeying him, a hatred of sin, and a sweetness of character in which fear has been cast out and an expectation of future glory is implanted. These are the 'right and title'[3] of the children of God in every age and circumstance. They glorify God and constitute the enjoyment of him.

iv. *The Seal of the Spirit*

The Puritan doctrine of assurance (like Owen's own teaching) possesses another dimension which needs to be examined, although, in Owen's view, it was 'very dark and difficult to be found out, few agreeing wherein it doth consist or what is the nature of it'.[4] He is speaking of the testimony of the Holy Spirit.

Calvin had laid great stress on the Spirit's testimony in his teaching on the authentication of Scripture,[5] and we will see that Owen followed very closely in his footsteps.[6] But, in fact, Calvin's emphasis on the ministry of the Spirit was resumed in his teaching on the Christian life.[7] He emphasized *the seal of the Spirit* in connection with both doctrines. In contemporary scholarship this has generally been discussed in relation to baptism, confirmation, or conversion,[8] but among the Puritans there was almost universal agreement that the significance of this expression lay in an *assurance* produced by a subjective experience of the Holy Spirit, often *after* conversion. Owen

---

[1]VI.605. [2]VI.164; cf. below p. 125ff. [3]V.405.
[4]VI.594. [5]*Institutes* I.vii. [6]Below, pp. 192ff.
[7]*Institutes* I.viii I.vii.5; III.i.1, cf. B. B. Warfield, *Calvin and Augustine*, Philadelphia 1956, p. 485.
[8]See G. W. H. Lampe, *The Seal of the Spirit*, London, 1951; Gregory Dix, *The Theology of Confirmation in Relation to Baptism*, Westminster, 1946; J. D. G. Dunn, *Baptism in the Holy Spirit*, London, 1970, respectively.

proved to be an exception, in a number of respects, to this rule, although the premise which lay behind it, that faith can exist without the experience of full assurance, was one with which he agreed.

The origins of this view are difficult, if not impossible to trace. Calvin had taught that the Spirit of God is himself the seal,[1] and this is associated with confirming the promise of God's word.[2] Indeed he virtually denied that it is possible to believe without this sealing. The later Puritans, however, faced with the lack of assurance in the lives of true Christians, tended to associate the 'seal of the Spirit' with the conscious experience of full assurance which often comes at a later point in the development of faith in Christ.[3]

Theodore Beza, Calvin's colleague and successor in Geneva, appears to have accepted his view in its totality, and wrote:

Nowe he maketh the Ephesians (or rather all the Gentiles) equall to the Jewes, because that notwithstanding they came last, yet being called by the same Gospel, they embraced it by faith, and were sealed up with the same Spirit, which is the pledge of election until the inheritance it selfe be seene.[4]

But by the time of William Perkins' influence in Cambridge, attention was already concentrated less on the sealing *of the believer* than on the distinctive *sealing of the promise to the believer* in experience: 'When God by his spirit is said to seale the promise in the heart of every particular beleever, it signifieth that hee gives unto them evident assurance that the promise of life belongs unto them'.[5] This meant that, for Perkins, 'the seal of the Spirit' was an *activity* in addition to his indwelling of the believer. This in turn opened the way for a further development of the idea of the seal in which the notion of its subsequence to conversion would come to the fore.

Perkins' successor, Paul Baynes, was clearly conscious of the dualism to which this teaching might lead, and in *An Entire Commentary upon the Whole Epistle of St. Paul to the Ephesians*[6] he

[1] Cf. Calvin's comments on 2 Cor. 1.21–2; Eph. 1.13–14.
[2] *Ibid.*   [3] Cf. *The Confession of Faith*, XVIII.iii.
[4] *The Geneva Bible* with annotations by T. Beza, many editions, *ad* Eph. 1.13.
[5] *A Discourse of Conscience*, in *William Perkins 1558–1602, English Puritanist*, ed. T. F. Merrill, Nieukoop, 1966, pp. 50–1.
[6] 1643, r.i. 1866.

attempted to reconcile the diverse interpretations:

'The seal, the Holy Spirit, that is, both the person of the Spirit dwelling in us, and the graces of the Spirit inherent in us.'[1] He regarded the sealing *of* believers and the sealing of the promise *to* believers as equivalent terms. Rather than conclude that the seal was an experience known by some Christians only, he went to the extent of stressing that a believer could be sealed and not know it.[2] In particular he suggested that the seal could be thought of as the developing fruit of the Spirit, and in these terms: 'This is comfortable, that I may assure my conscience while I stand, that I shall have redemption, because the graces of the Spirit which I find are God's mark, and the seal to me of my salvation.'[3]

Within a few years of Baynes' work on Ephesians being published, however, Richard Sibbes had taken hold of the doctrine of the sealing of the Spirit, and directed it into the tributary in which it was to flow for the succeeding decades. In *A Fountain Sealed*,[4] he had gone further than his father-in-Christ Baynes:

When we believe the promise of God in Christ – though it be by the help of the Spirit – we seal God's truth. And then God honoureth that sealing of ours by the sealing of his Spirit: 'After you believed you were sealed', saith the apostle, Ephesians 1.13; that is, the gracious love of Christ was further confirmed to them.[5]

Since he saw this as a 'superadded work',[6] Sibbes was forced into a position of suggesting that there are three kinds of Christians: those still under the spirit of bondage; those under the spirit of adoption who still fear; and those who are 'carried with large spirits to obey their Father'.[7] For him the sealing of the Spirit is a matter of degree, involving the enlarging of the heart, a new liberty, and producing a new humility and spirit of duty. It invariably draws out the affections towards future glory with Christ. If it is asked: 'how shall we know this witness from an enthusiastical fancy and illusion?', Sibbes' answer is, 'In whatever transfiguration and ravishment we cannot find

[1]*Ibid.*, p. 80.   [2]*Ibid.*, p. 81.   [3]*Ibid.*, p. 298.
[4]1637, in *The Works of Richard Sibbes*, ed. A. B. Grosart, Edinburgh, 1862–64 V.409ff.   [5]*Works* V.433–4.   [6]*Works* III.455.   [7]*Works* V.488.

Moses and Elias and Christ to meet – that is, if what we find in us be not agreeable to the Scriptures – we may well suspect it is an illusion'.[1]

Sibbes was instrumental in the conversion of John Cotton, and the latter was so indebted to him that, according to Cotton Mather, he kept a picture of Sibbes in a prominent place in his home.[2] Cotton was conscious, however, of some of the implications of Sibbes' teaching, and in the turmoil of what has come to be known as the Antinomian or Hutchinsonian Controversy,[3] was compelled to clarify his own position on the issue. He recognized the usual significance of a seal as distinguishing, confirming, or marking ownership by an image,[4] but he realized fully the diversity of applications of the idea to which this gave rise:

The Seale of the Spirit is taken by some good Divines to be the sanctification of the Spirit, as that which like a Seale:

1. Distinguisheth,
2. Consenteth,   }   the faithfull:
3. Confirmeth

Others take it for the Witnesse of the Spirit it selfe, as it is distinguished from our Spirit, Romans 6.18 [8.16]. In which sense it is commonly used by our Brethren in the Church: Though I my selfe doe generally forbeare to call it by that name, and do not usually call it the *Witnesse of the Spirit*, least I might give offence to any, who may conceive the Seale of the Spirit to be more generall.[5]

In the first sense mentioned by Cotton, the seal is common to all believers, but in the second sense, where it refers to 'evident assurance of our Adoption',[6] it cannot be thought of as a universal Christian experience.

---

[1]*Works* V.441.

[2]Cotton Mather, *Magnalia Christi Americana*, Hartford, 1853, I, p. 255.

[3]Cf. *The Antinomian Controversy*, 1636–1638, A Documentary History, ed. D. D. Hall, Middletown, Conn., 1968.

[4]John Cotton, *A Practical Commentary, or An Exposition with Observations. Reasons and Uses, upon The First Epistle Generall of John*, London, 1656, p. 199.

[5]*Severall Questions of Serious and necessary Consequence, Propounded by the Teaching Elders, unto M. John Cotton of Boston in New England. With His respective Answer to each Question*, London, 1647, p. 1. Question 1: 'What the seale of the Spirit is?'

[6]*Ibid.*, p. 2.

What Cotton felt reluctant to state, his convert John Preston affirmed without hesitation. He taught that the seal of the Spirit was a second work,[1] and was given exclusively to those who 'overcome'.[2] While it could be experienced, it was beyond definition:

You will say, what is the seale or witnesse of the Spirit? My beloved, it is a thing that we cannot expresse, it is a certain divine expression of light, a certain unexpressable assurance that we are the sonnes of *God*, a certaine secret manifestation, that *God* hath received us, and put away our sinnes: I say, it is such a thing, that no man knowes, but they that have it.[3]

In fact Preston admitted that were it not for the fact that contemporary Christians had experienced it, 'you might believe there were no such thing, that it were but a fancie or enthusiasme'.[4] But, he says, in a sentence replete with significance for his time, 'there are a generation of men that know what this seale of the Lord is'.[5]

Thomas Goodwin, who in his day was deeply influenced by both Preston and Cotton, provided the clearest and best-remembered exposition of this position.[6] While not conversant with the terminology involved in the language of contemporary scholarship on Paul's use of the coincident aorist participle in Ephesians 1.13,[7] Goodwin was nevertheless well aware of the translation this represented. Calvin and Piscator, he knew, both adopted it.[8] But he rejected this, as well as the view that the reference is to the sealing of the word of God. Instead,

---

[1]John Preston, *The New Covenant: or The Saints' Portion*. A Treatise Unfolding the all-sufficiencie of God, Man's uprightness, and the Covenant of Grace, London, 1634, p. 416.

[2]*Ibid.*, p. 417.

[3]*Ibid.*, pp. 400f., cf. Thomas Norton, *Forty-Six Sermons upon the whole eighth chapter of the Epistle of the Apostle Paul to the Romans*, London, 1674, p. 246 for a similar sentiment. Norton viewed the seal of the Spirit as a strengthening and confirming of our adoption, *ibid.*, pp. 249ff.

[4]Preson, *loc. cit.*

[5]*Ibid.*

[6]J. K. Parratt, 'The Witness of the Holy Spirit: Calvin, the Puritans and St. Paul', *The Evangelical Quarterly*, XLI.3, July-Sept. 1969, p. 163. Cf. Dunn, *op. cit.*, p. 1.

[7]Dunn, *op. cit.*, p. 87, 159.   [8]*Works* I.228.

alongside his teaching that faith is evidenced by good works, he taught that there is *also*

an immediate assurance of the Holy Ghost, by a heavenly and divine light, of a divine authority, which the Holy Ghost sheddeth in a man's heart (not having relation to grace wrought, or anything in a man's self,) whereby he sealeth him up to the day of redemption . . . the one way is discursive . . . the other is intuitive.[1]

It is 'a light beyond the light of ordinary faith'.[2] Goodwin found it illustrated in Psalm 51.12, where the psalmist, having received the *word* of forgiveness, seeks assurance of it in his heart by the Spirit.

Similar views were held by Richard Baxter as well as by other main-stream Puritans. Baxter understood 2 Corinthians 1.21-2 to refer not to the universal reception of the Spirit by believers, but to 'confirmation or universal establishment in Christ'.[3] Similarly on Ephesians 1.13-14, he says, 'Here it is evident that it is such a gift of the spirit . . . that is given to men, after they believe'.[4] He maintains 'there is to be an eminent gift of the Holy Spirit to be expected after our first believing, even such as ceased not with miracles.'[5] While recognising that some features of life in the Spirit were unique to the apostolic age, Baxter was unwilling to place the Spirit's sealing in that category. These sentiments could be duplicated from many other sources.[6]

Owen belonged inextricably to this tradition of Christian living. We have already seen that he had lacked assurance himself for an extended period of time in earlier years. But he became increasingly persuaded that it was a mistake to follow this exegesis of the 'seal of the Spirit'. In his earlier ministry he sensed a lack of certainty in his own exegesis. As late as 1657 he wrote: 'I am not very clear in the certain particular intendment of this metaphor' (i.e. the seal of the Spirit).[7] He rejected the

---

[1]*Ibid.*, p. 233.   [2]*Ibid.*, p. 236.
[3]Richard Baxter, *Practical Works*, IV, London, 1847, p. 308.
[4]*Ibid.*   [5]*Ibid.*
[6]e.g. Thomas Brooks, *Works*, ed. A. B. Grosart, Edinburgh, 1861–67, II.229ff. Cf. G. F. Nuttall, *The Holy Spirit in Puritan Faith and Experience*, London, 1946, pp. 138ff.
[7]II.242.

view which Calvin had suggested, that the Spirit is 'said to seal us, by assuring our hearts of those promises and their stability',[1] and insisted that it was not *promises* but *persons* who were sealed.[2] Instead of this, he argued, 'We are sealed to the day of redemption, when, from the stamp, image, and character of the Spirit upon our souls, we have a fresh sense of the love of God given to us, with a comfortable persuasion of our acceptation with him'.[3] His mind was not, at the time of writing, settled on one side of the question or the other. He was certainly reluctant actually to *deny* that the Holy Spirit might give such full assurance after conversion.[4]

In later years Owen came to a more settled exegesis. It is difficult to resist the view that he was consciously differing from the cherished opinions of close friends,[5] while expressing a more accurate statement of their communal convictions. In the posthumously published[6] concluding sections of his treatise on the Holy Spirit, he states that sealing is 'no especial act of the Spirit, but only an especial effect of his communication unto us'.[7] Again, he writes, 'The effects of this sealing are gracious operations of the Holy Spirit in and upon believers; but the sealing itself is the communication of the Spirit unto them'.[8] Owen realized this was not standard exegesis in the Puritan school:

It hath been generally conceived that this sealing with the Spirit is that which gives assurance unto believers, – and so indeed it doth, although the way whereby it doth it hath not been rightly apprehended; and, therefore, none have been able to declare the especial nature of that act of the Spirit whereby he seals us, whence such assurance should ensue. But it is indeed not any act of the Spirit in us that is the ground of our assurance, but the communication of the Spirit unto us.[9]

Owen's exposition is controlled by the theological principle that all spiritual blessings are communicated to the church in Christ – 'in him, in whom all things are conspicuous, we may learn the nature of those things which, in lesser measure and

---

[1]II.242 2–3.   [2]II.243. cf his later comments, IV.400.
[3]II.243.   [4]IV.405 'I do not deny such an especial work of the Spirit.'
Cf. XI.335.
[5]IV.400–1.   [6]1693.   [7]IV.400.   [8]IV.404.
[9]IV.405.

much darkness in ourselves, we are made partakers of'.[1] Since Christ is said to have been sealed by the Father,[2] the sealing of the Christian should be understood in that light. His sealing was, in particular, the communication of the Spirit to him in all his fulness.[3] Owen is therefore driven to the conclusion that the seal of the Spirit must be the communication of the Spirit to the believer. Assurance is the knowledge of the possession of the Holy Spirit:[4] 'this is to be the sole rule of your self-examination whether you are sealed of God or no.'[5]

What Owen has done, it is now clear, is to remove the suggestion of any theology of subsequence from his doctrine of the Christian life, without destroying the element of progression and development in experience of God. Elsewhere he is able to say that there is 'a twofold *coming unto Christ* by believing. The first is that we may have life. . . . . But, secondly, there is also a coming unto him by believers in the actual exercise of faith, that they may "have this life more abundantly," (John X.10)'.[6] So it is with the Holy Spirit.[7] He seals the believer by his personal indwelling. But the recognition and enjoyment of his presence is a matter concerning which no rules may be prescribed in terms of a single identifiable experience.

Owen does not deny that Christians may have 'special' experiences. He says so in a moving passage which summarizes the place the Spirit has in all his thinking about fellowship with God and the assurance of faith:

Now, sometimes the soul because it hath somewhat remaining in it of the principle that it had in its old condition, is put to question whether it be a child of God or no; and thereupon, as in a thing of the greatest importance, puts in its claim, with all the evidences that it hath to make good its title. The Spirit comes and bears witness in this case.[8] An allusion it is to judicial proceedings in point of titles and evidences. The judge being set, the person concerned lays his claim, produceth his evidences, and pleads them; his adversaries endeavouring all that in them lies to invalidate them, and disannul his plea, and to cast him in his claim. In the midst of the trial, a person of known and approved integrity comes into the court, and gives testimony fully and directly

---

[1]IV.401.   [2]Jn. 6.27.   [3]IV.403.   [4]IV.405.
[5]IV.406.   [6]I.396.   [7]XI.335.
[8]In keeping with the fundamental character of the witness of the Spirit, this testimony is 'sure and infallible in itself'. XI.154. See below, pp. 192ff.

on the behalf of the claimer; which stops the mouths of all his adversaries, and fills the man that pleaded with joy and satisfaction. So is it in this case. The soul, by the power of its own conscience, is brought before the law of God. There a man puts in his plea, – that he is a child of God, that he belongs to God's family; and for this end produceth all his evidences, every thing whereby faith gives him an interest in God. Satan, in the meantime, opposeth with all his might; sin and law assist him; many flaws are found in his evidences; the truth of them all is questioned; and the soul hangs in suspense as to the issue. In the midst of the plea and contest the Comforter comes, and, by a word of promise or otherwise, overpowers the heart with a comfortable persuasion (and bears down all objections) that his plea is good, and that he is a child of God. . . . When our spirits are pleading their right and title, he comes in and bears witness on our side; at the same time enabling us to put forth acts of filial obedience, kind and child-like; which is called 'crying, Abba, Father,' Gal. iv.6. Remember still the manner of the Spirit's working, before mentioned, – that he doth it effectually, voluntarily, and freely. Hence sometimes the dispute hangs long, – the cause is pleading many years. The law seems sometimes to prevail, sin and Satan to rejoice; and the poor soul is filled with dread about its inheritance. Perhaps its own witness, from its faith, sanctification, former experience, keeps up the plea with some life and comfort; but the work is not done, the conquest is not fully obtained, until the Spirit, who worketh freely and effectually, when and how he will, comes in with his testimony also; clothing his power with a word of promise, he makes all parties concerned to attend unto him, and puts an end to the controversy.

Herein he gives us holy communion with himself. The soul knows his voice when he speaks, 'Nec hominem sonat.' There is something too great in it to be the effect of a created power. When the Lord Jesus Christ at one word stilled the raging of the sea and wind, all that were with him knew there was divine power at hand, Matt. viii.25–27. And when the Holy Ghost by one word stills the tumults and storms that are raised in the soul, giving it an immediate calm and security, it knows his divine power, and rejoices in his presence.[1]

The reference to Matthew 8.25–7 recalls Owen's own coming to assurance, after, in his own case 'the cause' was 'pleading many years'.[2] His wise and patient exposition of assurance inevitably received flesh and blood from his personal search for assured acceptance before God.

[1]II.241–2.
[2]Above p. 2.

∾ 6 ∾

Conflict With Sin

For John Owen, sanctification has several constituent parts.[1] It involves the gradual renewal of our human nature, and the assistance of God's Spirit in the living of the obedient life. It also includes the assistance God gives, in temptation and trial, for the mortification of sin. This process is the maturation and growth of regeneration. It involves a radical cleavage from sin on the one hand, and the restoration of the image of God on the other. In Pauline fashion, Owen deals both positively and negatively with these aspects of the development of the Christian life.

i. *Sin's dominion ended*

When a person becomes a Christian, the *dominion* of sin is broken.[2] Owen builds his doctrine of sanctification on this foundation.

Sin is not primarily an activity of man's will so much as a captivity which man suffers, as an alien *power* grips his soul.[3] It is an axiom for Owen that while the *presence* of sin can never be abolished in this life, nor the *influence* of sin altered (its tendency is always the same), its *dominion* can, indeed, must be destroyed if a man is to be a Christian. This is the whole force of Paul's declaration in Romans 6.14: 'That sin which is *in you* shall not have *dominion over you.*'[4] The *nature* of sin does not change in regeneration or sanctification, but its *status* in us is radically

---

[1]I.177, cf. XXIV.270.　　[2]Rom. 6.14.　　[3]III.427, 431.
[4]VII.506.

altered.[1] Such a distinction is crucial for the understanding of Paul's teaching, and definitive of the very character of the Christian life.[2]

This raises some very basic questions which Owen answers in the course of a treatise on *The Dominion of Sin and Grace*.[3]

What is the *character* of indwelling sin's dominion? It is a '*usurped*' dominion. It has no *right* to rule in men, nor do men have the right to allow its rule. Under the law of God men have the legal authority to overthrow its reign, but they do not possess the power to accomplish such an end.[4] Nor do they have the will to do so, since the natural mind is at enmity with God; it *cannot*, and *will not* submit to the law of God.[5] Paul teaches that God may even resort to abandoning men to this predicament.[6] It is but righteous judgment when men continue their practice of known sin, ignoring the warnings of God and despising his word; when they relinquish their share in the means of grace, and take pleasure in deliberately associating with others who enjoy the profane treatment of Christian people.[7] Such are verging on the sin against the Holy Spirit. Sin is not only present, but *reigns* in their lives.

But Owen is quick to point out that the dominion of sin is more than a *force* in the life of man. It has the character of a *law*,[8] a notion he later expounds in greater detail. Where sin reigns, the consent of the individual's will is involved, and this leads to the total domination of the life of man by sin. Sin is alien to man *as man* but it is legally installed in man *as sinner*.[9] Only one principle may exercise supreme rule in a life: 'Grace and sin may be in the same soul at the same time, but they cannot bear rule in the same soul at the same time.'[10] Naturally such a dominion *exercises* its power in man, whether it be in repressing

---

[1] VI.177.

[2] This is expressed in the passage in Rom. 6.2 by Paul's use of *hoitines*. 'Paul does not use the ordinary relative (hoi – we who died) but a specialized form (hoitines) which gives the sense "We who in our essential nature, i.e. just because we are Christians, died." . . . *as Christians* we have died to sin.' C. K. Barrett, *A Commentary on the Epistle to the Romans*, London, 1962, p. 121. Owen does not make use of the linguistic emphasis in his discussions of Romans 6, but he grasped the point nevertheless.

[3] VII.499ff. [4] VII.509.

[5] VII.510. Owen is drawing on Rom. 8.7. [6] Rom. 1.24, 26, 28.

[7] VII.511–2. [8] VII.512; VI.163f. [9] VII.512. [10] VII.513.

the convictions of the mind towards good, or soliciting them towards evil and specific sins.[1]

Two practical, pastoral problems arise from this. The first is to convince those who are under sin's dominion that this is their predicament. The second is to convince others that they are not. It is to help resolve this problem that Owen further asks: *How do we know whether sin has dominion or not?*[2]

In some instances sin's dominion is clear and certain.[3] But what of less obvious cases? It is possible to experience much that *seems* inconsistent with the dominion of sin, and yet really to be under that dominion. To know the divine illumination; to experience a change in the affections; assiduously to perform external duties, like the Young Ruler in the Gospels; even to know a kind of repentance and resolve to live a new life in the future – all this is possible without sin being dethroned in the heart. Owen resolves the question thus: where there is the dominion of sin, it rules in the *whole* soul, and evidences its presence in every distinct aspect of our faculties.[4] It is universal and all-pervasive.

What then are the symptoms of this condition? Where sin has possessed the *imagination* and engaged the *thought process* this dominion may be found, whether the mental processes tend to thoughts of self-elation, or sensuality, or unbelief.[5]

Similar temptations and moral failures may appear in the true believer, but in his case they are the result of particular opportunities rather than a settled disposition. Further, this experience is a burden which afflicts him rather than a pleasure which delights him. The true believer detests the lusts he discovers in himself, and in fact may really be the victim of a satanic attack, 'surprising, furious, and irresistible'.[6]

Sin may also have dominion when it prevails in the *affections*.[7] The presence of the 'love of the world' suggests the absence of 'love for the Father' (1 Jn. 2.15).

Sin will also prevail when the duties of faith,[8] such as mortification of sin, and growth in the graces of the Spirit are

---

[1]VII.515–6.　　[2]VII.518.
[3]*Ibid*. Owen quotes Rom. 6.12, 13, 16.
[4]VII.518–9.　　[5]VII.520.　　[6]VII.524.
[7]*Ibid*.　　[8]VII.526.

ignored. It often reveals itself by a reluctance toward spiritual duties, leading first to unwillingness to fulfil them, and finally to a total neglect of them.[1]

Again, where the antipathy to sin is directed against only *one* known sin, and not to all sins and to sin *as sin*, the dominion of sin continues: 'Whatever impeacheth the universality of obedience in one thing overthrows its sincerity in all things.'[2]

Hardness of heart is also a symptom of sin's dominion,[3] and is frequently illustrated in Scripture. Owen treats it at some length.[4] He maintains it is either *total* or *partial*, either *natural* or *judicial*. Natural hardness of heart is present from birth, judicial hardness is either immediately from God, or from the devil acting with the permission of the divine will. When Scripture speaks of *God* hardening the heart, it implies that he withholds the light and understanding by which men see their need of his grace, and also the means which would bring them to repentance. This is a condition without remedy.

There is another hardness of heart, which is different from the first because it is *lamented* by those who suffer it. They experience a loss of tenderness of heart in response to the word of God, and find a diminished sense of his power in their lives; they no longer are aware of their need of forgiveness; they are not affected in the same way by the sins of others; they lose their sense of God's displeasure with sin.[5] Yet they realize this to be their condition; they are humbled in heart, *and this in itself is assurance that sin does not yet have dominion in them.*

Besides these, Owen maintains there is a kind of intermediate condition, in which it is impossible to affirm categorically that sin has dominion, but equally impossible to affirm that its dominion is broken. This condition is 'hardly reconcilable unto the rule of grace'.[6] It exists when a man can feel secure although he is guilty of sin; when that guilt does not incite him to be watchful against other sin; when he is satisfied with an empty profession of faith; and when he has fallen into such a deadness of spiritual power that he is *'not recoverable by the ordinary means of grace.'*[7] Such was David during the months between his adultery with Bathsheba and the birth of the child and the preaching

[1]VII.527.   [2]VII.533.   [3]*Ibid.*   [4]VII.533–42.
[5]VII.534–6.   [6]VII.537.   [7]VII.538.

[128]

of Nathan (2 Sam. 11–12). This condition tends to the dominion of sin.

There are, however, clear evidences where sin prevails. If these can be detected then sin's dominion is not in doubt and the issue certain: When the only restraints on sin are the *consequences* of the action, sin has dominion in the will. When men boast of their sin and approve of it; when they neglect private worship and spiritual duties and reveal an enmity to true godliness, despising the means of conversion, the person of Jesus, and the warnings of the Scriptures; when they know nothing of the sanctifying power of the gospel and are open apostates or persecutors of the faithful[1] – *then sin clearly has dominion*.

Owen was deeply concerned both with the clear-cut application of Scripture and with these marginal areas of spiritual experience, where discerning pastoral ministry was (and is) so necessary.

This pastoral concern leads him to explain why the Christian enjoys the assurance that sin will not have dominion over him. The reason given by Paul is that Christians are not under the law, but under grace. If men are 'under the law' the dominion of sin cannot be broken, because 'law *giveth no strength against sin*'.[2] It cannot provide liberty of any kind, nor even provide a sufficient encouragement to be quit with sin, because '*Christ is not in the law* .... we are not made partakers of him thereby. ... And he it is alone who came to, and can, destroy this work of the devil'.[3] The Pauline doctrine of the law is thus understood by Puritan theology.[4] It was never intended to set men free from sin's sway, but to direct, and even drive them, to the only source of that freedom – in grace, because in Christ. The law, according to the New Testament is the 'strength of sin' and not its destroyer.[5]

---

[1]VII.541.

[2]VII.542. Owen concedes that law does contain grace, but in this context he is thinking of the law as *commandment*.

[3]VII.551.

[4]Cf. John Flavel, *Works*, London, 1820 II.287–306. The main stream Puritans, like Owen, did not think of the law as in opposition to grace, but as ancillary to the work of grace in salvation-history.

[5]1 Cor. 15.56.

How does Christ set us free from the law? And how does that
freedom involve freedom from the dominion of sin? For Owen
the answers are clear: Christ sets us free from the curse of the
law by taking that curse himself[1] and he fulfils the demands of
the law for holiness for the believer by his perfect life. He is the
end of the law for righteousness for everyone who believes.[2] He
is the believer's righteousness.[3] But how does freedom from the
law entail freedom from the dominion of sin? It is because the
believer's union with Christ, which effects his freedom from the
law, *also* effects his 'death to sin', for he is united to Christ both
in his death *under the law* and his simultaneous death *to sin*.[4] The
two were inseparable in Christ, and through union with him,
they are also inseparable in the Christian.[5]

But there are inevitably those who will say: 'My experience
would suggest that this is not so; there is so much that is sinful in
my life that I cannot be free from sin's dominion'. Owen offers
counsel which is based on his earlier distinction between the
presence of sin and the *dominion* of sin. The Christian should be
clear in his mind about the nature of sin's dominion, and learn to
distinguish between the rebellion of sin and the dominion of sin.[6]
It is of fundamental importance to realize that this is an article of
faith before it becomes a fact of experience. This is the *'method of
the operation of divine grace'*.[7] *'It is the great interest of a soul conflicting
with the power of sin to secure itself against its dominion, that it is not under
its dominion'*.[8] Owen is not against subjective experience of divine
power, but, he argues, on a scriptural and theological basis, that
experience should be the fruit of faith, and faith rooted and
grounded in the spiritual realities to which Scripture bears
testimony.[9] When this is seen to be the method of grace, then the
privilege of freedom from sin's dominion will become a vital part
of the Christian's experience.

ii. *Sin's presence continued*

Freedom from the dominion of sin is not, as Owen stresses, the

---

[1]Gal. 3.13.   [2]Rom. 10.4.   [3]1 Cor. 1.30.   [4]VII.550.
[5]Cf. *The Confession of Faith*, XIII. Sanctification is 'through the virtue of
Christ's death and resurrection'. This is the heart of Owen's doctrine of
sanctification.
[6]VII.547–8.   [7]VII. 549.   [8]VII.556.   [9]*Ibid.*

same thing as freedom from its presence and influence. Indeed, the power of sin remains where the dominion has been banished, and though that power of sin 'be *weakened*, yet its nature is not *changed*'.[1] Owen concentrates his attention on this distinction in his work, *The Nature, Power, Deceit, and Prevalency of the Remainders of Indwelling Sin in Believers*,[2] which again draws on the Pauline teaching on sin and sanctification.

(a) *Indwelling sin is a law*.[3] 'Where there is a law there is power'.[4] In the Christian, the law of sin may yet have a real *domination* while its *dominion* has come to an end.[5] He cannot afford to have a slight view of sin precisely because sin is enmity towards God. As a law, sin retains its power to promote what it commands, through rewards and punishments, the 'pleasures of sin for a season' (Heb. 11.25).[6]

But what kind of law is sin? It is 'a law *inbred* in us'.[7] As an indwelling 'law', or principle in our lives, it is in permanent readiness to act. When it does so, it is with a certain ease, as the sin which so easily besets.[8] It will be noted that Owen's thinking about inherent sin moves in the same dimension as his teaching on received grace;[9] both are principles, both substantial, one might even say 'physical', in the sense of influencing the whole of man's *phusis* or nature.

Owen understood sin to be a power in man's life before it was a deed actively performed by him.[10] It is necessary to bear this in mind in order to appreciate the emphasis of his teaching on sanctification. He lays great stress on the duties the believer is to perform, and especially faith in Christ and the exercise of personal responsibility in mortification. But this is rooted in his exposition of the nature of grace and sin. The Christian life is possible only because the dominion of sin has been broken. But the nature of the Christian life is partly determined by the character of indwelling sin which has to be destroyed if he is to

---

[1]VI.164.   [2]VI.154ff.   [3]Rom. 7.21.   [4]VI.163.
[5]VI.164.   [6]VI.164.   [7]VI.165.
[8]Heb. 12.1–2. Owen wavers in his interpretation of this text between thinking of the 'sin' as indwelling sin in its entirety and, on the other hand, a particular sin to which the Christian may be prone. The two are not, of course, unrelated, the one is the manifestation of the other, as Owen shows, XXIV.239.
[9]See above, pp. 42ff.   [10]Above, p. 125ff.

be made like Christ, and to reach his high destiny recreated in the image of God. It is in this context that Owen discusses the way in which sin works.

Scripture teaches that the *seat of sin* is to be found in the heart of man. 'Temptations and occasions put nothing into a man, but only draw out what was in him before'.[1] All real sins proceed from the heart. But what does Scripture mean by the heart? Sometimes it means the mind and the understanding, sometimes the will or the affections, sometimes the conscience, or the whole soul.[2] Sin's strength in the heart lies in its unsearchable nature – there is always more there than can be discovered; it lies too in the deceitfulness of man's heart which is full of contradictions.[3] This makes mortification and a spirit of watchfulness imperative.

(b) The *nature of sin* is *enmity with God*.[4] Unlike the status of being an enemy, enmity, the thing itself, is not able to accept terms of peace. It must be destroyed, not accommodated. This explains Owen's later teaching on mortification, and indicates why sanctification should have a negative aspect, as well as the positive one of recreation and renewal. The nature of sin is unalterable: 'Whatever effect be wrought upon it, there is no effect wrought in it, but that it is enmity still, sin still.'[5] With a touch of characteristic realism, Owen comments: 'It is in vain for a man to have any expectation of rest from his lust but by its death; of absolute freedom but by his own.'[6]

The question may be asked, what led Owen to adopt this view of Christian experience? His doctrine of the Christian life is more closely associated with his interpretation of Romans than any other New Testament book.[7] He understands, the much discussed verses in Romans 7.14–25 to refer to *regenerate* man.[8] The believer then is a 'wretched man' (Rom. 7.24) as long as he lives. Consequently, the enmity of sin to God is both universal and constant. Any other view will lead to

---

[1]VI.169.   [2]VI.170. Cf. III.252.   [3]VI.171.   [4]VI.176.
[5]VI.177, cf. VI.164.   [6]VI.178.

[7]This remains true although the shape and form of his teaching was not so clearly influenced by the form of Romans as was Calvin's. See F. Wendel, *Calvin* (Eng. trans., P. Mairet), London, 1965, p. 115.

[8]VI.157, 189, 195, 199, 202.

superficial conceptions of sanctification, and correspondingly slight experiences of God's grace.

(c) *The pattern of activity of indwelling sin* shows a certain 'aversation in it unto God',[1] revealed most clearly in the secret duties of faith: *in the affections*, producing a weariness towards the works of faith; *in the mind*, producing weakness in the practice of meditation.[2] There is also a more direct opposition to God, which works by *force* and by *deceit*.[3]

The *force* of sin is described in Scripture, as a lusting, and as a fighting.

First, it lusts, stirring and moving inordinate figments in the mind, desires in the appetite and the affections, proposing them to the will. But it rests not there, it cannot rest; it urgeth, presseth, and pursueth its proposals with earnestness, strength, and vigour, fighting, and contending, and warring to obtain its end and purpose.[4]

Sin then leads captive the soul, and develops a 'rage' and 'madness in its nature'.[5] In this context also Owen understands Romans 7.14–25 to refer to the regenerate man, and to sin's temporary success in his life. Indwelling sin draws some of its energy from outside itself, either from Satan, or the nature of the temptation.[6] But there is also a violent pressure in sin itself, 'like an untamed horse, which, having first cast off his rider, runs away with fierceness and rage'[7] resulting in fearless contempt of the danger to which sin leads. This may be related to earlier yielding to sin, maintains Owen, and that, in turn emphasizes the necessity in mortification to 'Venture all on the first attempt'.[8]

Sin is not only *brutal*, it is *subtle* too, and works by *deceit*. Scripture speaks in several places of the *deceitfulness* of sin[9] and

[1]VI.182.
[2]VI.186. Owen gives some directions to help at this point: the Christian should learn to live by rule, and try to prevent the early development of this 'aversation'; he should carry a constant sense of humility because of his sin, and work to feed the mind with considerations of the beauty and excellency of spiritual things.
[3]VI.189.   [4]VI.195.   [5]VI.206.
[6]VI.207, 'Though sin be always a fire in the bones, yet it flames not unless Satan come with his bellows to blow it up.'
[7]VI.208.   [8]*Ibid.*
[9]Heb. 3.13; Eph. 4.22; 1 Tim. 2.13–14.

frequently sounds the warning, 'Do not be deceived'.[1] This deceit affects the *mind* particularly, for 'though the entanglement of the affections unto sin be ofttimes most troublesome, yet the deceit of the mind is always most dangerous.'[2] It consists in presenting sinful activities to the mind in other than their true colours. James 1.14–15 indicates how easily this may be done by degrees, and makes plain that the *end* of deceit is death and the *means* generally temptation.[3] Owen uses these verses as an analysis of the whole pattern of sinful deceit, in which he says there are five degrees.

(1) The mind is drawn away 'from attending unto that course of obedience and holiness which, in opposition unto sin and the law thereof, he is bound with diligence to attend unto.'[4] It is drawn away from a sense of sinfulness, which is itself a protection from sin. This may lead to antinomianism.[5] The mind is also drawn away from an appreciation of the Christian's position in the world.[6] When the Christian is young, affections are strong and easily wounded by the presence of sin; but in later years there may be less power, less sensitivity in them. There needs to be a growing mental conviction of sin if the believer is to remain stable in his profession. The mind becomes more important the older the Christian grows, for there is 'No sinner like him that hath sinned away his convictions of sin'.[7] Simultaneously the believer will discover that the mind is also drawn away from the duties which preserve him from sin, particularly meditation and prayer, by which the hidden presence and work of sin may be discovered, and steps taken to countermine its deceitfulness.[8] When this is the case, our weariness in our spiritual duties may be accompanied by satisfaction in the performance of certain good deeds as a compensation for the neglect of other duties, and promising a more diligent fulfilment of them in the future.[9]

It is axiomatic for Owen that sin darkens the mind,[10] and this inevitably leads to a loss of watchfulness in the Christian. He must learn to be more sensitive to the sovereignty of God, the

---

[1]Lk. 21.8; I Cor. 6.9; 15.33; Gal. 6.7; Eph. 5.6.
[2]VI.213.   [3]VI.215.   [4]VI.216.   [5]VI.218.
[6]VI.221.   [7]VI.222.   [8]VI.226.   [9]VI.229–30.
[10]III.248, 280; VI.109.

deceit of sin, the love and kindness of God, and especially to the
grace of the Lord Jesus in shedding his blood for the remission
of sins, the presence and power of the indwelling Holy Spirit.[1]
But the sin that darkens the mind by deceit brings slothfulness
to the soul, and mental watchfulness is dissipated. Sin destroys
by deceit; it draws us from the duties which keep us from
sinning; it engenders carelessness in mental watchfulness, and
leads to spiritual sloth.[2]

(2) When the *mind* is drawn from its duty, the *affections* are
enticed. This happens when the affections '*stir up frequent
imaginations* about the proposed object which this deceit of sin
leadeth and enticeth towards'.[3] As a direct result, vain
thoughts arise in the mind, and are met with 'secret delight and
complacency'.[4] Then the individual will discover himself seeking
'cheap grace' for his sin. Eventually, when the mind is drawn
away and deceived by the desirability of sin, the *dangers of sin*
will be altogether hidden:

sin . . . will use a thousand wiles to hide from it the terror of the Lord,
the end of transgressions, and especially of that peculiar folly which it
solicits the mind unto. *Hopes of pardon* shall be used to hide it; and *future
repentance* shall hide it; and *present importunity* of lust shall hide it;
occasions and opportunities shall hide it; *surprisals* shall hide it . . . *fixing the
imagination* on present objects shall hide it; *desperate resolutions* to
venture the uttermost for the enjoyment of lust in its pleasures and
profits shall hide it. A thousand wiles it hath, which cannot be
recounted.[5]

If only watchfulness in duties will safeguard the Christian
against the drawing away of the mind, he must also learn to
keep the heart if he is to be guarded from the enticing of his
affections into sin.[6] He must learn to set his affections *deliberately*
and *frequently* on the things that are above,[7] and make the cross
of Christ in a special way the object of those affections.[8]

(3) When deception succeeds thus far, the next step is *the
conception of sin*.[9] In this the *will* is necessarily involved: 'without

---

[1]VI.238–41.   [2]VI.242–5.   [3]VI.245.   [4]VI.246.
[5]VI.249.   [6]*Ibid.*   [7]Col. 3.2.
[8]This, for Owen, is part of what Calvin had earlier designated central in
Christian experience, namely bearing the Cross. Cf. *Institutes* III.viii.
[9]VI.251.

the consent of the will sin cannot be committed'.[1] It is the root of our obedience or disobedience to God. How does sin produce consent in the will? The will consents only to what possesses an appearance of good.[2] In temptation, the mind is deceived into thinking that there is very little difference between: (i) there is pardon from sin that men may be free from sinning, and (ii) there is pardon from sin. Thus deceived the mind may impose on the will what is absolutely evil under the guise of an apparent good. When the will is thus fertilized by the mind and affections, sin is conceived.

(4) Sin will then be brought to actual accomplishment. Two things are needed for this: the power to commit sin, and the perseverance of the will in a purpose of sinning until the sin has been committed.

God's mercy will, at times, obstruct sin's birth, but this does not alleviate the *guilt* of sin, since it has already been conceived in the will. But it does obviate the external *fruit* of sin in society. God may do this in two ways: *by his providence*, obstructing the power of man to sin; or *by his grace* transforming and liberating the will of man from sin.[3]

God obstructs the power of man to sin in a number of ways. He may do so by cutting life short, or by cutting off some power in life.[4] Frequently he provides some external hindrance,[5] or, even removes the object of temptation altogether,[6] or diverts men's thoughts in some other direction.[7]

God also diverts sin inwardly, working on the will of the individual in restraining or renewing grace.[8]

Restraining grace usually involves 'certain arguments and reasonings presented to the mind of the sinner, whereby he is induced to desert his purpose, to change and alter his mind, as to the sin he had conceived.'[9] These may include the difficulty of performing the sin, or the inconvenience which may result, or

---

[1]*Ibid.* It is interesting to note Owen's order here. The *mind* is drawn, the *affections* entangled and sin conceived in the *will*. The will is the final fulcrum of man's responsibility and freedom.

[2]VI.254.   [3]VII.261.

[4]E.g. 2 Kings 18.35; 19.28, 35; Ex. 15.9–10; Gen. 6.12–13.

[5]I Sam. 14.45.   [6]Acts 12.1–11; Jno. 8.5–9; 10.39.

[7]Gen. 37.24; I Sam. 23.27.

[8]VI.258–70.   [9]VI.271.

the unprofitableness of it – all these are scriptural motives.[1] Or God may appeal to the conscience. He reminds his people

of their *wounding* the Lord Jesus Christ, and putting him to shame, – of their *grieving* the Holy Spirit, whereby they are sealed to the day of redemption, – of their *defiling* his dwelling place; minds them of the reproach, dishonour, scandal, which they bring on the gospel and the profession thereof; minds them of the *terrors*, darkness, wounds, want of peace, that they may bring upon their own souls.[2]

Renewing grace restrains sin in the unbeliever by conversion,[3] the great example of which, according to his own testimony, is Paul:[4] 'His heart was full of wickedness, blasphemy, and persecution; his conception of them was come unto rage and madness, and a full purpose of exercising them all to the utmost', and then, 'In the midst of all this violent pursuit of sin, a voice from heaven shuts up the womb and dries the breasts of it, and he cries "Lord, what wilt thou have me to do?"'[5] Renewing grace also gives fresh help to the Christian. This is part of Christ's work as Mediator, and one of the ways he enables us to escape from temptation.[6] This grace may be shown in affliction too, so that the Christian is able to say, 'Before I was afflicted I went astray; but now I obey your word.'[7]

(5) Sin finally erupts, and consequently produces declension in obedience to God. Owen finds this a frightening fact because it has so often been true of the greatest believers, like Noah, Lot, and David, 'not men of an ordinary size, but higher than their brethren, by the shoulders and upwards, in profession, yea, in real holiness.'[8] These were men who fell, not at the beginning of their lives, but when they had experienced the riches of God's grace. Thus Lot

saw, as one speaks, '*hell coming out of heaven*' upon unclean sinners; the greatest evidence, except the cross of Christ, that God ever gave in his providence of the judgment to come. He saw himself and children delivered by the special care and miraculous hand of God; and yet

[1]Matt. 14.5; Rom. 2.14–15; Gen. 37.26–7.
[2]VI.274.   [3]VI.275.   [4]I Tim. 1.16.
[5]VI.276.   [6]VI.277; cf. I Cor. 10.13.
[7]VI.278; Ps. 119.67.   [8]VI.279.

whilst these strange mercies were fresh upon him, he fell into *drunkenness and incest*.[1]

No man possesses an automatic immunity from the power of sin.

Owen had suggested that this eruption of sin may lead to a declension in obedience to God, an '*obdurate course* in sinning, that finisheth, consummates, and shuts up the whole work of sin, whereon ensues death or eternal ruin.'[2] He sees an example of this in King David, whose life reveals such a declension from the early years until his latter end.[3] It is a declension in zeal for God, in delight in the ordinances of religion, and in any conscientious loyalty to duties. All this is the result of the power of indwelling sin. But how does this pattern develop and take form in a man's life? It happens in two ways: indwelling sin dams the flow of grace which gives the Christian his sense of God's pardon, and it takes '*men off from their watch against the returns of Satan*.'[4] It does the former by producing sloth and negligence and by setting the mind off-balance, 'so that it shall have formal, weary, powerless thoughts of those things which should prevail with it unto diligence in thankful obedience.'[5] It may then introduce false ideas which corrupt the simplicity of the gospel, and the clear apprehensions the Christian formerly had of free grace and assured forgiveness through the love of Christ.[6]

Distraction from watching against the adversary the devil is a more complex matter.[7] Sin will entangle the soul in the things of this world.[8] This makes the soul negligent[9] so that it is no longer 'sober' or 'watchful'.[10] When this happens, the argument, 'This way, this course of walking, doth well enough with others; why may it not do so with us also?'[11] seems to carry a new force. Owen therefore issues a warning couched in the most direct and vigorus language:

Take heed, Christians; many of the professors with whom ye do converse are sick and wounded, – the wounds of some of them do stink

---

[1]VI.280.   [2]VI.216.   [3]VI.281.   [4]VI.294.
[5]VI.292.   [6]*Ibid.*   [7]VI.294.
[8]Calvin also likens Satan to Pharaoh, *Institutes* IV. xv. 9.
[9]VI.296.   [10]I Peter 5.8.   [11]VI.297.

and are corrupt because of their folly. If you have any spiritual health, do not think their weak and uneven walking will be accepted at your hands; much less think it will be well for you to become sick and to be wounded also.[1]

Christ warned his disciples against such hypocrites, for 'all that have oil in their lamps have it not in their vessels'.[2] The professing Christian is wise to make sure he does not share their condemnation.

Sin also operates in the cherishing of a particular lust in the heart. David kept himself from this in his earlier days, and could say, 'I was blameless before him, and I kept myself from guilt'.[3] But this was not the case when he yielded to indwelling sin; he discovered that *one* unmortified lust weakened grace *in every way*, and destroyed confidence in God in prayer, darkening the mind, numbing the conscience, fighting in the will for dominion, disturbing the thoughts, and breaking out in scandalous sins.[4]

The pattern is such that sin 'becomes to the soul like a moth in a garment, to eat up and devour the strongest threads of it, so that though the whole hang loose together, it is easily torn to pieces.'[5] It works by encouraging the neglect of private worship and devotion to God, drawing the soul away from the fountain of all spiritual blessing and bringing decay and corruption to the Christian's gracious relationship with God. In this context Owen gives expression to a thought often repeated in later evangelical piety: 'what a man is in secret, in these private duties, that he is in the eyes of God and no more'.[6] But there is an even greater deceit than this, for we can grow in understanding the truth of the gospel without our lives showing consistency with its teaching. A man may be 'puffed up' instead of being 'built up':[7] 'like a man that hath a dropsy, we are not to expect that he hath strength to his bigness'.[8] Elsewhere Owen distinguishes between knowing the *truth* of the gospel, and experiencing the *power of the truth* in the heart.[9] Similar decays in grace may be produced by carnal wisdom, (which teaches a man to trust in himself, while grace teaches him to trust in Christ), or by unconfessed and unrepented sin.[10]

[1]VI.298. [2]VI.297. [3]VI.298; cf. Ps. 18.23.
[4]VI.299. [5]*Ibid.* [6]VI.300. [7]I. Cor. 8.1.
[8]VI.301. [9]V.413; VI.387. [10]Cf. David, Ps. 38.5.

Owen has thus dealt with the nature of sin, its location in man's life, and its outworking in his experience. He also considers the *power* of sin in order to impress upon us the necessity of watchfulness.

The power of indwelling sin is no less real in the believer than it is in the unbeliever.[1] It does violence to the nature of man,[2] leading him into a life that is, ultimately, unreasonable and irrational. It keeps him from faith in the gospel, though this be reasonable,[3] profitable,[4] and necessary for salvation and the enjoyment of spiritual blessings.[5] It eventually leads to apostasy.

The power of sin is seen with greater clarity in the amount of opposition it is able to withstand from God's law. For his law shows the true nature of sin; it judges the sinner and shows him the consequences of his sin; it disquiets the soul and brings to it the terror of God; it even 'slays the soul' (*cf.* Rom. 7.9). Yet none of this deprives sin of its power. Rather than lose its strength it seems to thrive on such opposition, so that its rebellion is increased. At times sin may even seem to be conquered and defeated, but actually may be welling up, ready to break forth in another area of a person's life, sometimes dangerously in the sin of self-righteousness.[6] It has not been conquered, only diverted:

As a traveller, in his way meeting with a violent storm of thunder and rain, immediately turns out of his way to some house or tree for his shelter, but yet this causeth him not to give over his journey, – so soon as the storm is over he returns to his way and progress again; so it is with men in bondage unto sin.[7]

The law has no power to condemn sin, since it is weak through the flesh (Rom. 8.3).

But sin is assailed not only by the law; men themselves may make massive attempts to curb it without reference to Christ; by 'pilgrimages, penances, and self-torturing discipline'.[8] But all to no avail. The nature of sin cannot be changed, as Owen

[1]Above, pp. 125ff.
[2]VI.306 where sin is 'that inbred traitor', cf. V.430.
[3]VI.307. [4]*Ibid.* [5]VI.308. [6]VI.313-7.
[7]VI.317. [8]VI.321.

consistently maintains. Only the destruction of its *dominion* by regeneration, and the erosion of its *influence* in sanctification will protect us from its power and presence.

iii. *Temptations abound*

We have already seen that the means generally employed by indwelling sin are temptations.[1] Owen takes up this theme in a series of sermons preached in Oxford,[2] on the words of Jesus: 'Watch and pray that ye enter not into temptation'.[3] He not only deals with this particular text, but also gives a summary of his view of temptation, and especially explains what it means to *enter* into it.

'*Temptation*' is used in two different senses in Scripture. In a morally neutral sense, it means to test or to try: 'temptation is like a knife, that may either cut the meat or the throat of a man; it may be his food or his poison, his exercise or his destruction.'[4] More particularly, it indicates a leading into evil and sin. It is this more sinister meaning that Owen is concerned to expound, where temptation has 'an *active efficiency towards sinning*'.[5] To enter into temptation then is: '*any thing, state, way, or condition that, upon any account whatever, hath a force or efficacy to seduce, to draw the mind and heart of a man from its obedience, which God requires of him, into any sin, in any degree of it whatever*'.[6]

This has three different, and frequently concurrent sources: the world, which provides the theatre for temptation, and its opportunities; the flesh, in its natural tendency to sin; and the devil, who is the ultimate and sometimes the only source of the evil to which the individual is drawn. His 'fiery darts are prepared in the forge of his own malice, and shall, with all their venom and poison, be turned into his own heart for ever.'[7]

What is involved when a man is led into temptation, or enters

---

[1] W. Haller speaks of temptation as 'The central experience of Puritan morality'. *The Rise of Puritanism*, New York, 1938, p. 153.

[2] See VI.150 where the sermonic style is very clearly evident.

[3] Matt. 26.50.

[4] VI.92–3. Temptation itself is not sinful. Cf. IX.27 'Steadfastness in believing doth not exclude all temptations from without. When we say a tree is firmly rooted, we do not say that the wind never blows on it.'

[5] VI.95.   [6] VI.96.   [7] VI.95.

into it? It is not to be tempted *simpliciter*. Men can never be freed from that, even by watching and praying. Nor is it an ordinary work of the devil that is involved; nor does it mean to be conquered by temptation, for a man may enter into it without giving way to it. 'Whilst it knocks at the door we are at liberty; but when any temptation comes in and parleys with the heart, reasons with the mind, entices and allures the affections, be it a long or a short time, do it thus insensibly and imperceptibly, or do the soul take notice of it, we "enter into temptation."'[1] When a man falls into temptation, Satan is more insistent than usual in his tempting work, having taken an advantage against the soul. Or, it may be, a man's lusts meet with a special degree of external provocation. When this happens, it is the 'hour of temptation',[2] when temptation has come to a head.

This 'hour' may be the result of the long solicitations of sin. It is recognized by the fact that when temptation gains control of those around the Christian, he no longer feels a dislike and horror of it, or a sympathy for those who are entangled by it.[3] Owen notes that at its height temptation is marked by a restless urgency: 'When a temptation is in its hour it is restless; it is the time of battle, and it gives the soul no rest.'[4] There is a

conjunction of *affrightments and allurements*, these two comprise the whole forces of temptation. When both are brought together, temptation is in its hour. They were both in David's case as to the murder of Uriah. There was the fear of his revenge on his wife, and possibly on himself, and fear of the publication of his sin at least; and there was the allurement of his present enjoyment of her whom he lusted after. Men sometimes are carried into sin by love to it, and are continued in it by fear of what will ensue upon it.[5]

Christ teaches two means of guarding against this danger, namely *watching* and *praying*: 'these two comprise the whole endeavour of faith for the soul's preservation from temptation'.[6]

We are taught to pray, 'lead us not into temptation, but deliver us from evil'.[7] If a man will only face up to the issues, he

---

[1]VI.97.   [2]Rev. 3.10.   [3]VI.99.   [4]VI.100.
[5]*Ibid.*   [6]VI.101.

[7]Owen takes the second phrase of the petition as explanatory of the first, since 'if we are led into temptation, evil will befall us, more or less.' VI.101.

will quickly realize his need to listen to the teaching of Jesus; he will realize that he is '*weakness* itself',[1] and that neither his love of honour in the world, nor his sense of shame at open sin, will save him from temptation's power. If he considers the power of temptation, he will realize it darkens his mind and gives fuel to his lusts: 'It will lay the reins on the neck of a lust, and put spurs to the sides of it, that it may rush forward like a horse into the battle.'[2] Its power is displayed both publicly and privately, and its aim is the dishonour of God and the ruin of men's souls. If only a man will consider his own past temptations, and his record of success and failure, he will soon learn the importance of the injunction of Jesus Christ to pray.[3]

How then do we *know* that we have entered into temptation?[4] James 1.14 suggests it is when we are drawn into sin. But this process may take place in stages. It appears first when 'the heart begins secretly to *like the matter of the temptation*';[5] it grows when lust meets with temptation and is stimulated by opportunities for its exercise, and when formality begins to creep into duties.

It is at this point that the exhortation to 'watch and pray' is so relevant. The danger of the situation needs to be recognized, for, says Owen, 'I scarce ever knew any come off without a wound; the most have had their faith overthrown.'[6] But let there be prayer also, for it is not within the power of the strongest Christian to preserve himself; he is kept only by the power of God's grace: 'he that would be little in temptation, let him be much in prayer.'[7]

We must learn to take note of the times and seasons in our lives when there is the possibility of entering temptation. These are manifold: times of prosperity go hand in hand with temptation, indeed prosperity itself is a kind of temptation; times of neglected communion with God,[8] and by contrast times of great spiritual enjoyment, which are turned, by the weakness of our own hearts and the malice of Satan, into seasons of danger; times of self-confidence and self-comparison, as when Peter boasted that his faith was superior to that of the rest

[1]VI.104.   [2]VI.110.   [3]VI.114.   [4]VI.117.
[5]VI.119.   [6]VI.123.   [7]VI.126.   [8]VI.127-8.

of the disciples, and yet was the one to deny his Master.[1] All this emphasizes the need for the 'watching' commended by Christ.

Watching implies understanding one's individuality and guarding against personal moral weakness.[2] Let the Christian 'be acquainted with his own spirit, his natural frame and temper, *his lusts and corruptions*, his natural, sinful, or spiritual weaknesses, that, finding where his weaknesses lie, he may be careful to keep at a distance from all occasions of sin.'[3] If the first principle of this spiritual warfare would be, for Owen, *Know your enemy*, the second would certainly be, *Know your limitations*. The Christian must be aware of the situations in his own life which are peculiarly means of temptation *to him*.[4] Further, he ought to make advance provision for such times. Thus, 'If Satan, the prince of the world, come and find our hearts fortified against his batteries, and provided to hold out, he not only departs, but, as James says, he flees'.[5] Joseph, for example, had, stored in his heart, such a sense of the love of God that 'temptation could not stand' before it.[6] Protection is also available from the *law* of God: 'fear of death, hell, punishment, with the terror of the Lord in them,'[7] though the believer must realize that this is only of secondary and ancillary value. On its own, it can never provide adequate protection against temptation. So Owen stresses all the more:

Store the heart with a sense of the love of God in Christ, with the eternal design of his grace, with a taste of the blood of Christ, and his love in the shedding of it; get a relish of the privileges we have thereby, – our adoption, justification, acceptation with God; fill the heart with thoughts of the beauty of holiness, as it is designed by Christ for the end, issue and effect of his death; – and thou wilt, in an ordinary course of walking with God, have great peace and security as to the disturbance of temptations.[8]

When this is done, the Christian will be more awake to the first approach of temptation,[9] and will realize that the purpose of Satan is to beguile like a serpent and to devour like a lion.[10]

Temptation, therefore, should be met with faith directed towards Christ crucified. This is 'the shield of faith'. Our

---

[1]VI.129–30.   [2]VI.131.   [3]*Ibid.*   [4]VI.132.
[5]VI.133.   [6]VI.134.   [7]*Ibid.*   [8]VI.134.
[9]*Ibid.*   [10]VI.135.

attitude towards the sins to which we are tempted should be: 'Christ died for these, I will not live for them!'[1] If we are taken by surprise, we should look to God in Christ for help and succour in the hour of need; we should also diagnose the cause of the breach in our spiritual life, and block up our defences again.[2] This will help us to keep the word of Christ's patience, and in turn we will be kept in the hour of temptation.[3]

iv. *Mortification required*

Owen preached a further series of sermons in Oxford on the theme of mortification which were published in 1656 when he was still Vice-Chancellor of the University. The published work consists of only some eighty pages,[4] and is an exposition of Romans 8.13, 'If through the Spirit you mortify the deeds of the body you shall live.' It proved to be one of his most popular works, passing through several editions before the end of his own lifetime.

Mortification is characterized by Paul as a duty belonging to Christians, effected by the Spirit, and containing a conditional promise of life on its performance. '*The choicest believers, who are assuredly freed from the condemning power of sin, ought yet to make it their business all their days to mortify the indwelling power of sin*'.[5] The Spirit is the principal efficient cause of this work. It cannot be accomplished by man-made means. Indeed, 'Mortification from a self-strength, carried on by ways of self-invention, unto the end of a self-righteousness, is the soul and substance of all false religion in the world.'[6]

As to the duty itself, Paul's expressions require some definition:

'*Body*' in this context Owen takes to be the same as the 'flesh', the corruption and depravity of man's nature of which the body is the seat and instrument, its very members being made the servants of sin. Here as elsewhere Owen equates the 'body of sin' with the 'old man'.[7]

The *deeds* which are to be mortified are not only outward actions, but inner motivations.[8]

[1]*Ibid.*   [2]VI.136.   [3]VI.138; Rev. 3.10.   [4]VI.5–86.
[5]VI.7.   [6]*Ibid.*   [7]VI.7.   [8]VI.8.

'*Mortify*' is 'a metaphorical expression, taken from the putting of any living thing to death. To kill a man, or any other living thing, is to take away the principle of all his strength, vigour, and power, so that he cannot act or exert, or put forth any proper actings of his own; so it is in this case.'[1]

The well-being of the Christian depends on mortification: sin must be put to death in him, if he is to enjoy the comfort of the gospel and energy in his spiritual life.[2] Having cleared the ground with these definitions, Owen now proceeds to investigate the work of mortification itself. He treats it as a duty of believers, performed through the Spirit; he emphasizes its importance, and he outlines what is involved in it and how it is exercised.

(1). *Mortification is the duty of Believers*

When Paul enjoins mortification on the Colossian church, he addresses them as those who have been united to Christ in his death, burial, resurrection and ascension.[3] They are Christians, and as such share in the identity of being united to Christ; this is the foundation in grace for mortification. The branches are to draw upon the power of the Vine in his death, resurrection and exalted authority.[4]

Mortification is necessary because of the nature of indwelling sin.[5] We have seen that the *dominion* of sin is broken through regeneration, but that the *presence* of sin remains, or, as Owen now expresses it, 'We have a "body of death," Romans vii.24; from whence we are not delivered but by the death of our bodies'.[6] Sin is not only present, but active, and if not mortified 'will *bring forth great, cursed, scandalous, soul-destroying sins.*'[7] But, since '*Exercise* and *success* [in mortification] are the two main cherishers of grace in the heart',[8] 'let not that man think he makes any progress in holiness who walks not over the bellies of his lusts.'[9] Perseverance is needed. 'Notwithstanding . . . the real foundation of universal mortification laid in our first conversion, by conviction of sin, humiliation for sin, and the

---

[1]*Ibid.*   [2]VI.9.   [3]*Ibid.* cf. Col.3.1ff.   [4]VI.10.
[5]*Ibid.*   [6]VI.10–11.   [7]VI.12.   [8]VI.13.
[9]VI.14.

implantation of a new principle opposite to it, and destructive of it',[1] there needs to be advance throughout the Christian life.

It is also necessary because of the dangers of failure to mortify sin: 'To use the blood of Christ which is given to *cleanse* us, 1 John i.7; Tit. ii.14; the exaltation of Christ, which is to give us *repentance*, Acts v.31; the doctrine of grace, which teaches us to *deny all ungodliness*, Tit. ii.11–12, to countenance sin, is a rebellion that in the issue will break the bones.'[2] It will also bring disgrace on the Christian testimony and harden others against the gospel when they see such a contrast between profession and reality.[3]

(2). *Mortification is accomplished through the Spirit*

The Holy Spirit is the only *efficient* means of true mortification.[4] Owen believed the greater part of Roman Catholic religion consisted in using wrong means to deal with sin: 'Their vows, orders, fastings, penances, are all built on this ground; they are all for the mortifying of sin. Their preachings, sermons, and books of devotion, they look all this way.'[5] But they are not appointed by God, or, if so appointed, they are not used according to divine direction in Scripture. These things may be the stream of mortification but they should not be confused with the fountain of it, for they are directed to the natural man, instead of to the corruption of the old man – 'upon the body wherein we live instead of the body of death.'[6]

Mortification is a gift of the Crucified, Risen, Ascended Christ, and is mediated through the Spirit. He works in three ways. He causes the heart to abound in grace and in the fruit of the Spirit.[7] The antidote to corruption is being filled with the Spirit. But he also acts in 'a *real physical efficiency* on the root and habit of sin, for the weakening, destroying, and taking it away.'[8] This is done as 'He brings the *cross of Christ* into the heart of the sinner by faith.'[9] Owen means by 'the cross' the power of Christ's dying and rising which is ours through union

---

[1]*Ibid.*

[2]VI.15. This is a favourite expression with Owen, drawn from Pss. 51.8; 31.16.

[3]*Ibid.*   [4]VI.16.   [5]VI.16–17.   [6]VI.18.

[7]VI.19.   [8]VI.19.   [9]*Ibid.*

with him.[1] This union, as we have seen,[2] is founded on his union with us, in our nature,[3] in which he destroyed the work of the devil, in the sense of drawing out his authority and sting. There is not only death *for the guilt* of sin in Christ, but death *to its reign* too, which is the root of the ultimate death of its *presence*. Even when sanctification is negatively expressed, it has its origin in union with Christ.

Of course, this work of the Spirit is also the duty of the believer; these are not mutually exclusive. As with every grace, we engage in the duty of mortification through the Spirit, who works in us for obedience – '*in us* and *with us*, not *against us* or *without us*.'[4]

(3). *The Importance of Mortification*

Owen has already suggested that the continuation of spiritual well-being depends on mortification. He amplifies this by noting that this does not involve a mechanical cause and effect sequence. The metaphors in the Bible for spiritual progress are vital rather than mechanical. Hence, a man may perpetually mortify sin, yet not 'enjoy a good day of peace and consolation'.[5] Here Owen is stressing the sovereignty of God rather than what appears at first sight to be a rather dismal view of the life of the Christian. The duty of mortification is our responsibility, but the blessing is God's to bestow. The opposite is, however, an inevitable truth of experience. Unmortified sin will *weaken* the spirit, it will 'drink up the spirit, and all the vigour of the soul, and weaken it for all duties.'[6] It will *darken* the soul too, by hiding the love of God and removing the sense of adoptive privileges. By contrast, 'Mortification prunes all the graces of God, and makes room for them in our hearts to grow.'[7]

(4). *The Practice of Mortification*

The question now is:

Suppose a man to be a true believer, and yet finds in himself a powerful indwelling sin, leading him captive to the law of it,

---

[1]See III.516–7.   [2]Above, p. 32ff.   [3]See I.70.   [4]VI.20.
[5]VI.21.   [6]VI.22.   [7]VI.23.

consuming his heart with trouble, perplexing his thoughts, weakening his soul as to duties of communion with God, disquieting him as to peace, and perhaps defiling his conscience, and exposing him to hardening through the deceitfulness of sin, – what shall he do?[1]

In his answer, Owen defines true mortification, and provides both general and particular instruction to achieve it.

He first expounds what mortification is *not*: it does not mean to root out and utterly destroy sin. This is what is aimed at, but it cannot be accomplished in this life.[2] Nor is it the dissimulation of sin, for then a man has 'got another heart than he had, that is more cunning; not a new heart, that is more holy.'[3] Nor is mortification the development of a restful and quiet nature; such 'may seem to themselves and others very mortified men, when, perhaps, their hearts are a standing sink of all abominations.'[4] Nor is it the mere diverting of sin, as when Simon Magus's sorcery was diverted to covetousness.[5] Nor do the occasional conquests of sins amount to the mortifying of them – men may do this when sin has erupted in them – 'The whole man, spiritual and natural, being now awaked, sin shrinks in its head, appears not, but lies as dead before him'.[6]

Rather, mortification involves the habitual weakening of sin, and constant fighting against it with a measure of success.[7] The battle needs to be perpetual because each manifestation of sin contains the seeds of sin's evil dominion, and inclines to the same end. There is a necessary universal[8] crucifying of the flesh by which sin is weakened. Owen describes the scene:

As a man *nailed to the cross*; he first struggles, and strives, and cries out with great strength and might, but, as his blood and spirits waste, his strivings are faint and seldom, his cries low and hoarse, scarce to be heard; – when a man first sets on a lust or distemper, to deal with it, it struggles with great violence to break loose; it cries with earnestness and impatience to be satisfied and relieved; but when by mortification the blood and spirits of it are let out, it moves seldom and faintly, cries sparingly, and is scarce heard in the heart; it may have sometimes a dying pang, that makes an appearance of great vigour and strength,

---

[1]VI.24.
[2]VI.25. 'Its not being is the thing aimed at'.
[3]*Ibid.*   [4]*Ibid.*   [5]VI.26.   [6]*Ibid.*
[7]VI.28.   [8]XXIV.231.

but it is quickly over, especially if it be kept from considerable success.[1]

The believer must therefore constantly battle against sin. He must learn its strategy in relation to his own life – its 'ways, wiles, methods, advantages and occasions of its success',[2] and must daily exercise himself in this spiritual warfare, so that he may succeed.

We have seen that mortification is the *duty* of the believer.[3] It is of course true that it is every man's duty, but not necessarily his primary duty: 'mortification is not the *present* business of *unregenerate men*. God calls them not to it as yet; *conversion* is their work.'[4]

Mortification is therefore a work of faith, which purifies the heart.[5] But this must be coordinated with sincere and universal obedience if it is to prove successful.

There is no value in healing an individual sore in the body (argues Owen), if a man 'leave *the general habit of his body* under distempers'.[6] This kind of mortification really proceeds from motives of self-love and not from the hatred of sin and love of the cross. Christ bled for all our sins – 'Why dost thou not set thyself against them also?'[7] The work of mortification 'consists in *universal obedience*'.[8]

With this in mind, we can now consider the directions Owen gives preparatory to mortification, and for the work itself. What may the Christian do in a preparatory fashion? There are nine things to take in to account:

(1) We should, first, examine the symptoms of sin and their attendant dangers – is there a 'deadly mark'?[9] If so, then extraordinary measures will be needed as a remedy.

What is such a 'mark'? If a sin has long characterized our lives without any effort being made to deal with it, it may be impossible to distinguish this condition from the *dominion* of sin. Whenever we tolerate sin, we minimize its seriousness: 'a man searches his heart to see what evidences he can find of a good

---

[1]VI.30.
[2]VI.31. Owen quotes Ps. 51.3, which probably conveys a different meaning, although Owen's point remains valid.
[3]Above pp. 71ff.   [4]VI.35.   [5]Acts 15.9.   [6]VI.41.
[7]*Ibid.*   [8]*Ibid.*   [9]VI.43.

condition, notwithstanding that sin and lust, so that it may go well with him'.[1] We grant ourselves self-created pardon for such conditions. But to 'apply mercy, then, to a sin not vigorously mortified is to fulfil the end of the flesh upon the gospel.'[2]

Another such mark is the frequent consent of the will to sin, even if the external action is never consummated;[3] or, when we fight sin only because of the result of it – using only the *law* against it, and not the weapons of the gospel.[4] Other marks are judiciary hardness and sin against which some special work of God has not so far prevailed.

(2) '*Get a clear and abiding sense upon thy mind and conscience of the guilt, danger, and evil* of that sin wherewith thou art perplexed'.[5] We must remember that the breaking of sin's dominion aggravates the guilt of sin's commission in our lives. We should recall that sin hardens the heart by deceit, erodes our sense of peace, weakens our strength, and always leads to eternal destruction. No one thus entangled with sin can have a clear sense of scriptural assurance, for sin grieves the Spirit of God,[6] wounds Christ afresh, and mars the usefulness of our service.

(3) The *conscience* should be 'loaded' with the guilt of sin.[7] Sin should be brought into the light of the law and the gospel respectively, in the prayer that sin may be seen in the true light of God's holiness, grace and love, and the sacrifice of Christ for it. Then we will learn to tremble before the patience of God with those who have thus offended him.[8]

(4) We should pray for a new and constant desire to be delivered from the power of sin:[9] 'Assure thyself, unless thou *longest* for deliverance thou shalt not have it.'[10] This will make us look for opportunities of success against sin.

(5) The question should be asked: Is this sin related to my natural temperament and disposition?[11] This does not relieve the guilt of it; it may accentuate it, as in David's meditation in Psalm 51.5. But if this is the case, the only possible remedy is that of the apostle Paul, keeping the body in subjection with special reference to this natural disposition and catalyst of sin.[12]

[1]VI.44–5.   [2]VI.46.   [3]*Ibid.*   [4]VI.47.
[5]VI.50.   [6]VI.55–6.   [7]VI.56.   [8]VI.57–8.
[9]VI.59.   [10]VI.60.   [11]*Ibid.*   [12]VI.61. Cf. 1 Cor. 9.26–7.

(6) Care should be taken to analyse the *occasions of sin*. 'He that dares to dally with occasions of sin will dare to sin.'[1]

(7) 'Rise mightily against *the first actings*'[2] of sin. Sin cannot be contained, it must be slain.

(8) We must direct our meditation to what will promote self-abasement, for example, the majesty of God and the poverty of our knowledge of him,[3] remembering that 'our God is a consuming fire'.[4]

(9) We must listen to God's voice rather than our own, and not allow peace to enter our conscience until *God* speaks it.[5] It is his sovereign pleasure to do so, and Christ's prerogative to voice it to us by his word and Spirit.

Here Owen raises a vital pastoral question: *How may the voice of Christ be distinguished from our personal inclinations?* The voice is that of our personal inclinations if it is not accompanied by a genuine hatred of sin,[6] and not evidenced by a waiting patiently upon God, for 'self-healers, or men that speak peace to themselves, do commonly make haste.'[7] It is man's voice and not Christ's, if peace is spoken easily, or spoken to a heart that harbours sin contentedly,[8] or when the humiliation which attends a normal work of grace in such instances is absent.[9] But if Christ speaks, he does good to the soul which recognizes his voice because there is 'a secret instinct in faith, whereby it knows the voice of Christ when he speaks indeed; as the babe leaped in the womb when the blessed virgin came to Elisabeth, faith leaps in the heart when Christ indeed draws nigh to it.'[10]

This brings Owen to mortification proper. His exhaustive discussion thus far enables him now to confine his exposition to a few summarizing remarks: it is accomplished through faith in Christ, and in stages by the Holy Spirit.

'Set faith at work on Christ for the *killing* of thy sin. . . . Live in this, and thou wilt die a conqueror'.[11] We need to know the *provision* that has been made in Christ for this very purpose,[12] and that purging grace is received through abiding in him.[13] This will lift up our hearts for promised relief, to Christ as High

---

[1]VI.62. [2]*Ibid.* [3]VI.63. [4]VI.70, Heb. 12.29.
[5]*Ibid.* [6]VI.71. [7]VI.75. [8]VI.76.
[9]VI.77. [10]*Ibid.* [11]VI.79. [12]*Ibid.*
[13]John 15.3.

Priest, sympathizing with us and procuring grace for us. We will look to Christ's mercy and to his faithfulness to receive help, and with that expectation we will fulfil the duties of mortification previously outlined, and put ourselves in the way of Christ's help.[1]

Faith will be directed towards '*the death*, blood and cross of Christ; that is, on Christ crucified and slain. Mortification of sin is pecularily from the death of Christ.'[2] This is the reason why he died,[3] as Owen is never tired of emphasizing. Such faith will look to Christ for power to mortify sin, and for *grace* to be conformed to him in his death.

Mortification can never be thought of as separated from the ministry of the Spirit. He brings the work to a consummation. He convinces of sin in the first place,[4] and reveals the help that is in Christ.[5] He establishes the heart to expect relief, and he 'alone brings the *cross* of Christ into our hearts with its sin-killing power; for by the Spirit we are baptized into the death of Christ'.[6] He is both Author and Finisher of sanctification. His presence gives support in this essential work.

---

[1] VI.80–83.

[2] *Ibid.* Cf. Calvin: 'Paul referred explicitly to the cross in order to show more distinctly that the only source of our mortification is our participation in the death of Christ'. *Commentary on Romans*, p. 125.

[3] Titus 2.14; Eph. 5.25–7; I John 1.7; Heb. 1.3; Rev. 1.5.

[4] VI.95.   [5] VI.86.   [6] *Ibid.*

∽ 7 ∽

The Fellowship of the Saints

In any account of reformed theology the doctrine of the church demands treatment. This is all the more so in the theology of John Owen, in view of the definitive influence which Puritan ecclesiology had upon the whole character of its adherents' lives. For them, ecclesiology was a vitally important aspect of consistent Christian living. Since the church is the sphere of Christian experience in Owen's thought, there is an inextricable relationship between the teaching he provides on ecclesiology and the whole ethos of his doctrine of the Christian life and character.[1] The ancient maxim that there is no salvation outside of the church lies at the heart of his soteriology, so long as salvation is taken in its full New Testament sense.

Frequently, in this context, the regulative principle of the whole Christian life is applied to fellowship in the church: only what God has commanded in his word should be regarded as binding; in all else there may be liberty of action. Thus, while in soteriology, Owen defended the liberty of God in the sovereign exercise of his grace, in ecclesiology we find him contending for the liberty of the Christian man.[2] This is essentially a liberty to obey God and the teaching of Scripture.

Owen saw a very direct relationship between the covenant of God with his people, and the analogous church covenants by which Christians mutually bind themselves to him and one another.

The idea of the church covenant, while arising in the context of the federal theology, did not originally seem to be integrated

[1]XV.323.
[2]XV.213-4, 320, 401 and with respect to schism, XV.401.

[154]

with it in early Congregationalist thought.[1] Sometimes the congregational covenant obscured the covenant of grace, or at least was not happily married to it. Owen however sees the church covenant as the local application of the one covenant of grace, and for that reason marries his ecclesiology more successfully to his soteriology, and also expounds the doctrine of the church without an overbearing emphasis on the necessity of the congregational covenant.[2] Since union with Christ is the heart of the covenant,[3] and fellowship is based on union, the divine and human covenants belong together, so that the one is the foundation of the other.[4]

God's covenant with his people is the foundation of every church-state, of all offices, powers, privileges, and duties thereunto belonging. They have no other end, they are of no other use, but to communicate, express, declare, and exemplify, on the one hand, the grace of God in his covenant unto his people, and, on the other, the duties of his people according unto the tenor of the same covenant unto him.[5]

What we find in Owen's teaching is that the covenant of grace becomes the objective ground for the consecration of the individual believer, or congregation, to God and his kingdom. The congregation by virtue of its very constitution is objectively founded (in grace) rather than subjectively (in faith); it is upward looking (to God), rather than inward looking (to self-created communion); it is outward looking (because it exists to defend, exemplify and share the grace of the covenant) rather than holiness-orientated (concerned only to preserve itself

---

[1] Richard Rogers, in his *Seven Treatises* makes no mention of covenant theology, but speaks of the local covenant in the fifth treatise. Cf. I. Morgan, *Puritan Spirituality*, London, 1973, p. 36.

[2] See XV.486; 488; 489 for a striking lack of emphasis on church covenant. On the other hand, on Dec. 5, 1679, Owen preached a sermon (unpublished) on the renewal of the church covenant in interesting and unusual circumstances. He had, at an earlier date, proposed to his congregation that they should *review* their church covenant. This met with a lack of understanding from some, and opposition from others! When he faces the objection that this idea is not present in the New Testament, Owen simply replies that it is a duty of nature: 'Do you think that every Duty is exemplified in the New Testament?'

[3] XV.462.   [4] XVI.28.   [5] XV.329, cf. XVI.23.

unspotted from the world). It is undoubtedly this covenant foundation which, however unconsciously, meant that Owen's congregation in London consisted in large measure of men and women who were involved in this world,[1] as well as waiting for the world to come. It is significant that when Owen preached to them on texts now usually understood to refer to the events of the end-time, his exegesis and application of them was usually to the tumults of the present world rather than to the future kingdom.[2]

Two areas of investigation will lead to an appreciation of the doctrine of the church as the sphere of the Christian's experience. In the first place we must examine the nature of the church in general terms, and then, secondly, the relationship between the individual and the church in particular.

1. The Nature and Government of the Church

Owen's approach to the doctrine of the church is primarily *theological*.[3] In keeping with his distinction between the covenant of works or life, and the covenant of grace,[4] he regards the church-state as one which is founded in the light of nature.[5] This is important in view of his defence of the regulative principle, that only what is commanded in Scripture, *or agreeable to the light of nature* is acceptable in worship.[6] This latter concessive clause in the principle of purity of worship was necessary to any defence of it over against the Anglican view that whatever was not explicitly forbidden was permitted.

The foundation of the church lies in the fact that man was created by nature to worship God, and for a life of fellowship with others.[7] Hypothetically the church would have existed if man had never fallen, and the light of nature would have encouraged him to be receptive to further divine illumination.

[1]R. Tudur Jones, *Congregationalism in England* 1662–1962, London, 1962, pp. 40–1. *Transactions of The Congregational Historical Society* 1, pp. 28–9.
[2]VIII.247–9; IX.173–9.
[3]See XV.77ff., and XV.269–70 for his discussion of etymology.
[4]See above, pp. 22ff.
[5]XV.231.
[6]XV.402; XVII.451f.; XXI.550. Cf. *The Confession of Faith*, XXI.1, vii.
[7]XV.228.

Owen goes so far as to suggest that in this primitive church-state the trees in the Garden of Eden may be thought of as a '*sacramental* addition'.[1]

In the post-Edenic dispensation there is a special redemptive revelation, to which the church is peculiarly related. Yet the light of nature, however fragmented by man's sin, still shines, and continues to play a significant, if not determinative part, in the doctrine of the church. Thus, for example, Owen refutes the suggestion that the New Testament church took its pattern from the worship of the extra-scriptural pattern of the synagogue. Any elements common between the two flow from the light of nature.[2]

Three general conclusions may be drawn about the relationship between the light of nature and the church-state. Firstly, it is the natural duty of men to meet together for the worship of God, and to this man is restored by the gospel.[3] Secondly, whatever is required by the light of nature must be regarded as of divine institution.[4] Thirdly, general rules may be found in Scripture for applying the light of nature to the church-state, so that all may be done decently and in order.[5] It would be wrong therefore, Owen asserts, for the Christian to look for express command for all the practices of the worshipping community. Nonetheless, the approach to the so-called '*adiaphora*' should still be governed by the application of general biblical principles, and not merely by natural reason.[6]

It follows, in terms of the covenant structure of Owen's theology, that the new humanity, the elect of God, the church as now understood, is not simply founded on the light of nature and the covenant of works. It is the community of the new covenant, and fundamentally structured on the covenant of grace.[7] The church then becomes the sphere of the covenant of grace, in Owen's theology. Indeed it is only in these terms that the Spirit is himself covenanted to the church, and it becomes the dwelling place of God in the Spirit.[8] Since this covenant is

---

[1] XV.229; cf. T. Goodwin, *Works* X.8; XI.41.
[2] XV.246–7. This view was itself necessitated by Owen's adherence to the regulative principle.
[3] XV.243.   [4] *Ibid.*
[5] XV.244. Unfortunately Owen does not list them.
[6] *Ibid.*   [7] XV.329.   [8] IV.501.

founded in Christ, 'the Lord Christ is this single rock and foundation of the church'.[1] This is true both doctrinally (since it is the doctrine of Christ which animates and constitutes the church), and mystically (since membership involves a real and substantial union with him in his death and resurrection).

In historical terms, this church, founded upon Christ, has passed through a number of epochs. It was 'under age' during the 'old' dispensation of the one covenant of grace,[2] but in the 'new' dispensation in Christ it reaches its *teleiōsis* or *maturity*.[3] But this condition is itself brought about by a sequence, in which the 'extraordinary' officers of the church, specially called, gifted, inspired and commissioned, exercised their ministry antecedent to the founding of the new dispensation of the church, before giving place to the 'ordinary' officers of the church, to whom *it* [the church] is antecedent.[4]

i. *The Lord's congregation*

What then is the church? Owen offers a number of descriptions and definitions, in catechetical instruction, preaching, and theological writing, and it is of interest to record each of these:

1. In his *Greater Catechism* (1645), in answer to the question, What is the church? he defines it as:

The whole company of God's elect, called of God, by the Word and Spirit, out of their natural condition, to the dignity of his children, and united unto Christ their head, by faith, in the bond of the Spirit.[5]

2. In a sermon (preached in 1650, when he travelled north with Cromwell's army) on the words of Isaiah 56.7, 'Mine house shall be called a house of prayer for all people', he states:

By the church of Christ I understand, *primarily*, the whole multitude of them who antecedently are chosen of his Father, and given unto him; consequently, are redeemed, called, and justified in his blood. . . .

---

[1]I.33.   [2]Cf. IV.1ff.   [3]XV.232–3; XXII.394ff.

[4]XV.249, 492. Cf. Calvin's distinction, *Institutes* IV. iii. 5, employed by Owen XV.489. Owen tends to speak of the church in the New Testament dispensation as 'the evangelical church state', XV.232–3.

[5]I.485.

And, *secondarily*, also every holy assembly of mount Zion, whereunto the Lord Christ is made beauty and glory, – every particular church of his saints, inasmuch as they partake of the nature of the whole, being purchased by his blood.[1]

3. In *A Brief Instruction in the Worship of God*, first published anonymously in 1667, he defined a church as:

A society of persons called out of the world, or their natural worldly state, by the administration of the word and Spirit, unto the obedience of the faith, or the knowledge and worship of God in Christ, joined together in a holy band, or by special agreement, for the exercise of the communion of saints, in the due observation of all the ordinances of the gospel.[2]

4. In *An Inquiry into the Original, Nature, Institution, Power, Order, and Communion of Evangelical Churches* (1681), in response to a question about the church-state instituted by Jesus Christ. He defines the church as:

an especial society or congregation of professed believers, joined together according unto his mind, with their officers, guides, or rulers, whom he hath appointed, which do or may meet together for the celebration of all the ordinances of divine worship, the professing and authoritatively proposing the doctrine of the gospel, with the exercise of the discipline prescribed by himself, unto their own mutual edification, with the glory of Christ, in the preservation and propagation of his kingdom in the world.[3]

The main themes of Owen's teaching are then as follows: essentially the church consists of the 'chosen, called and faithful', in a universal sense. To be a Christian, by definition, is to be within the church. But the church has a specific manifestation: a congregation constituted in a particular form[4] and marked by four characteristics: the ministry of the word, the celebration of the sacraments, the exercise of discipline,[5] and the work of evangelism.[6] The church is then defined in universal and local terms. As to the former it is possible to think of it as 'invisible', since constituted by election, calling and

---

[1]VIII.286.   [2]XV.479.   [3]XV.262.
[4]That is, it is congregational.   [5]XV.262.
[6]Cf. John Cotton, *The Keyes of the Kingdom of Heaven*, London, 1644, p. 20, where evangelism is explicitly, if not exclusively, the work of elders.

faith; as to the latter it is visible, as the recipient of gifts by which it is organized and disciplined in its structure.[1] But Owen appears to hesitate to *define* the church in these terms, and this is of significance for the rest of his doctrine.[2]

It is already apparent that Owen's understanding of ecclesiology leaves room for only a universal and local expression of the church.[3] By local he means *congregational*. While he insists that, 'Salvation depends absolutely on no particular church-state in the world; he knows not the gospel who can really think it doth',[4] yet he does not sit lightly, as some later evangelical traditions were to do, to properly regulated order. His use of the adverb 'absolutely' serves as a reminder that the salvation bestowed in the work of regeneration and the declaration of justification, is to be worked through the whole of life in conversion and sanctification. In this sense, properly regulated church life is one of the duties of salvation and responsibilities of discipleship.[5]

At this point Owen exemplifies two features, characteristic of Puritanism, which have often suffered neglect at the hands of its evangelical descendants. He stressed the importance of ecclesiastical order for true Christian living, and he refused to draw an unhelpful distinction between the form and the content of the church, as though the latter could survive in strength without the former.[6] For him congregationalism was much closer to the *esse* of the church than its *bene esse*. He also believed wholeheartedly in a 'divine right' congregationalism, which not even his views on toleration diminished. Biblical scholarship was not yet at the stage of rejecting the whole notion of a specific form of government possessing 'divine right' in the early church, and Owen certainly shared with many of his contemporaries (within and beyond congregationalism) the view that this was the essence of any debate about the nature of the church.[7]

---

[1] IV.427.

[2] It would appear, by way of contrast, that *The Confession of Faith*, XXV, defined the church in terms of this distinction.

[3] XV.77ff.; 269–70. [4] XV.324. [5] XV.320.

[6] Cf. J. R. de Witt, *Jus Divinum, The Westminster Assembly and the Divine Right of Church Government*, Kampen, 1969, *passim*.

[7] For the lengths to which this could go, *ibid.*, p. 200.

Owen's congregationalism is essentially a truncated form of presbyterianism.[1] This, he believes, is the divinely appointed means of rule and government in the Christian church, because it is the institution of Christ and the apostles,[2] governed by the precepts and examples of the New Testament:[3] 'it is in congregational churches alone that these things can be done and observed'.[4]

The basis for this congregationalism is found in the twofold reference of the term *ekklēsia* in the New Testament, to either the invisible and universal church, or to a particular congregation. According to Owen it is in the local, congregational sense that the word is employed in the Gospels,[5] and it was such a church which was planted throughout the ancient world by the work of the apostles. Even in small areas many churches were planted and elders with deacons appointed.[6] This contention Owen believed to be substantiated by the history of the early church, and by the fact that, '*in no approved writers for the space of two hundred years after Christ is there any mention made of any other organical, visibly-professing church, but that only which is parochial or congregational*'.[7] Given this presupposition, along with the Puritan principle, that, this being the teaching of Scripture it is perpetually obligatory on the church, it becomes clear *why* the teaching of Owen on the church involved both non-conformity and the repudiation of the charge of schism which was so often brought against Puritans. We will see below[8] that Owen believed, with what may now appear to be a remarkable naïvety, that rather than beget schism, congregationalism was the one safe pathway to the true unity of the church, by a reduction to scriptural essentials.

This had not always been Owen's precise position. One of his earliest works, *The Duty of Pastors and People Distinguished* (1643), had been published as a defence of the *presbyterian* position, with this qualification that 'The conceptions delivered in the treatise were not (as appears in the issue) suited to the opinion of the one party nor of the other, but were such as occurred to mine own naked consideration of things, with relation to some

---

[1]XV.433.   [2]XV.194.   [3]XV.223.   [4]XV.268.
[5]But see Matt. 16.18!   [6]XV.269–70.
[7]XV.277.   [8]See p. 170ff.

differences that were then upheld in the place where I lived'.[1]
At that time Owen viewed congregationalism as a *'democratical
confusion'*[2](!) in which the people were ascribed 'primarily all
ecclesiastical power for the ruling of the congregation'.[3] In
effect he had confused the extremes of Brownism[4] with the
'middle-way . . . between that which is called Brownisme, and
the Presbyteriall-government, as it is practised',[5] and was
'unacquainted with the congregational way'.[6]

Shortly afterwards, Owen gave himself to an extended
study of the whole question of church government, and as a
foil for his work (he said that he had never *met* a congregationalist, and had only once *seen* one!),[7] he read John
Cotton's *The Keyes of the Kingdom of Heaven, and Power thereof,
according to the Word of God.* Cotton was then minister of the
church in Boston, New England, and a divine of prodigious
reputation. By a remarkable providence, ten years before,
Thomas Goodwin had consulted him, and 'Cotton made him
an independent'.[8] He was one of the three New England
theologians invited to the Westminster Assembly. But Cotton
made Owen an independent, not so much by changing his
views, as by this written demonstration to Owen that the
views he already held were closer to congregationalism than
contemporary presbyterianism! So much was this the case
that Owen admitted that his

principles were far more suited to what is the judgment and practice
of the congregational men than those of the presbyterian. . . . So that
when I compare what then I wrote with my present judgment, I am
scarce able to find the least difference between the one and the other;
only, a misapplication of names and things by me gives countenance
to this charge.[9]

[1]XIII.222–3. [2]XIII.5; cf. XIII.223. [3]XIII.5.

[4]After Robert Browne (c.1553–1633) whose *Treatise of Reformation without
Tarrying for Anie*, Middleburgh, 1582, summarized separatist views and
brought him much abuse. He is known as the 'father of English congregationalism'.

[5]*The Keyes of the Kingdom of Heaven*, Epistle to the Reader, by Philip Nye and
Thomas Goodwin, p. 5 (pages not numbered).

[6]XIII.223. [7]*Ibid.*

[8]*D.N.B.*, VIII, p. 148. The same appears to have been true of John
Goodwin.

[9]XIII.223.

In this congregationalism we find that Owen takes the covenant principle one step further. Just as the universal church is founded historically on the covenants of life and grace, the local manifestation of the *ekklēsia* of God is founded on a particular covenant, or a *'mutual confederation'*, of the people.[1] This Owen finds illustrated in 2 Corinthians 8.5 where the early Christians gave themselves to the Lord *and* to the apostles. He takes this to be an action of covenantal significance, involving a divine appointment demanding a solemn engagement on the part of the gathered people of God, who receive the annexation of God's special promises to them. While this is obviously not the covenant of grace, it is, for Owen, a 'gospel duty in the covenant of grace'.[2] Owen's exegesis loses sight of the relationship between these words and the collection for the saints at Jerusalem, which tends to cut the theological nerve of his emphasis. But his reasoning is that the context in which it is set gives the church relationship the character of a covenant.

Owen's view was really a more refined one than John Cotton's, which relied heavily on the development of the church covenant throughout the Old Testament. In *The Way of the Churches in New England*,[3] Cotton failed to provide *any* New Testament evidence for the church covenant position. Thomas Goodwin employed a similar argument.[4] It was not surprising that John Goodwin placed his finger on a weakness of this position when he asked where any mention of a church covenant could be found in the language of the New Testament.[5] Owen's view had this merit that, if it were possible to move from the explicitly revealed covenant of grace to a surmised covenant with Adam, it might also be possible to move from a church covenant in the old dispensation to another in the new.

The virtue of Owen's position was that he was able to see the

---

[1]XVI.25. [2]XVI.27. [3]1645, pp. 2–4.
[4]T. Goodwin, *Works* XI.490.
[5]*A Quaere concerning the Church-Covenant practised in the separate Congregations.* Sent with a Letter thereunto annexed from J.G. to T.G. Wherein it is proved that there is much evill and manifold inconveniences in the exacting and urging such a covenant, London, 1643.

church covenant as the result and application of the one covenant of God's grace.

ii. *Order in the church*

Owen envisioned congregations of a moderate size. In fact he saw the growth of congregational size and the consequent neglect of the real pastoral oversight of the flock to be one of the causes of spiritual decline in the early church.[1] He suggests that, ideally, a congregation should be not less than one hundred, and not more than five hundred,[2] if all the ordinances and mutual duties of congregational life are to be sustained. Obviously Owen believed this could be determined by the light of nature and a wise application of the New Testament.[3]

How then is a congregation constituted? Owen mentions two things in his brief discussion:[4] believers give themselves to the Lord and engage '*to do and observe all the things which Christ hath commanded* to be done and observed in that state . . . their so doing hath the nature of a divine covenant included in it',[5] and further:

They must give up themselves unto one another, by the will of God; that is, they must agree, consent, and engage among themselves, to observe all those mutual duties, to use all those privileges, and to exercise all those powers, which the Lord Christ hath prescribed and granted unto his church.[6]

The primary rule for such a properly constituted congregation is edification, which is ministerial, and consists in 'an *authoritative declaration* and application of the commands and will of Christ unto the souls of men'.[7] This thought leads us to consider Owen's view of the structure of ministry within the congregational life.

---

[1]XVI.201ff.   [2]VIII.51.

[3]It is interesting to note that when Owen's church united with Joseph Caryl's in 1673, Caryl's church had 136 members, and Owen's had 35. Within the next decade another one hundred or more members were received. Cf. P. Toon, *God's Statesman*, p. 154.

[4]XVI.25–30.   [5]XVI.27–28.   [6]XVI.28.

[7]XVI.33, cf. IV.514.

iii. *Office in the church*

Owen adopted the traditional reformed distinction between the 'extraordinary' officers listed in the New Testament, and the 'ordinary' officers who exercise their gifts throughout the whole of the Christian dispensation.[1] He held that it could be conclusively demonstrated that the office, gifts, and ministry of apostles, prophets and evangelists belonged exclusively to the founding of the church.[2] They combine an extraordinary call with extraordinary gifts, and are, in a certain sense, antecedent to the church's catholic formation.[3] Only the 'ordinary' offices of bishops or elders, and deacons continue. An examination of these not only clarifies Owen's teaching on the government of the church, but indicates the way in which the individual Christian is edified, and grows in grace, through the exercise of these ministries.

Bishops or elders, according to Owen, have authority to teach, administer the sacraments and rule. Or, more accurately, those elders who are pastors and/or teachers may do so. He finds another kind of elder whose function is regulatory rather than didactic, although such rule is clearly another form of the one ministry of the word.[4]

The role of the pastor is of fundamental importance to the whole experience of the life of the individual Christian (for Owen). He feeds and rules the flock of God[5] and must do so with love, care and tenderness. He is called outwardly by the church to exercise gifts which have been bestowed on him by God. He must therefore possess the necessary spiritual gifts for his task. He should be marked by his compassion and a prayerful and constant concern for the flock in all his public and private ministry; he should have a zeal for the glory of God, and in all these things have a degree of eminence. In this the pastor will simply reflect the character and gifts of the Chief Shepherd. The whole office is of Christ's appointing for the ordering and rule of the church, and carries his own authority. No man

---

[1] IV.438–53, cf. the beautiful illustration in Cotton's *Keyes of the Kingdom*, p. 20 where he describes the King giving gifts on his coronation which are not so lavishly distributed in ordinary government.
[2] IV.446.   [3] XV.258; 492.   [4] XVI.42–3.   [5] 1 Pet. 5.3.

should take the office to himself, but only those appointed to it according to the rule of Christ.[1]

Owen is not oblivious to the necessity that others should share in ministry, not by virtue of office, but 'in a way of *charity*'.[2] Spiritual gifts may very well be exercised without office, although, for the sake of the orderliness and decency of Christian fellowship, regular exercise of a preaching gift should be accompanied by office. This at least is the ordinary rule and should be followed in a mature and settled community of Christians.

How then is a man called to this ministry? His spiritual gifts should be tested and tried, and weighed for their qualities of edification.[3] His election to the pastoral office should be by the whole church, and should involve the congregation in which his ministry will be exercised. Here, following Calvin,[4] Owen draws attention to the use of the verb *cheirotoneō* in Acts 14.23, arguing that the election of a pastor is by congregational agreement, and not by external, or even internal imposition by special authority.[5] This choice does not *confer* power, in Owen's view; it is simply an instrumental means of *instating* in the authority given through the ordination of Christ. Here Owen believes he is at one with Clement, Ignatius, Tertullian, Cyprian and Origen.[6]

Thus the pastor is solemnly set apart for his duties, of which Owen lists eleven! His first responsibility is to feed the flock of God, as we have seen. This the pastor will do from the word of God, first of all studying and applying its teaching to himself, and then sharing this with his people: 'a man preacheth that sermon only well unto others which preacheth itself in his own soul';[7] 'If the word do not dwell with power *in* us, it will not pass with power *from* us.'[8] Clearly a man of spiritual wisdom, insight into human needs, and skilled in the exposition of Scripture is required to meet these standards for the pastoral and teaching ministry. It is a work of such moment that the example of the apostles, who devoted themselves to the study of

---

[1]XVI.49–53.   [2]XVI.53.   [3]XVI.55.

[4]*Institutes* IV. viii. 15; *Commentary on The Acts of the Apostles*, 14–28, trans. J. W. Fraser, ed. D. W. & T. F. Torrance, Edinburgh, 1966, p. 19. Cf. Cotton *Keyes*, p. 12 and *Way*, p. 42.

[5]XVI.61. Cf. XV.495.   [6]XVI.69.   [7]XVI.76.   [8]*Ibid*.

God's word and to prayer, is to be closely followed.

Prayer is another major responsibility of the pastor; he will pray for the preaching of the word, for, 'To preach the word . . . and not to follow it with constant and fervent prayer for its success, is to disbelieve its use, neglect its end, and to cast away the seed of the gospel at random'.[1] But the pastor will also pray for the whole congregation, and for individual members of it, as well as for the presence of Christ in the worship and for the preservation of the people in their faith.[2] He will also be responsible for the proper administration of the sacraments, preserving the truth of the gospel and defending it against attacks, and meanwhile do the work of an evangelist, directing his preaching of the word to conversion as well as edification.[3]

In personal work pastors will comfort and strengthen the tempted, a work for which they are fitted 'by diligent study of the Scriptures, meditation thereon, fervent prayer, experience of spiritual things, and temptations in their own souls, with a prudent observation of the manner of God's dealing with others, and the ways of the opposition made to the work of his grace in them'.[4] The pastor will suffer with his flock, care for the poor and visit the sick,[5] rule the church with other elders, have a care for fellowship with other churches, and all the while live a life that is exemplary in its humility and holiness. It is hardly a surprise to discover Owen thereafter treating two subsidiary matters: one, the calling of a colleague to help in the work, and the other the question of a pastor demitting his charge.

In the light of this high calling, it becomes clear how central a figure the pastor was in the life of the Puritan Christian, particularly when, as Owen suggested, a congregation is of sufficiently compact size for this kind of caring ministry to be exercised.[6] He is, in effect, trying to strike a balance in his teaching on the ministry between the two things held out in the New Testament as truly edifying in Christian experience and character, namely, the teaching of the word, and the exercise

[1]XVI.78. [2]*Ibid.* [3]XVI.80, 83.
[4]XVI.86. [5]XVI.87–8.
[6]XV.460. It is in the context of speaking of the work of Christ's servants in Eph. 4.11–16 that Owen speaks of increase of grace, communion with Christ, and experience of his love.

and reception of genuine love. Knowledge on its own puffs up, but love builds up, and it is this which is Owen's real concern. Thus, when he is speaking elsewhere of communion with Christ, the experience of his love, and growth in grace, it is natural for him to do so in the context of the central apostolic teaching on the function of the ministry.[1]

Owen accepted the commonly adopted view of his contemporaries that the work of teacher could be distinguished from that of pastor.[2] But his distinction was a different one from that made by Calvin,[3] who viewed the teacher as a lecturer who would not normally administer the sacraments. For Owen the teacher or doctor was also a ruling elder, and shared in the administration of the sacraments, since his office was of the same kind as that of pastor, while his special responsibility, according to his own distinctive gifts, was to teach the truth and confute error. Writing to Robert Asty, the father of his early biographer, Owen put the matter succinctly: 'I know no difference between a pastor and a teacher but what follows their different gifts; – the office is absolutely the same in both; the power the same, the right to the administration of all ordinances every way the same'.[4] Replying to similar questions from the same Robert Asty at the same time, Thomas Goodwin had given a similar reply: 'the distinction of officers arises from the distinction of gifts'.[5]

Alongside these elders are to be found ruling elders.[6] For Owen, all elders rule, and none but elders.[7] Thus in the New Testament church it was *as elders* that apostles held rule in the congregations with which they were associated.[8] This work is to be distinguished from the rule which is exercised in the teaching of the pastor, and requires different gifts. Indeed Owen thought it very rare to find the pastoral and ruling gifts

[1]*Ibid.*

[2]Cf. The Westminster Assembly's *Form of Church Government.*

[3]For Calvin's distinction between the pastor and teacher, see *Commentary on Romans*, pp. 269f; *Commentary on Galatians-Colossians*, p. 179. See also *Calvin: Theological Treatises*, trans. and ed. J. K. S. Reid, London 1954, *Draft Ecclesiastical Ordinances*, p. 58, 62 and the *Reply to Sadolet*, p. 222.

[4]I.cxix.   [5]*Works* XI.542.

[6]XVI.115–6.   [7]XVI.106.

[8]Church power resides first, of course, in Christ XV.500–1, 514.

combined in any one man.[1] What is noteworthy here is Owen's emphasis that elders received their authority from Christ and not from the congregation:[2] 'Though they have their power *by* the church, yet they have it not *from* the church'.[3] It was this kind of sentiment which made Richard Baxter hope (in vain) that his presbyterianism and Owen's congregationalism might one day be united.[4]

All rule in Owen's church is ministerial, in the fundamental sense of the term; it is a form of service, and it is exercised only in a spiritual manner in spiritual matters. The authority is always Christ's, and never man's.

In general the elders watch over the flock, motivated by love.[5] They encourage, visit and care for the members, and preserve peace and order in the flock. In this way the individual Christian and his family are cared for within a recognized structure of human fellowship.[6]

A well regulated congregation will also have *deacons*.[7] Owen sees the foundation for this office in such passages as John 12.8 (cf. Deuteronomy 15.11), and suggests that the responsibility for the work of the deacon originally fell upon the shoulders of the apostles as the first and only officers of the churches. Thus the traditional foundation of the deacon's work is found in the setting apart of the seven in Acts 6.1–6.[8] He notes that it is only the care of the work of mercy, i.e. the actual execution of it, which is the responsibility of deacons. There is no *authority* or *rule* involved in their service, and its function, apart from the administration of help, is to set others free for the ministry of the word. The diaconate is not, for Owen, the first step to the presbyterate. These offices are distinct in the work involved and the gifts specially required.[9]

Deacons also administer the contributions of the church,[10] and so it is in this context that Owen deals with the question of Christian liberality. He regarded the question of tithing as problematical: 'Herein, I confess, so many circumstances are in particular cases to be considered, as that it is impossible any

---

[1]XVI.108–9.   [2]XV.131.   [3]XV.501.
[4]See Goold's note, XV.446.   [5]XVI.135.   [6]XVI.138–143.
[7]XVI.143; XV.506.   [8]IX.434; XV.506.   [9]XVI.147–9.
[10]XVI.147ff.

one certain rule should be prescribed unto all persons'.[1]
Certainly, 'The precise law of tithing is not confirmed in the
gospel'.[2] But certain New Testament principles are clearly
applicable. The Christian should contribute weekly[3] and
bountifully,[4] according to his abilities[5] and as God has
prospered him,[6] willingly and freely.[7]

The deacons' ministry in this area is to make known to the
congregation what the existing and projected needs are, and to
encourage them in the ministry of giving, and admonish any
who may be negligent.[8] Owen displays a marked sense of
conscience about the use of such contributions, and in his view
the deacons have a further responsibility to familiarize themselves with the precise condition of the poor who may receive
help from the congregation. The 'means test' is not only
financial; it is moral: 'That in other things they walk according
unto rule'.[9] The ministry of the deacons is correspondingly
spiritual, since they are 'To comfort, counsel, and exhort them
unto *patience*, submission, contentment with their condition,
and thankfulness'.[10]

iv. *Unity of the church*

We have now traced Owen's exposition as it develops the idea
of the church in redemptive-historical terms, and then in
congregational and structural terms. His teaching raises the
question of the unity of the church on earth. In what way is it
manifested if churches are specifically congregational and
independent in their structure? The question was all the more
pressing for Owen in view of the appearance independent
churches gave of fragmenting the unity of the church in
England in the seventeenth century. These issues must be
raised again when we turn to consider the individual's relation
to the church, and particularly Owen's justification of membership outside the established communion.

In fact, however, Owen viewed congregationalism as a

[1]XXII.326.   [2]*Ibid.*   [3]I Cor. 16.1–2.
[4]2 Cor. 9.5–7.   [5]2 Cor. 8.13.   [6]I Cor. 16.2–4.
[7]2 Cor. 8.12. See XVI.147ff. where Owen uses these texts.
[8]XVI.148.   [9]*Ibid.*   [10]*Ibid.*

means of unity rather than division. He regarded it as the primitive church-state, and consequently the condition in which the original unity of the church consisted. Hence his view of church unity is simply that 'all churches should endeavour to reduce themselves unto the *primitive pattern*'.[1] He therefore maintains that the cause of unity is highly valued by non-conformists. Love and forbearance will bring a desire for the unity which is required and desired by Christ. It will be maintained by a due application of the rule prescribed by Christ:[2] '*this rule in general is the rule of faith, love, and obedience contained and revealed in the Scripture; and in particular, the commands that the Lord Christ hath given for the order and worship that he requires in his churches.*'[3] This is the unity which concerns the Christian[4] and only in terms of this rule can a man be guilty of schism: '*It is unity of Christ's appointment that schism respects as a sin against it, and not uniformity in things of men's appointment.*'[5] Even so, Owen longs for mutual forbearance which will lead to 'sedate conferences'![6]

Lest the conclusion be drawn that Owen is saying, in effect, that he need not face the theological questions involved in church unity and fellowship, simply because the established Church had gone (in his opinion) far astray from the commands of Christ, it should be remembered that 'Churches so appointed and established in order as hath been declared ought to hold communion among themselves, or with each other'.[7] Such communion involves an equality of power and order if not of gifts and usefulness (the abuse of which brought disorder in the early church).[8]

In such a union of churches as this, two things are involved: the relation of each congregation to Christ the head of the church, and the character of their relationship to each other.[9] Both must share the same faith in the doctrine of the gospel. Unity is in Christ and in the truth which is found in him, so that each congregation is to be a pillar and ground of the truth. Unity also involves the mutual fellowship of prayer, administration of the sacraments, and a professed submission to

[1]IV.478.   [2]XV.212.   [3]XV.213.   [4]XV.214.
[5]*Ibid.*   [6]XV.215.   [7]XVI.183.   [8]XVI.184, 189.
[9]XVI.190.

Christt.[1] This union is held together by love.[2]

Beyond this, Owen recognized the validity of a synod,[3] at which delegates meet to discuss and determine matters of mutual importance. They may be called to prevent divisions and avoid offences against mutual love; to advance the cause of the gospel by a joint confession of faith; to testify against current errors, and to advise those churches which find themselves in difficulties.[4] Consequently, there is scope for fellowship and for a general unity within the independent-congregationalism Owen adopted, and indeed, according to the regulative principle, this fellowship and general unity is *required* of such congregations by the gospel.

2. *The Individual in the church*

Having given attention to the general tenor of Owen's thinking about the nature of the church itself, we now turn to what he has to say about the relationship of the individual Christian to this church. Owen did not write a treatise on church member-ship. Nevertheless we may glean from his various ecclesio-logical writings a good deal of information about what kind of church the Christian should join,[5] about the duties which Christians share in the fellowship of the church, and also about individual discipline and excommunication.

i. *Valid Church life*

'What sort of churches the disciples of Christ may and ought to join themselves unto as unto entire communion'?[6] Owen replies

It is the duty of every one who professeth faith in Christ Jesus, and takes due care of his own eternal salvation, voluntarily and by his own choice to join himself unto some particular congregation of Christ's institution, for his own spiritual edification, and the right discharge of his commands.[7]

Here are hints of Owen's congregationalism: the Christian joins a 'particular' congregation, and does so 'voluntarily'. It must be one 'of Christ's institution', which indicates his

---

[1]XVI.191–2.   [2]XVI.195.   [3]XVI.196.   [4]XVI.195ff.
[5]XV.334.   [6]XV.334.   [7]XV.320.

insistence that only the command of Christ through his word is able to create a genuine spiritual duty.

In *An Inquiry Concerning Evangelical Churches*, these points are further elucidated. *Negatively*, the believer should not bind himself to a church where any fundamental article of faith is denied or rejected in its confession, nor where teaching is given which hinders biblical holiness and obedience. In terms of practice, he should avoid a church where the fundamentals of worship are overthrown, or where the true rule of worship (divine institution) has been altered.[1] Similarly where fundamental principles of ecclesiastical order or practice have been destroyed, where the ministry is not one accepted by the congregation[2] or qualified by true spiritual gifts and graces;[3] or where the discipline of Christ is not exercised.[4]

Positively, the believer should look for a church in which the fundamental truths are gladly accepted and recognized,[5] and Christ-ordained worship is celebrated and enjoyed.[6] Here he is at liberty to bear with differences from, and perhaps even additions to the apostolic prescriptions (although in this case he has no obligation of conscience to remain in fellowship).[7] He will look for a fully biblical exercise of ministry,[8] and the implementation of proper discipline.[9]

In this context, the Puritans have sometimes been heavily criticized as ecclesiastical perfectionists. But what Owen sought was not perfection so much as truly universal adherence to the principles of Scripture (hence his frequent quotations at this point). He was aiming at *scripturalness rather than perfection*.

It will be clear that the Christian who adopted Owen's teaching did not readily become a member of the national church! The fact that Owen's Christian life is non-conformist is an important practical factor in the whole of his thought at this point, and some consideration should be given to it.

Owen well expresses a common grievance of non-conformity when he writes: 'Men are forced by their interest to lay more weight on a few outward rites and ceremonies, which the world and the church might well have spared, had they not come into

[1]XV.335–6.   [2]*Ibid.*   [3]XV.337.   [4]*Ibid.*
[5]XV.339.   [6]XV.340.   [7]XV.340–1.   [8]XV.341.
[9]XV.343.

the minds of some men none know how, than upon the most *important graces and duties* of the gospel.'[1] What at first sight may seem to be a rather Philistine objection to the dignity and symbolism of a form of worship antithetical to the simplicity of non-conformity had, for Owen, much deeper implications.

What concerns Owen is that *these things are made obligatory without scriptural and dominical warrant*, and by that token ought not to have a place in the true worship of God, far less be imposed upon the consciences of Christian men. They offend, he believes, the genuine reformation principle, that 'nothing ought to be so imposed that is not prescribed in the Scripture'.[2]

Two further objections to conformity play a large part in the development of Owen's teaching. The *first* of these is his objection to *episcopacy*, and to the current doctrine of apostolic succession.[3] He argues that the church is *before* all its ordinary officers,[4] of which a bishop is one, and therefore the continuation of the apostolic church cannot be dependent upon them. Successive ordination there may be, but within Owen's exposition of the scriptural doctrine the power of such ordination, under Christ, lies in each congregation. Further, the doctrine of episcopal succession is built upon false presuppositions. It assumes, wrongly in Owen's view, that all ordination of bishops was originally apostolic, and that by virtue of it they received power to ordain others and commission them by a communication of power. It also assumed that this power cannot be forfeited by crime or error. He will not accept that such ordination can be regarded as valid, especially when men have been guilty of heresy, nor that those who have received such ordination have been *divinely* ordained and gifted.[5] It cannot be held, he argues, that power and authority in the church is a result of such ordination.

The results of this whole system, and their lack of correspondence with the New Testament pattern, are sufficient evidence to Owen of the error of this whole doctrine, a fact which he believes should be evident to all who have a true understanding of the doctrine of authority in the church.[6]

[1]XV.395.   [2]XV.401.   [3]XV.257.
[4]XV.258. See above, p. 165.   [5]XV.528–9.   [6]XV.260.

The *second* objection to conformity involves the worship of the episcopal church. Owen stresses that a complete separation ought to be made from the established church by every Christian whose aim is to 'live according to Scripture'.[1] Attendance at Prayer-Book services should be discouraged, as contrary to the general principle of Galatians 2.18, to refrain from building again what the gospel has destroyed. It is also contrary to the great rule that whatever is not of faith (which in Owen's theology is dependent upon the teaching of Scripture) is *sin*.[2] Further, it contravenes the principle that we are to bring our best to God[3] and that all things are to be done for edification.[4] But more than this, it would align the Puritan with those who persecute his brethren, and possibly encourage others to follow his example, thus, for all practical purposes, justifying the episcopal position and its condemnation of non-conformity as schism.

Characteristically Owen also believed that a 'reading ministry'[5] excluded the continuing gifts of the Holy Spirit. For similar reasons the non-conformist should avoid participating in the Lord's supper in the established church. To do so would involve him in an incorporation, both ecclesiastical and spiritual,[6] which would tend to justify the episcopal church-state as acceptable and biblical.[7]

ii. *The Charge of schism*

Is this not precisely the schism with which Owen and his fellows were charged? Does it not imply that the whole nature of such a Christian life is schismatic, and ultimately destructive of Christian love, the edification of the church and its unity? Can such a Christian escape the inevitable judgment that there is something incomplete, even immature about his Christian life and the whole ethos of his fellowship with the people of God? Owen was at great pains to vindicate himself and those like him from this charge of schism.

[1] I Cor. 4.1 (R.S.V.).
[2] XVI.241–2.   [3] Mal. 1.13f.; XVI.242.   [4] XVI.243.
[5] XVI.245.   [6] XVI.245–6.
[7] XVI.247. Cf. Thomas Goodwin's grudging acceptance of the legitimacy of occasional communion, *Works* XI.308.

He makes it clear that the separation (an expression which Owen differentiates from schism) of non-conformists is not an exercise in which they engage with any pleasure.[1] On the contrary, he argues that 'a reconciliation amongst all Protestants is our *duty*, and *practicable*'.[2] Indeed, he confesses, 'I would rather, much rather, spend all my time and days in making up and healing the breaches and schisms that are amongst Christians than one hour in justifying our divisions'.[3]

The crux of the defence of the non-conformist Christian against the charge of schism is essentially that 'schism' is an inappropriate term. In the true sense of the word, the non-conformist is not guilty of schism, and the odium which commonly accompanies the charge is therefore misapplied. Owen's demonstration of this follows an etymological and theological line, based on the recurring principle that 'we may abide solely by that discovery and description which is made of it in Scripture, – that that alone shall be esteemed schism which is there so called, or which hath the entire nature of that which is there so called. Other things may be other crimes',[4] but they cannot be regarded as the spiritual crime of schism.

The defence, in essence, is quite simply that the non-conformists (at least of the Owenian variety) can only be charged with the guilt of schism when presuppositions different from their own, and (Owen would argue) different from Scripture, are applied. If it were to be said in reply that Owen can only escape the charge of schism by the adoption of an entirely novel presupposition, he would reply that it is the mark of *conformity* to have adopted novelty, and the mark of the *truly* reformed tradition to have rejected it.[5]

In the ordinary or political sense, 'schism' indicates '*differences of mind and judgment, with troubles ensuing thereon, amongst men met in some one assembly, about the compassing of a common end and design*'.[6] In the spiritual sense, the expression is used only by Paul, and involves a division over *unnecessary* things. In his writings, schism takes place in an individual congregation, and does not involve separation. There is certainly no suggestion

---

[1]XVI.94.   [2]XIII.95.   [3]*Ibid.*   [4]XIII.99.
[5]XV.207–8.   [6]XIII.101.

that it involves a withdrawal of obedience from bishops or rulers.

Rather, schism consists in *'causeless differences and contentions amongst the members of a particular church, contrary to that exercise of love, prudence, and forbearance, which are required of them to be exercised amongst themselves, and towards one another'*.[1]

It follows from this that certain elements must be present in any activity which is rightly judged to be schism. It must involve members of the same congregation, and concern causeless differences with others, related in particular to the worship of God.[2] This Owen finds vindicated in Augustine's view that 'schism' refers only to those who share the same doctrine and worship, but choose to meet separately.[3] The then-current definition of schism as a rending of the seamless robe of Christ,[4] a sin against charity, and a rebellion against the church[5] he regarded as unscriptural, vague, and unacceptable. Since Owen views his own definition as scriptural, it follows that the Roman Church is the most schismatic of all![6] But then, according to his own principles, the Church of Rome, by virtue of its confession of faith, cannot be regarded as a true church at all.[7] Thus, according to Owen, departure or secession from it, on proper grounds, cannot be regarded as schism; it is obviously permissible.[8] The refusal of one church to hold fellowship with another, or the departure of an individual from the communion of a church, on sound principles, cannot be judged to be schismatic action. As far as the Church of England is concerned, Owen refuses to regard it as a church, as such, in terms of its constitution, since he believed Christ appointed no 'national church' in this sense.[9] The conclusion of the matter would seem to be that schism is only possible within the local congregation or at least in terms of it. It is perhaps not surprising that the attack on his position was not only taken up by the Dean of St Paul's, Dr Edward Stillingfleet,[10] but also by the

---

[1]XIII.108.   [2]XIII.108–9.   [3]XIII.109.
[4]XIII.110.
[5]XIII.111.   [6]XIII.114.
[7]XIII.115.
[8]XIII.199; XV.424.   [9]XIII.117–8.
[10]*D.N.B.* LIV, 375–8.

presbyterian Daniel Cawdrey,[1] of Billing in North-amptonshire! It is in his reply to the latter that Owen gives some personal insight into his own pilgrimage from Pres-byterianism to Independency.[2]

iii. *Church membership*

The qualifications for membership of the church are well defined in the Puritan tradition. Fundamental to them is the notion that it is not sufficient to be a citizen whose life is outwardly beyond reproach. The Puritans stood for a clear-cut distinction between decency and regeneration, regarding the latter as essential to adult church membership.[3] Regeneration is not baptism, as we have seen, but an inward and powerful work of the Spirit, of which baptism may properly be regarded as the sign. While true regeneration is a matter which only God can judge, yet a judgment is given to the church, to assess 'its evidences and fruits in their external demonstration, as unto a participation of *the outward privileges of a regenerate state*, and no farther, Acts viii.13'.[4] A number of things are involved in this judgment. Only those who answer the scriptural description of Christian character can be admitted, even to the visible church.

As far as Owen is concerned it must always be remembered that what is visible is the *church*, and that the church is in fact *visible*, if imperfectly, and can therefore be delineated and recognized. Robert Bellarmine, the Roman Catholic theolog-ian, must therefore be regarded as being in grave error when he says that 'no internal virtue or grace is required unto the constitution of a church in its members'.[5] An open and visibly acceptable confession of subjection to Christ and his authority must be required of aspiring members. The candidate for membership should have a competent knowledge of the

---

[1] *D.N.B.* IX, 377. He wrote, *The Inconsistency of The Independent Way with Scripture and Itself*, London 1651 and *Independency a Great Schism*, London, 1657, in which he 'assailed both the principles and the character of Dr. Owen in no very measured terms'. (Goold, *Works* XIII.208). Andrew Thomson calls Cawdrey 'a stormy petrel' (I.lxxiv). For another view, see J. Reid, *Memoirs of the Westminster Divines*, Paisley, 1811, I.219–20.

[2] XIII.223.   [3] XVI.13.   [4] *Ibid*.

[5] XVI.14 quoted from R. Bellarmine (1542–1621), *De Ecclesia*, III.2.

gospel, and particularly of the person and offices of Christ;[1] he must profess his subjection to Christ in the fellowship of the church. For adults this will be done at baptism; for those baptized in infancy it will be done when they profess 'consent unto and abiding in that covenant whereunto they were initiated'.[2] Further, potential members must be instructed in, and consent to '*the doctrine of self-denial and bearing of the cross*, in a particular manner; for this is made indispensably necessary by our Saviour himself unto all that will be his disciples, Matthew x.37–9; Mark viii.34, 38; Luke ix.23; Phil. iii.18; Acts iv.10, 11, 20; xxiv.14'.[3] Such aspiring members should have experience of the conviction and confession of sin, and of the power of Christ to deliver from its dominion, and will walk constantly and consistently in all the known duties of true religion, carefully abstaining from all known sins. This, in fact, is a brief summary of Owen's exposition of the work of the Spirit in the individual, with his resulting experience and duties. In short, candidates for membership must show evidence of regeneration by the profession of their lips and the practice of the new life.[4]

When candidates are regularly accepted into the fellowship of the congregation, there are certain obligations which they share with fellow-members that govern their mutual relationships. These Owen outlines in *Eshcol; A Cluster of the Fruit of Canaan . . . or, Rules of Direction for the Walking of the Saints in Fellowship, according to the Order of the Gospel*,[5] a work on which Goold comments, 'Owen is here, for once, a master in the art of condensation'![6]

The fundamental rule of Christian fellowship is affectionate and sincere love for fellow Christians.[7] This is 'the fountain, rule, scope, aim, and fruit of gospel communion'.[8] It naturally leads to prayer for the church and for the protection of God.[9] Members ought to strive, principally by the study and

---

[1]Hence the two Catechisms on Christ, I.463–94.
[2]XVI.16.
[3]*Ibid*. For the centrality of this theme in Calvin, see *Institutes* III.vii.8.
[4]XV.525–7. Compare the later emphasis on *experience* within Congregationalism, G. F. Nuttall, *Visible Saints, The Congregational Way*, 1640–1666, London, 1957, p. 112.
[5]XIII.53–87.　　[6]XIII.52.　　[7]XV.517.
[8]XIII.62.　　[9]XIII.64.

right application of the Scriptures, for the purity of the congregation and its enjoyment of all the covenant privileges promised in the gospel. Then, since union is 'the main aim and most proper fruit of love',[1] it follows that members will be concerned to preserve it, by prayer, by marking the first beginnings of strife and dealing with them, and by seeking together to be conformed to the mind of Christ.

It is also the duty of members belonging to the fellowship to be separated from the world[2] – not in the sense of breaking the bonds of natural and familial love, or neglecting to care for the whole of society, but rather in the whole tenor of lives transformed by the renewing of the mind rather than conformed to the thought patterns of the present age.[3] To promote this, frequent spiritual fellowship is necessary.[4] This naturally leads to the further obligation of bearing the infirmities of other Christians and also their burdens[5] – not only their weaknesses of a physical nature, but their failings in spiritual things.

Each member of a congregation is further duty-bound to contribute to the needs of the poor in the same fellowship,[6] to avoid every possible cause of division in it, and cheerfully share in its prosperity or affliction.[7] He will make no distinction between persons in worldly terms:[8] 'Men in the church are considered as saints, and not as great or rich. All are equal, all are naked, before God'.[9] Therefore if any one is persecuted, the whole church will share in humbling and prayer; if any sins, the whole church will be concerned. All should therefore have a caring watchfulness and pastoral concern for one another and engage in mutual admonition.[10] In such a context the final duty, exemplary Christian living, will follow naturally.[11] Mutual forbearance will be the keynote of the whole fellowship.[12]

These are indeed 'puritan' rules and principles of membership. It would not be too difficult to detect in them the possibility of situations emerging which, in view of the weakness of the best Christians, might result in the destruction

[1]XIII.66.   [2]XIII.68.   [3]Romans 12.1.   [4]XIII.69.
[5]XIII.70.   [6]XIII.74.   [7]XIII.79.   [8]XIII.80.
[9]XIII.81.   [10]XIII.83; XV.517; XXIV.524f.   [11]XIII.85.
[12]XV.215.

of fellowship rather than its promotion. But the rather remarkable fact is that to vindicate and expound these propositions, of which there are fifteen, Owen quotes from no less than two hundred and seventy parts of Scripture.[1] It is clear that, from his own point of view, he is doing no more than seeking to establish a truly scripturally-governed fellowship.

iv. *Discipline*

Since the authority of the church includes admission to the fellowship, it also includes the power of exclusion from it. Owen taught that the act of excommunication involves the whole church and is administered by the elders. The church has a duty to exclude those whose offences bring scandal to the name of Christ, who obstinately persist in sin, despite both private and public admonition, and also those who disrupt the peace and unity of the church.[2] Naturally this whole process is one that should be characterized by love,[3] patience,[4] and a forgiving spirit. But should the member involved remain intransigent, excommunication should be administered, accompanied with the prayer that what is done on earth might be ratified in heaven.[5] All this should be done with a genuine sense of mourning, and a consciousness of the future judgment of Christ. It should also be administered as a corrective, and not vindictive, judgment, since it is an ordinance for healing rather than destruction.[6] Owen argues that this discipline is necessary to the health of the body of Christ, even if at times it *seems* to cause more trouble than it cures. But the watchword is patience; no person who is charged with sin should thereby be excommunicated without careful and considerate investigation, and time for repentance, except perhaps when there is an obvious threat of public scandal otherwise.[7] Owen's answer to the question whether a person who repents should still receive the sentence of excommunication is simple and genuine: 'It would be publicly to *reject them* whom they

[1]XIII.53–87.
[2]XVI.165. Owen intended, but failed, to develop this point, p. 167 fn.
[3]XV.518.   [4]XV.520, 523.   [5]Matt. 16.19.   [6]XV.519.
[7]XV.516.Cf. Calvin, *Institutes* IV.xii.3.

acknowledge that *Christ doth receive.*'[1]

Discipline is to be administered sparingly and is not to be employed in dubious cases.[2] To zealots who ask whether those who leave the fellowship without its consent, and those who leave to join the parish church, should be excommunicated, Owen answers in the negative.[3] Even for those suspected of erroneous doctrine or practice, 'a considerable season or *space of time*'[4] should be allowed to elapse before the decree of excommunication is pronounced, and then only after considerable prayer on the part of the whole church. An excommunicated person should still be permitted and, indeed, encouraged to attend the congregation to receive the ministry of the word.[5]

What then *is* the deprivation involved in excommunication? Owen suggests it is the ordinary fellowship with an excommunicated person which is made by choice rather than occasion. It involves secular matters rather than spiritual, since the excommunicated individual is still to be admonished and helped. It does not involve the suspension of natural relationships, but any other fellowship not rendered necessary by such a relationship.[6]

The function of discipline is *to restore the offender*, so that he may be received, on repentance, *internally* with meekness, compassion, love, and with joy, and *publicly* on his repentance, with the consent of the church-covenant, through the auspices of the elders of the congregation.[7] This is so despite the fact that, for Owen, excommunication is proleptic of the last judgment of Christ;[8] the point being that without repentance that last judgment will finally vindicate the lesser pronouncement of the church. Because this is so the offending brother should continually be prayed for and admonished by the other members of the congregation, with a view to his re-engagement in their mutual covenant with God.[9]

It is in these last thoughts that we discover Owen returning to the covenant motif once again, for the church is the elect of God, covenanted to the Son in the counsel of redemption,

[1]XVI.176.   [2]XVI.182.   [3]XVI.178.   [4]*Ibid.*
[5]XVI.180.   [6]*Ibid.*   [7]XVI.181.   [8]XV.522.
[9]XV.523.

established in the beginning through the covenant of nature,
and sustained by the covenant of grace. It is within that
covenant, the new covenant in Christ's blood, that the principle
of fellowship and membership, or exclusion and excommunication operates, as a man specifically walks in the duties of the
covenant of grace, and consistently sustains the responsibilities
of the church covenant. To turn from these is inevitably to
share in the curse of the covenant, which is the obverse of its
promise, and in Pauline terms, to experience judgment rather
than salvation.[1]

The church then is simply the sphere in which the man who
has been brought into the covenant of grace, continues to
experience the benefits of that covenant, and expresses his
obedience to its duties by walking in fellowship according to the
command of Christ, and, as we have seen, 'according to
scripture'.[2]

[1] I Cor. 11.29.
[2] I Cor. 4.6 (R.S.V.).

➣ 8 ➣

Scripture and Ministry

John Owen's theology was carved out of a tradition which employed the philosophical categories of means and ends to describe the work of salvation: 'The end is the first, principal, *moving cause* of the whole';[1] 'the *means* are all those things which are used for the attaining of the end proposed'.[2] Within this context, the death of Christ was seen as the means to satisfy divine justice.[3] The same categories hold good for Owen throughout Christian experience as well. As God has employed *means* for our justification, so he employs means for our sanctification. These are the 'means of grace'.[4]

Owen distinguishes between 'outward means of grace'[5] and the means which are made effectual by the Holy Spirit. The bare use of means does not *guarantee* the end – they are not mechanical (*ex opere operato*) in nature.[6] Rather they are given as *covenant* pledges. It is only through the response of faith that 'we may attain the effect directly expressed, of being carried on in the increase of spiritual light and knowledge'.[7] God's wisdom provides means which are appropriate to the sanctifying end he has in view; his power makes the means efficacious.[8] For Owen, *every* duty of the Christian life is, therefore, a means of grace. But God has provided particular *ordinances* which are the chief 'means of grace'. Four of these call for special attention because they help to provide the structure of the Christian life. In this chapter we will examine the roles of Scripture and Ministry.

[1]X.160.   [2]X.161.   [3]X.162.   [4]IV.417.
[5]XXI.82ff., 566; XXII.128.
[6]XXI.84ff.   [7]XXII.14.   [8]XXII.475.

1. *Scripture*

It is apparent from the exposition of Owen's teaching thus far that his great concern was to work out a biblical pattern of Christianity. He constantly appeals to the authority of Scripture. Some account of his doctrine of Scripture will therefore illuminate the general trend of his approach to Christian living.

Owen's doctrine was forged in the fires of contemporary debate.[1] On one hand he faced the Roman Catholic insistence on the teaching office of the Church, and the importance of tradition;[2] on the other the growing movement towards a thorough-going rationalism among Protestants; and in opposition to both of these approaches, the development of the Quaker movement, and the doctrine of the 'Inner Light' in which the Christ of Scripture was replaced by the Christ within.[3] But Owen's keen intellect breaks through the merely controversial, as he endeavours to lay bare the foundations of a reformed approach to the Bible.

'That the whole authority of the Scripture in itself depends solely on its divine original,[4] is confessed by all who acknowledge its authority.'[5] These words are the foundation on which Owen builds his doctrine. They are written, strictly speaking, in theological shorthand. Owen knew that in theory, Scripture could have some kind of authority irrespective of its origin. The New Testament, for example, could carry authority (as it does for Owen in a secondary sense) simply because it was authoritatively promulgated by the apostles. But what Owen is intent to stress is that the Scriptures cannot validly carry the authority they claim for themselves unless they are in fact of divine origin, and have a nature in keeping with that origin. In

[1]See, for example, his biting words VIII.518–9.

[2]For his summary of the differences between the Roman and Reformed dogma, see VIII.502–4; IV.121.

[3]Cf. G. F. Nuttall, *The Holy Spirit in Christian Faith and Experience*, pp. 1ff. The Latin Edition of Robert Barclay's *Apology for the true Christian Divinity* had appeared in 1675. Owen published his *Reason of Faith* in 1677.

[4]He means Scripture's origin in God, not the original manuscripts or *autographa*.

[5]XVI.297.

this sense his view of both the *authority* and *canonicity* of Scripture is dependent on his doctrine of the *inspiration of Scripture*.[1] It is because God spoke *to* men in order to speak *by* men, because the material of Scripture was not in the first instance from men but from God, that the Bible has authority. If we would understand authority, therefore, we must first examine inspiration.

i. *The Inspiration of Scripture*

The inspiration of Scripture is, for Owen, part of a larger category of revelation, and in turn the source of all individual illumination. Indeed, inspiration and its product in the Scriptures is now the only form in which special revelation is extant, since 'God hath gathered up into the *Scripture* all divine revelations given out by himself from the beginning of the world, and all that ever shall be to the end thereof'.[2] Thus 'The Scripture is now become the *only external means of divine supernatural illumination*, because it is the only repository of all divine supernatural revelation'.[3]

Biblical revelation is given by inspiration.[4] Owen describes the experience of the biblical writers in these terms: 'Their tongue in what they said, or their hand in what they wrote, was . . . no more at their own disposal than the pen is in the hand of an expert writer';[5] 'they were but as an instrument of music, giving a sound according to the hand, intention, and skill of him that strikes it.'[6] Thus, commenting on Peter's words, 'no prophecy of scripture' (*graphēs*) in 2 Peter 1.20–1, Owen suggests that it is not merely the doctrine which is inspired, but the *graphē* itself, the doctrine *in written form*.[7] This is somewhat modified, or clarified, when he says, 'Though their mind and understanding were used in the choice of words, (whence arise all the differences – that is, in their manner of expression . . .) yet they were so guided, that their words were

---

[1]IV.19, cf. XVIII.28f.   [2]IV.11.   [3]IV.12.
[4]XIV.38.   [5]XVI.298.   [6]XVI.299.
[7]XVI.300, cf. III.144; XXIV.255 'The words spoken by Solomon, were spoken by God himself'. Cf. Calvin's comments on Jeremiah 15.18, *Commentaries on the Book of the Prophet Jeremiah and the Lamentations*, trans. John Owen, Edinburgh, vol. II, 1850, p. 290.

not their own, but immediately supplied unto them.'[1] There is then no suggestion that it is the doctrines of Scripture which are inspired, *rather than* the words. Owen certainly held to a verbal inspiration.[2] On the one hand, he guards himself against some of the more extreme conclusions of this view, and made room for the individualities of the penmen, if not for their frailties and sins. It would be wrong to categorize this as a 'Dictation Theory of Inspiration', since the writers are not at all regarded as inanimate objects. But on the other hand, Owen's view necessitates the dictation theory for those parts of Scripture which claim to have been written down at God's dictation! Indeed, the development of the canon begins with God's own writing in Exodus 31.18: the tables of the law 'written with the finger of God', which were then committed to Moses in the writing of the first books of the Bible.[3]

Three elements are involved in inspiration: the minds of the writers were inspired with the knowledge of the things communicated to them; words were provided to express these apprehensions of God's revelation; and their tongues or pens were guided in the setting down or telling forth of what had thus been revealed. By these means the Scriptures were kept from human imperfection:[4] 'Thus is it [Scripture] from God – entirely from him. As to the doctrine contained in it, and the words wherein that doctrine is delivered, it is wholly his; what *that* speaks, *he* speaks himself. He speaks in it and by it; and so it is vested with all the moral authority of God over his creatures.'[5]

Owen's view, as we have already suggested, was formulated against the background of an ever-increasing Protestant rationalism, and in the context of the strongly scholastic influence of many of the continental Calvinists. His doctrine of the Christian life cannot properly be judged without asking how deeply he was influenced by this trend, and to what extent he managed to remain faithful to the biblical and theological

[1]XVI.305, cf. III.144.
[2]III.143–4; XVI.434.
[3]*Ibid.* Owen believed Moses was also the most likely author of Job, III.143.
[4]III.144.
[5]XVI.306, cf. VIII.528; XIII.496; XIV.41; XXI.21, 575; XXIV.255 for the illustration of this.

insights of the Reformation, and the exposition of Calvin in particular. That he recognized the significance of the *testimonium internum* will later become evident. Here it will be sufficient to note that he also employed Calvin's doctrine of accommodation.[1] Brian Armstrong has maintained that this principle 'practically disappeared in orthodox Calvinism; at least I have not found a single example in seventeenth-century orthodox writers'.[2] But Owen both recognized the principle,[3] and employed it.[4]

In stressing the inspiration of Scripture it was not his purpose to deny its humanity.

ii. *The Authority of Scripture*

Owen believed that the authority of Scripture is the authority of God.[5] The character of this authority is a correlate of the character of God, and also of the role of Christ as Prophet in the covenant of redemption. Owen defines it as 'a power of commanding or persuading, or, as some phrase it, "convincing," arising from some excellency in the thing or person vested with such authority.'[6] The logic of inspiration means that the authority of Scripture must be of an *infallible* nature, that is without error. Owen's position is that 'there is no possibility of error or mistake in what is declared unto us'[7] since, 'To suppose that any thing which is not absolutely true can proceed from him, is to deny him to be God'.[8] More positively, the Scriptures are 'divine and infallible' and contain 'no human imperfection'.[9]

The Scriptures also possess this quality because by and through them Christ continues to exercise his ministry as the Prophet of the Church. Since he is an infallible Prophet, his word bears this character too.[10] It does so *necessarily*, not only because of his perfect character and knowledge, but because he is 'the image of the invisible God, the express image of the

---

[1] *Institutes* II. xi. 13; II. xvi. 2. See also H. Jackson Forstman, *Word and Spirit, Calvin's Doctrine of Biblical Authority*, Stanford 1962, pp. 13ff.
[2] B. G. Armstrong, *Calvinism and the Amyraut Heresy*, Madison, 1969, p. 173.
[3] IV.414.   [4] XVI.464.   [5] XVI.303.   [6] VIII.500.
[7] I.94.   [8] XXI.575.   [9] III.144.   [10] I.94.

person of the Father; and the principal end of the whole Scripture, especially of the Gospel, is to declare him so to be'.[1] It is necessary for him to be perfectly revealed in Scripture in order to produce assurance in the believing heart. Owen is not here denying the agency of the Spirit in bringing such assurance, but, because it is produced by the testimony of the Holy Spirit in and by the word[2] the practical outworking of Scripture's infallibility and the ministry of the Spirit are coordinate.

The authority of Scripture, then, is *infallible*. It is also *permanent*, as the 'everlasting rule of faith',[3] and *unique*: '*There is a certain fixed rule and measure of this obedience. . . . This is the revealed will of God in the Scripture*'[4] so that 'Whatever pretends to exceed the direction of the Word may safely be rejected – cannot safely be admitted'.[5]

Owen comments further on other aspects of the nature of scriptural authority, including its *sufficiency*. It contains all that is necessary for the ends of religion[6] and for its own purposes[7] as well as to vindicate its own claim of divine inspiration.[8]

In treating its *perspicuity* Owen attacks the Roman insistence on an authoritative ecclesiastical interpretation.[9] He affirms that, when divinely ordained means are used, Scripture is intelligible to all, and abundantly perspicuous. This does not mean that every text or passage is easy to understand. Scripture represents itself otherwise,[10] for the doctrine of perspicuity does not deny the necessity of illumination. The point is, according to Owen, that all *necessary* truth is plain.

Scripture is also characterized by a certain *fulness*, which evokes a lyrical passage from Owen's pen:

O heavenly, O blessed depositum of divine grace and goodness! . . . Hence, although every humble soul may learn and receive from it what is absolutely sufficient for itself on all occasions, with respect to its own duty and eternal welfare, yet the whole church of God, neither jointly nor severally, from the beginning to the end of the world, have been, are, or shall be, able to examine these stores to the bottom, and

---

[1]I.74, cf. XX.519; XXII.436.   [2]See above, p. 161ff.
[3]I.90.   [4]III.469.   [5]I.143.   [6]XV.402, cf. XV.449–50.
[7]IV.196.   [8]IV.8.   [9]XIV.38–41, especially his words on p. 41.
[10]XIV.39. Cf. 2 Pet. 3.15–16.

to find out perfectly all the truths, in all their dimensions, concerns, and extent, that are contained therein.[1]

iii. *The Preservation of Scripture*

What makes this whole discussion possible is, of course, the church doctrine of the *preservation* of Scripture under the providential hand of God. It was on this theme that Owen published *Of the Integrity and Purity of the Hebrew and Greek Text of the Scripture*, and entered the fray against some of the sentiments expressed in Brian Walton's *London Polyglott*.[2] Owen has been much criticized for his position[3] but in some ways he was simply drawing his *a priori* of preservation to a logical, if mistaken conclusion.

Owen's reasoning was as follows: If God gave the Bible to men, inspiring the very words in which it was written, surely he would preserve it in a substantially static form? Here Owen argued for the inspiration of the original autographs of Scripture, *and also* for their entire preservation in the transcription of the best manuscripts of the time. On this basis, he opposed three particular suggestions of the *Polyglott* which seemed to prejudice his position: (1) that the pointing of the Hebrew text was the work of the Massoretes and not original;[4] (2) that translations, and the marginal *Kere* and *Kethib*, have considerable authority for determining the true text; (3) that conjectural emendations based on internal textual considerations may carry authority even if unsupported by external,

---

[1]XXI.309.

[2]The *Biblia Sacra Polyglotta Londinii* appeared in 6 folio volumes (1655–57), and contained, besides the texts and translations, the first systematic collection of variant readings, in volume VI, and an extensive *Prolegomena* in volume IV, including over 100 pages by Walton himself. A seventh volume was projected, but did not materialize.

[3]By Andrew Thomson, *Works* I.lxxiv–lxxvi; Thomas Chalmers, *Institutes of Theology*, Edinburgh, 1849, I.287; F. F. Bruce, *Tradition, Old and New*, Exeter, 1970, pp. 154–162; B. B. Warfield, *The Westminster Assembly*, New York, 1929, p. 278. See also Orme, *Memoir*, pp. 271–3.

[4]In Walton's reply, *The Considerator Considered*, or a Brief view of certain Considerations upon the *Biblia Polyglotta*, the *Prolegomena* and *Appendix* thereof, London 1659, p. 233, Walton claimed Calvin shared this view and drew attention to his commentary on Zechariah 11.7.

objective evidence. Owen particularly objected to the vast number of variant readings in which this resulted. He argued that, since the majority could be readily discounted, the publication of them could only detract from the ordinary Christian's confidence in the text which lay behind the Bible he read.[1]

The laurels in this debate have been almost universally awarded to Walton. Owen did not give sufficient consideration to Walton's insistence on the integrity of Scripture, and its authority for faith. Walton had unequivocally maintained that in every thing related to faith and morals, all of the ancient texts are in agreement.[2] He was also right to draw attention in his reply to the fact that Calvin had held the view that the pointing was *not* original. But it is doubtful if Owen's response merits the epithet 'illiterate'[3] which Thomas Chalmers applied to it. For one thing, Owen had on his side John Lightfoot,[4] one of the greatest Hebraists of his time, and himself a contributor to the London Polyglott.[5]

Walton ridiculed Owen's critique, and virtually charged him with blatant dishonesty. He emphasized that, while the Polyglott's *Prolegomena* was in Latin, and intended for scholars (i.e. there was no danger that it would 'corrupt' the masses), Owen's reply had been written in English and was clearly intended to reach ordinary intelligent Christians, despite its scholarly appearance. He further believed Owen had mounted little more than a personal attack on him.[6] This was unworthy of such a great scholar, and it was also to miss the point. Owen's great concern was not scholarship, but religion and faith. He was concerned, for example, that a late date for the pointing of the Hebrew text would necessitate the pointing being done by

---

[1] XVI.364.
[2] 'In rebus omnibus, quae fidem et mores spectant, omnes codices convenire'. *Prolegomena* vol. IV, 1657, p. 35. Cf. pp. 36, 42, for similar sentiments.
[3] *Op. cit.*, p.287.
[4] D.N.B. XXXIII.229–231.
[5] XVI.383–4. For Walton's Correspondence with Lightfoot, see *The Whole Works of the Rev. John Lightfoot D.D.*, ed. J. R. Pitman, London 1824, Volume XIII, pp. 348–364.
[6] Walton, *Considerator Considered*, pp. 2ff.

unbelieving Jews.[1] His anxiety was that the publication of so many textual variants, most of which he regarded as unnecessary, could only be a stumbling block to many Christians who might see them, or hear about them, without possessing the equipment to understand their real (and limited) significance.[2] He would have been less anxious had the readings been reduced to 'a less offensive and less formidable number'.[3] In any case, since 'it was no less crime of old to be *traditor libri* (one who distorts the Book) than to be *abnegator fidei* (one who denies the faith)'[4] Christians could have great confidence in the careful transmission of the original text.

From Owen's point of view, therefore it was important to say *in English*, 'if all the errors and mistakes that are to be found in all the rest [i.e. manuscripts] should be added to the worst of all, every necessary, saving, fundamental truth, would be found sufficiently testified unto therein'.[5]

Owen's concern was essentially a pastoral one, and arose from the conception he entertained of the pastoral ministry as involving the protection, as well as the feeding, of the flock of Christ.

We must turn now to consider Owen's treatment of one of the most important of all the questions related to Scripture.

iv. *The Attestation of Scripture*

In Owen's own words, the question is: 'Why, or on what account, do you believe the Scriptures, or books of the Old and New Testament, to be the word of God?'[6]

It is in discussing this issue that Owen provides the first systematic and comprehensive treatment of the experimental authentication of Scripture.[7] He has this to say about believing the Bible to be God's word: 'God requires of us that we believe them [the Scriptures] to be his word *with faith divine, supernatu-*

---

[1]XVI.382. He is here following Lightfoot's principle, 'The pointing of the Bible savours of the work of the Holy Spirit, not of wicked, blind, and mad men.' Quoted, XVI.383.

[2]XVI.364.   [3]XVI.366.   [4]XVI.300.

[5]XVI.302, cf. Walton's *Latin* words, quoted above p. 191, fn.2.

[6]XVI.306–7.   [7]See Goold's comments, IV.4.

ral, and infallible'.[1] An analysis of this statement will bring us nearer to Owen's resolution of the question.

By 'infallible faith', Owen does *not* mean 'an *inherent quality* in the subject, as though he that believes with faith infallible must himself also be infallible; much less do we speak of infallibility absolutely, which is a property of God, who alone, from the perfection of his nature, can neither deceive nor be deceived'.[2] 'Faith infallible' means a faith built upon infallible testimony. Such divine, infallible testimony is already available in the revelation of God, and this 'renders the faith that rests on it and is resolved into it infallible also'.[3] Only *the authority and veracity of God* evokes faith which is 'divine, supernatural and infallible'. If we then ask how we know that Scripture provides infallible testimony, Owen answers:

It is *solely* on the evidence that the Spirit of God, in and by the Scripture itself, gives unto us that it was given by immediate inspiration from God; or, the ground and reason whereon we believe the Scripture to be the word of God are the authority and truth of God evidencing themselves in and by it unto the minds and consciences of men.[4]

Scripture then is not only *theopneustic* (God-breathed), it is also, necessarily, *autopistic* (self-authenticating).[5]

Owen, in keeping with the direction of the reformed tradition, is not denying the value of external and supportive arguments.[6] They are of use to confirm faith 'against temptations, oppositions, and objections',[7] and they provide a 'moral certainty'.[8] In this way some value is to be found in the arguments from the antiquity of the writings, their preservation, their design, and the testimony of the church.[9] These are not to be despised.[10] But moral certainty is an inferior kind of knowledge; it has only a preparatory value, and it does not require the testimony of the Holy Spirit.[11]

---

[1]IV.15. Cf. Calvin, *Institutes* I. vii. 1,4,5.
[2]IV.17.   [3]*Ibid.*   [4]IV.20.
[5]Cf. Calvin, *Institutes* I. vii. 2, 5.
[6]But to rely on these would be, for Owen, as for Calvin, 'doing things backwards', *Institutes* I. vii. 4.
[7]IV.20.   [8]IV.21.   [9]See VIII.503; 528; 537.
[10]VIII.541–2.   [11]IV.56.

It might be thought that Owen is here taking refuge in an esoteric experience by appealing to a subjective work of the Spirit. He is conscious of this,[1] and of the circularity that is involved in his whole approach; but he believes this circularity is justified by the very nature of the case. The self-authentication of the Scripture is part of the gospel, and belongs to the objective given-ness of Scripture.[2] If it be said that this is presuppositional reasoning, Owen again replies, 'Unless we intend so to wander, we must come to something wherein we may rest for its own sake, and that not with a strong and firm opinion, but with divine faith.'[3]

What then is the autopistic nature of Scripture? Owen explains by arguing that every revelation of God, *ipso facto*, is self-authenticating.[4] He is revealed in the works of creation, in the consciences of men, and in the word of the gospel. In fact everything that God does is a self-revelation and 'hath such an impression of his authority upon it, as undeniably to evince that it is from him'.[5] What is true of the genus is also true of its species in the Bible. The Scriptures, Owen argues, are like *light* – they are self-evidencing.[6] But *light* is not *eyes*, and it does not remove the blindness of men. In a similar way, the Scriptures are God's light, but in and of themselves they cannot remove the blindness of man and illuminate his inner spiritual darkness. This is Owen's answer to the objection that all men apparently do not recognize what he claims to be self-evident. That is no fault of the Scriptures, nor, for him, does it detract from their self-evidencing power. While this is a deductive argument, it is entirely consistent with the nature of its own first principles, and with the concept of a divine revelation being given by God.[7] It is also inductive, being based on the *entire* teaching of Scripture.

This self-evidencing quality does not simply belong to the Scriptures as a special kind of literature however. It belongs to

---

[1]IV.61, hence the appendix he adds to confirm his teaching from church authorities, lest he 'be charged with singularity', IV.115. See IV.111, 112.

[2]IV.55–6.

[3]IV.71, cf. XVI.427. Note Owen's belief that here he is one with Calvin, *Institutes* I. vii. 5; IV.68–9.

[4]XVI.310.   [5]XVI.312.   [6]VIII.505, 525.

[7]See VIII.497–543, especially pp. 505f.

them as the instrument of the Holy Spirit, and Owen seeks to
hold together in unity the witness of the word and of the Spirit.
Here we come to his understanding of the *Testimonium Spiritus
Sancti Internum*,[1] and his careful statement of it. The Holy Spirit
does not speak *of* the word and give separate testimony; he
speaks *by* the word, *in* it, and *through* it.[2] His work is therefore
not the production of a subjectively-orientated, non-rational
certainty. Rather it involves the removal of men's spiritual
blindness through the testimony he gives to the mind in and by
the word, persuading men of its truth and its authenticity as the
word of the living God. In this way men 'hear and understand
the *voice of God* in it; and, by that Spirit which is promised unto
them, discern it from the *voice of a stranger*'.[3] Thus the Spirit
gives testimony to the word, 'imparting to it virtue, power,
efficacy, majesty, and authority'.[4]

Owen finds this to be a self-consistent position.[5] Divine
testimony leads to supernatural and infallible faith. Rather
than regard this as a poor substitute for a more natural
knowledge of the nature of the Bible, he maintains (following
the distinction of the Schoolmen between an assurance of
evidence and an assurance of adherence), that a more certain
conviction comes from *faith* than from *science*.[6] Here assent is
given to the testimony of God himself, and this, being the inner
work of the Spirit by the word, is an assurance of a different,
and more sublime kind.

Owen anticipates a number of further objections to his
thesis. If the rational arguments for belief in Scripture are not
emphasized, does this not open the floodgates to error, and
make a genuine apologetic impossible?[7] He answers that there
are two ways of convincing an unbeliever: the method of the
apostles, when they *preached* the word, and that of learned
Christian men, by the employment of rational *argument* only.
Owen is not opposed to rational argument, if the arguments are
cogent, and are not substituted for faith. But his view seems to
be that the method of the apostles sprang from the inner logic of
the gospel itself.[8] But if there is such an abundance of rational

[1]Calvin, *Institutes* I. vii, viii.
[2]See XXIV.255.   [3]XVIII.57.
[4]XVI.328.   [5]IV.100.
[6]IV.101.   [7]IV.102.   [8]IV.103.

argument on behalf of the Scriptures, does this not presuppose the sufficiency of reason to recognize them as God's word?[1] Owen answers negatively, for the assurance which results from the Spirit's testimony is of a different order altogether.

Owen is also conscious of the continuing Roman Catholic objection to the supposed circularity of his argument: 'we shall run in a round, which is no lawful way of arguing'.[2] But his position is that such a retort has missed the point, namely, that faith in Scripture finds its *motive* cause in Scripture itself, and its *efficient* cause in the testimony of the Spirit. It is the Roman argument, he contends, which is really circular, since it maintains Scripture's authority is from the church. But the authority of the church derives from Scripture, not vice-versa.[3]

But all these arguments are of little value (as Owen admits), unless the content of the divine revelation is understood.[4] To this aspect of the doctrine of Scripture he devoted considerable attention and care, particularly in his *Sunēsis Pneumatikē, or The Causes, Ways, and Means of Understanding the Mind of God as revealed in his Word, with assurance therein; and a Declaration of the Perspicuity of the Scriptures, with the external means of the interpretation of them.*[5]

v. *Understanding Scripture*

A genuine understanding of the message of Scripture is available to every believer, who may,

> in the due sense of the means appointed of God for that end, attain unto such a full assurance of understanding in the truth, or all that knowledge of the mind and will of God revealed in the Scripture, which is sufficient to direct him in the life of God, to deliver him from the dangers of ignorance, darkness, and error, and to conduct him unto blessedness.[6]

In this work of the Spirit, the fulcrum of understanding Scripture is a right use of the mind, to which the message of the Bible is addressed, as the 'leading, conducting faculty of the soul'.[7] Understanding, then, does not come by immediate revelation (there is no repetition of the phenomenon of Scripture), nor from ecclesiastical authority; but neither does it

[1]IV.105.   [2]VIII.524.   [3]VIII.527.   [4]VIII.119.
[5]IV.121ff.   [6]IV.122–3.   [7]III.330.

come from *unaided* reason,[1] but from a continuing work of the Spirit in *illumination* through the divinely ordained means.

This illumination by the Spirit lies at the heart of any true understanding of God's word.[2] The depravity of the human mind makes it necessary. Thus the Spirit is promised as the Spirit of truth, to guide Christ's disciples into the truth.[3] Owen argues that this is only partially fulfilled in the experience of the apostles on the day of Pentecost and later through the inspiration of their writings. This promise characterizes the whole ministry of the Spirit who 'leads us into all truth, by giving us that understanding of it which of ourselves we are not able to attain'.[4] This is the 'unction from the Holy One'[5] which brings with it illumination and assured knowledge. Owen places considerable emphasis on such assured knowledge:[6]

The word, rightly and legitimately interpreted is the word of God. And that interpretation in so far as it does not depart from the analogy of faith, is infallible. . . . And so, all true interpretation is infallible, that is, it sets forth infallible truth; not by reason of the infallibility of the interpreter, absolutely considered, but by reason of the rightly interpreted word.[7]

It may be objected that men can and do understand the Scriptures without any reference to this spiritual illumination. Owen dissents from such a judgment. A certain intellectual understanding may be possible, but not a genuine spiritual knowledge.[8] Only the latter will genuinely edify. Thus the Jews understood the grammar of the Old Testament, and yet they were unable to grasp its real message and meaning.[9]

Illumination is then an opening of men's spiritual eyes, which 'consists in the communication of spiritual light unto our minds by the preaching of the word'.[10] By it we come to a new understanding of God and of our relationship to him through Christ. It therefore heals the natural depravity of the mind, and works upon the corrupt affections through the word, communicating spiritual light, removing inward darkness, and bringing

[1]IV.125.   [2]XVI.439.   [3]Jn. 16.13; IV.142.
[4]IV.144.   [5]I Jn. 2.20, 27.   [6]IV.150, cf. IV.18; 122–3.
[7]XVI.452 (Latin material omitted from 1965–68 reprint).
[8]IV.155.   [9]IV.156.   [10]IV.162.

comprehension.[1] In this way, the process of coming to understand the mind of God in Scripture is a miniature of the whole
Christian experience. The fruit of this exercise, which in turn
becomes the qualification for further illumination, is '*meekness,
humility, godly fear, reverence, submission of soul and conscience* unto
the authority of God, with a *resolution* and readiness for and unto
all that obedience which he requireth of us'.[2]

This thought, that the Christian continues to depend on the
work of the Spirit for illumination of inspired Scripture, gives
Owen the clue to the actual form which revelation takes, and
illumination must follow. The Bible is not a system of divinity,
even though Owen believed it contains such.[3] The form in
which revelation comes is a reminder that God does not place
the premium on 'men's *accurate methods* as they may imagine
them to deserve, nor are they so subservient unto his ends in the
revelation of himself as they are apt to fancy'.[4] Rather,
revelation is suited to the growth and development of the
church throughout the ages, to make men humble, holy and
wise. The manner in which revelation is given is subservient to
this end.[5] The very character of the Bible makes God's church
dependent upon *ministry* through weak and frail men, and thus
glorifies God's name.[6] The people of God are to seek him in
Scripture day by day, thus promoting a continuing relationship
of dependence on him.[7]

What are the means by which the word is understood? Owen
stresses the necessity of frequent reading, bringing a general
knowledge of the biblical message, and a more distinct
knowledge of the individual books and doctrines. This gen-
erates right conceptions of God, and encourages heavenly
thoughts; it exposes the Christian to divine instruction, and
enables his senses to be exercised to discern good and evil.[8]

Alongside this, Owen indicates three other means:
Spiritual means. The Christian must pray personally for the
teaching ministry of the Spirit to be effective in his own life, if he
is to learn the *power* as well as the *truth* of God's word.[9] He must
pray that he will have a desire to receive such impressions from

---

[1]IV.162–3.   [2]IV.185–6.   [3]IV.188.   [4]*Ibid.*
[5]IV.189.   [6]Cf. Calvin, *Institutes* IV. iii. 1.
[7]XX.187–9.   [8]IV.200.   [9]IV.203.

God,[1] and exercise himself in practical obedience, with a continuing desire to grow in the knowledge of the truth.[2] The disciplines of the general ordinances of God will be a stimulus to this whole work.[3]

Intellectual means. The believer depends entirely on the work of the Spirit. But Owen indicates that the Spirit himself uses means to bring understanding of the word. Thus knowledge and skill in the original languages, while in itself a matter of moral and spiritual indifference,[4] can be of inestimable value when used for spiritual ends.[5] Further, a knowledge of history, geography and chronology can be an advantage in understanding the progress of revelation and interpreting the significance of prophecy.[6] Skill in intellectual disciplines, when subjected to the reasoning of Scripture itself, can aid the understanding of the sense of a passage.[7]

Ecclesiastical means. Owen had no patience with the concept of standardized authoritative interpretations of Scripture. The idea was wholly alien to his entire approach to the nature of the Bible. Catholic, Patristic, and other interpretations, *as such*, have little value.[8] The insight and illumination that has been given to any man who has depended on the Holy Spirit will be of help, and particularly if he is Calvin, Beza or Peter Martyr![9]

In practical terms, Owen's advice is as follows: Come with a humble, prayerful spirit; aim in your study at the ends for which God has given the word: to reveal himself, to provide a guide to direct men's ways, to bring consolation and hope, and to assure believers of eternal life.[10] Be guided in interpreting by the analogy of faith[11] and the self-consistency of Scripture. A consideration of the general nature of a difficult passage will help explain its meaning, as will a review of the ordinary grammatical sense of the language used.

All this has, for Owen, a practical goal.

vi *The Influence of Scripture*

The continuing union of the Spirit with the word has very

[1]IV.205.　　[2]IV.206–7.　　[3]IV.207–8.　　[4]IV.216.
[5]IV.210.　　[6]IV.219.　　[7]IV.223.　　[8]IV.226–7.
[9]IV.228–9.　　[10]XXI.313–4.
[11]XVI.449; XXI.315, cf. Calvin, *Institutes* IV. xvii. 32.

practical consequences. It means that God continues to speak
in and through Scripture as his living voice: 'Whatever was
given by inspiration from the Holy Ghost, and is recorded in
the Scripture for the use of the church, he continues therein to
speak it to us unto this day'.[1] There is therefore an 'immediate
speaking of God' and an 'impression of his authority'[2] for those
who continue to read the Bible or to hear it expounded. This is
what Owen elsewhere describes as its 'secret *energy*'[3] although
he is careful to indicate that this power 'for the subjecting of the
minds of men unto its intention in all things',[4] depends on the
Spirit's presence. This power is irresistible. God's work never
fails to accomplish its purpose.

In brief, the word fulfils four functions:

(1) It teaches the necessity of regeneration, and in order to do
so is accompanied with a *'powerful persuasive efficacy'*[5] which is
part of the work of God in regeneration. This touches the mind,
will, and affections and demands a response to God who is the
'most noble object for our affections'.[6] We thus learn to respect
the word, and indeed to tremble before it, and to submit mind
and conscience to it.[7]

(2) The word dwells in us, as the 'ingrafted word'.[8] As such it
'is to be brought into the soul'.[9] 'And to that purpose room is to
be made for it, by the casting out of such things as are apt to
possess the mind and leave no admittance for the word'.[10] The
word then has a sanctifying effect. It is compared to a seed
which bears a harvest; it is an ingrafting whose fruit is the
reproduction in human experience of the doctrine of the word
(Rom. 6.17).

(3) Scripture is also a source of spiritual nourishment. It is so
by union with Christ through his word, in which he is found to
be the Bread of Life.

(4) The word finally preserves us in temptation as we treasure
it in the heart. It is a word of grace and mercy to save, and not
simply to justify. It has power to deliver, and to bring us an
enjoyment of liberty. In times of trial it is a word of consolation
to preserve and support the church in hope, since it reveals the

---

[1]XXI.21. [2]XXIII.495. [3]XVIII.55. [4]*Ibid.*
[5]III.304. [6]III.305. [7]XXI.558–9. [8]James 1.21.
[9]XXI.249. [10]*Ibid.*

character of God[1] and his purposes of goodness and grace.[2] In fact these are all elements in Owen's doctrine of sanctification and indicate the primary role Scripture plays as a means of grace.

In this way, with the prayer that God the Spirit will open their eyes to behold wonderful things out of the word – a prayer for 'the immediate work of the Holy Ghost'[3] – the people of God discover that

In those very *fords* and appearing *shallows* of this river of God where the *lamb* may wade, the *elephant* may swim. Every thing in the Scripture is so plain as that the *meanest believer* may understand all that belongs unto his duty or is necessary unto his happiness; yet is nothing so plain but that the wisest of them all have reason to adore the depths and stores of divine wisdom in it.[4]

2. *Ministry*

We have already seen that ministry has a central place in the Christian life because it is a major source of spiritual edification.[5] But in order to share in this edification the church requires gifts for ministry, and, in order to participate in Christian service, the individual Christian must first of all be gifted. In this sense, Owen views all ministry as charismatic; a divine *grace-gift* is a necessary prerequisite for every stated office in the church, and for every exercise of ministry in worship or service. His categories cut the Gordian knot of the contemporary debate within the church about 'charismatic revival'. For Owen the categories in which we interpret the significance of spiritual gifts are not *charismatic* and *non-charismatic*, but *temporary* and *permanent*.[6]

All gifts, for Owen, are grace-gifts, but not all grace-gifts are given to the church in every generation or epoch.

Spiritual gifts are the 'powers of the age to come'[7] and are received from Christ in his office as Mediator.[8] They are not natural but spiritual endowments. Yet the fact that Christ

[1]VI.638.   [2]VI.639.   [3]XXI.312.   [4]IV.193.
[5]Above, pp. 165ff.   [6]See XX.281ff.; III.44; IV.363-4, 420.
[7]IV.421; XX.281; XXII.83. Cf. Hebrews 6.5.   [8]IV.422.

bestows them in his divine-human capacity, as the exalted Man at the right hand of God, is also indication that while supernatural and spiritual, they are not *unnatural* nor ought they to prove distortive of a truly human personality. Rather these gifts are related to the in-breaking of the powers of the future age, making it a present reality and conveying that reality in the context of the life of the flesh. They are the work of the Holy Spirit: *diakonia*, ministration; *energēmata*, effectual workings; *phanerōsis tou pneumatos*, manifestations of the Spirit.[1]

i. *Gifts and graces*

Owen distinguishes the *gifts* of the Spirit from the *grace* of the Spirit. This is a key thought in his analysis of genuine spiritual experience and true faith. It enables him to resolve the apparent failure of Christians to persevere in faith. Gifts should not be identified with grace, nor do they secure those who have them from the danger and possibility of apostasy.[2] Nevertheless Owen recognizes that there are similarities between the two. Both are purchased by Christ for the church;[3] both share the same immediate efficient cause in the power of the Holy Spirit; both are given for the good and blessing of the church, so that as 'grace gives an *invisible life* to the church, gifts give it a *visible profession*'.[4] They also bear a similar relationship to Christ, since every grace is his gift, and every gift is of his grace.

Nevertheless, Owen finds substantial differences between the two. Graces are the fruit of the Spirit and are the evidences of his personal indwelling of the Christian; gifts are '*effects* of his operation *upon* men, not *fruits* of his working *in* them'.[5] Further, while saving grace and the graces it produces, both proceed from the electing love of God in eternity,[6] Owen maintains that spiritual gifts are the effect of a merely temporal and functional election. This might appear to be suggesting that there is some kind of contradiction in God's purpose, but Owen's point is that there is election in the sphere of *personal salvation*, and there is a temporary election which operates in the sphere of *function* in the divine purposes.[7] Those elected for salvation are also

---

[1]IV.424. [2]VII.251. [3]IV.425. [4]IV.428.
[5]IV.429. [6]*Ibid.* [7]IV.429–30.

objects of this functional election. They fulfil temporal roles in the fellowship of the church. But in this case, God's election to function is separable from his election according to saving grace.

Owen sees this illustrated in Saul in the Old Testament, and Judas Iscariot in the New. Both enjoyed the privileges of election to service without experiencing the fruit of an eternal election in regeneration, repentance, and faith in Christ.[1] Owen makes a further distinction: saving faith is the effect of the covenant of grace, while gifts belong to the outward administration of the covenant in the church. Or, again, saving grace is the result of Christ's ministry as Priest, in obedience, sacrifice, and intercession, exercised only for the elect. But the gifts of the Spirit are the fruit of his exaltation as King, in which office he exercises a universal ministry.[2]

Gifts and graces also differ in their *outcome*.[3] Gifts may be removed, but graces, even though they decay, remain. Paul's words in Romans 11.29 might be thought to contradict this view: 'For the gifts and calling of God are irrevocable'[4] (especially when the word Paul uses for 'gifts' is *charismata*!). Owen nowhere discusses this text. However, the context of Paul's statement suggests that the reference is not to the spiritual gifts listed elsewhere in the New Testament, but those which mark the outworking of the history of redemption. Thus C. K. Barrett parallels the similar use in Romans 5.16, and translates it as 'acts of grace'.[5] Perhaps this was Owen's view.

Gifts also differ from graces in their *overall purpose* since they are primarily for the benefit of others.[6] But this, as Owen admits, is simply a matter of degree. More important is the difference in *nature* that is involved. Spiritual gifts are seated and located in the *mind*, in a rational rather than a practical way. The foundation of most of them lies in illumination. This is why it is possible that 'they *change not the heart* with power, although they may reform the life by the efficacy of light'.[7] Grace by contrast possesses and transforms the whole soul. Owen is here leaning on his analysis of Hebrews 6.4–6.[8] The

---

[1]*Ibid.* [2]IV.431–2. [3]IV.434. [4]R.S.V. translation.
[5]C. K. Barrett, *op. cit.*, p. 114. [6]IV.436.
[7]IV.437. [8]See below, pp. 232ff.

possibility of being illuminated without being converted is very real.

Owen may appear to be on weak ground when he represents the working of spiritual gifts as rational rather than affectional. Paul speaks of his understanding being unfruitful (*akarpos*) when he uses the gift of tongues. It is commonly held that this gift, at least, was not regarded as dominantly rational.[1] But Owen is surely correct when he stresses that a higher unity between graces and gifts is possible, so that 'Grace influenceth gifts unto a due exercise, prevents their abuse, stirs them up unto proper occasions, keeps them from being a matter of pride or contention, and subordinates them in all things unto the glory of God.'[2] After all, gifts are *charis*-mata. Here Owen is feeling after the balance of the apostle Paul: gifts need grace (love) in order to be exercised for the good of others, and not simply for self-seeking ends. 'Are we glad of gifts whereby we might be lifted up; and care little for grace, whereby we may be humbled?'[3] But graces (love) need gifts, in order to give expression to their concern to do good to others.

We have already noted that Owen divides the gifts of the Spirit into two categories, and we must consider what he has to say about each.

ii. *Extraordinary gifts*

The New Testament relates the experiences of special endowments of power in the apostolic period. These Owen sees as differing *only in degree* from the more ordinary gifts, which are essentially of the same kind. There are nine gifts to be regarded as extraordinary.

The word of wisdom was given particularly to the unlearned in view of the situations in which they were called to preach the word and defend the gospel. It is exemplified, for example, in Peter and John in Acts 4, and Stephen in Acts 6. It is 'that

[1] 1 Cor. 14.14. See, however, R. B. Gaffin, Jr., *Perspectives on Pentecost*, Phillipsburg, N.J., 1979, pp. 73ff. for a different exegesis and understanding of these words.
[2] IV.438.
[3] *Ibid*. Where there is grace, gifts are 'a means to cause the savour of it to flow forth', VII.291; cf. XV.264.

especial gift of spiritual wisdom for the management of gospel truths unto the edification of the church of Christ'.[1] Owen indicates the principles which should govern the use of this gift: the recognition of personal insufficiency, prayer for its provision, meditation on Christ as the pattern of wisdom, shunning habits which would stifle its growth and development, and pursuit of the gifts and graces which accompany wisdom, namely, humility, patience and constancy.

This suggests that it is easy to move from the realm of the extraordinary to that of the ordinary gift. Owen himself seems to recognize this: 'I suppose the wisdom here intended is not absolutely confined thereunto, [i.e. an 'especial kind of wisdom'] though it be principally intended'.[2] This kind of gift is a special improvement of the natural faculties rather than an altogether different category of human experience.[3] Here Owen underlines the principle that temporary and permanent gifts often differ only in degree.

The word of knowledge is 'a peculiar and especial insight into the mysteries of the gospel, as whereby those in whom it was were enabled to teach and instruct others'.[4] It is this kind of knowledge which will 'pass away'[5] but for which Paul so frequently prayed: 'it is still communicated in such a measure unto the ministers of the church as is necessary unto its edification.'[6] In fact, for Owen, this gift is a necessary endowment for the Christian ministry.[7] Here again the 'extraordinary' is related to the 'ordinary'. Elsewhere Owen admits that the only real difference lies 'in persons . . . and not in the things'.[8]

Faith is always a gift of God but Owen draws a distinction between saving or justifying faith, and the faith which is a special endowment of God. The latter is the principle of all the miraculous operations of the Spirit.[9] If it involves more than this, then it is 'a peculiar confidence, boldness, and assurance of mind in the profession of the gospel and the administration of its ordinances'.[10] In this sense it seems to mean simply boldness or full assurance of faith.[11] Here again, Owen sees the dif-

---

[1]IV.455.   [2]*Ibid.*   [3]IV.456.   [4]IV.460.
[5]1 Corinthians 13.9–12.   [6]IV.461.   [7]*Ibid.*
[8]VII.291.   [9]IV.461.   [10]*Ibid.*
[11]In *this* sense, Owen was prepared to attribute the *gift* of faith to Luther.

ferences between temporary and permanent gifts as a matter of degrees of experience. This is less so with respect to those that follow:

Healing. Owen notices that in 1 Corinthians 12, the gift of healing is mentioned in the plural, and he raises the question as to how it is to be distinguished from 'miracles' which follow. His answer is that miracles are signs to those who do not believe, healings to those who do believe, that the kingdom of God has come.[1] But further, healing represents God's universal kindness, and is evidence of his general love, for 'Men may have their *bodies* cured by *miracles* when their *souls* are not cured by *grace*.'[2] Indeed, healings are to be distinguished from miracles because they were normally accompanied by outward means and tokens of the healing itself, such as the laying on of hands, and anointing with oil. These were signs of an infallible healing, Owen maintains,[3] and therefore have fallen into abeyance, although the duty of elders to pray for the sick, and of the sick to call the elders, remains.

Miracles. Miracles are not powers inherent in those who work them. Instead, they involve a special act of *faith*. This 'had always a *peculiar, immediate revelation* for its warranty and security in the working of any miracle.'[4] This, Owen argues, always consists in the elevation of faith in order to take hold of divine power. Even in the apostolic period there is no question of a man himself possessing miraculous powers. Such power is not given to men, but can only be drawn upon through grace and faith.[5]

Prophecy involves immediate revelation from God, but also the declaration of the mind and will of God from the Scriptures. Even in the apostolic period, Owen argues that predictive prophecy (fore-telling) was comparatively rare, and proclamation of the divine will (forth-telling) more common. With this two-fold form goes a two-fold use, to convict and convert the unregenerate, and to edify the church.[6]

It is of interest that Owen does not equate prophecy with

---

[1]IV.463. Cf. Lk. 10.9; Matt. 11.4–5; Is. 53.4–5 with 1 Pet. 2.24 and Matt. 8.16–17.
[2]IV.464.   [3]IV.465.
[4]IV.466.   [5]*Ibid.*   [6]IV.469.

preaching, *simpliciter*. Both may legitimately be regarded as forms of the ministry of the word, and consequently must be intimately related in form and content; nevertheless there is a sense of immediacy about the idea of prophecy which is not necessarily present in the idea of preaching.[1]

Discerning of spirits. The rule in the church of Christ has always been the word. But, because of the weakness of the infant church, Owen believed that God gave the special gift of discerning spirits to contend against the 'mischief done in the church'.[2] In view of the abundance of spiritual gifts then operative, and the ease with which they might be counterfeited, this was clearly a necessary and much valued gift.[3] But then 'upon the ceasing of extraordinary gifts really given from God, the gift also of discerning spirits ceased, and we are left unto the *word alone* for the trial of any that shall pretend unto them.'[4] Yet, Owen would not argue that this gift has vanished *in toto*, since while all Christians have the word, evidently some in particular have a special insight into its meaning and application in a manner similar *in kind* if not so immediate *in degree* as the New Testament gift of discernment.

Tongues and their interpretation. Owen had several observations to make about the gift of tongues. Those on the day of Pentecost signify the universality of the covenant of grace and the means by which men may enter it, namely, the spoken word of the gospel.[5] *In the church* tongues are for the praise and magnifying of the name of God, and are a sign for unbelievers.[6] In and of itself however the gift of tongues is of little use. In his whole discussion it is evident that Owen regards these 'tongues' as foreign languages and not ecstatic utterances.[7]

Some of these gifts belonged, says Owen, only to the apostles. Miracles functioned as 'signs of a true apostle'[8] to vindicate their divine office in the sight of men.[9] Others existed in the church until the end of the apostolic period.

Owen does *not* imply that miracles have ceased. God continues to work them if he pleases, a matter Owen considers

---

[1]Cf. Calvin's striking remarks, *Commentary on 1 Corinthians*, trs. J. W. Fraser, ed. D.W. & T. F. Torrance, Edinburgh, 1960, pp. 263, 271.
[2]III.32.   [3]IV.471.   [4]III.35.   [5]IV.473.
[6]1 Cor. 14.22.   [7]IV.473-4.   [8]2 Cor. 12.12.   [9]IV.36.

to be 'not unlikely'.[1] But as a regular endowment to the church, as a form of ministry, these gifts have been withdrawn.

It might therefore seem to be pedantic to mention Owen's views on the matter at all, since for him these gifts could have no regular place in the contemporary church life. But in fact this discussion does have certain values. It provides an orientation for the kind of Christian experience Owen is concerned to expound. It might, for example, be assumed that, were Owen to witness the current revival of interest in spiritual gifts, not least in the historic denominations, he would immediately change his view of their cessation, and this in turn would influence his doctrine of the church and the fellowship of Christian experience. But this does not follow. Owen knew well that Christians through the centuries had claimed to receive again these apostolic gifts.[2] But this claim disguised the existence of a deep delusion, as far as Owen was concerned, as his constant attacks on 'Inner Light' theology demonstrate.

In Owen we see the beginnings of the argument which later become part of reformed orthodoxy, that these extraordinary gifts were 'signs of the apostles', vindicating their ministry and mission, just as miracles had testified to the divine origin of God's servants and prophets, Moses, Joshua, Elijah, Elisha, Daniel, and Christ.

iii. *Ordinary gifts*

The second category of gifts contains those which Owen regards as 'ordinary'. They are to be distinguished from those which surpass the natural powers of the human soul, and Owen believed they continue in the ordinary state of the church. Such gifts are 'nothing but a spiritual improvement of our natural faculties or abilities; and a man cannot speak or utter any thing but what proceeds from his rational faculties, by invention or memory, or both, managed in and by his thoughts, unless he speak by rote and that which is not rational.'[3]

These ordinary gifts are seen by Owen as particularly

[1]IV.475.   [2]III.35.   [3]VII.284.

valuable for the work of the pastorate. Spiritual gifts do not make a minister, any more than they make Christians, since they can be present where saving grace is absent. But a man cannot be a minister without them; they represent the *sine qua non* of his office.[1] So firmly is this view held that he is even able to say, 'There may be a true ministry in some cases where there is no sanctifying grace; but where there are no spiritual gifts there is no ministry at all'.[2] Owen is not here adopting the position that regeneration is not essential as a qualification for ministry. He is rather employing the distinction common in the reformed theology between the decretive will of God and the preceptive will of God. God is able to use the agency of the unregenerate to minister to the needs of the regenerate, but that is not to be the principle on which we act. This is consistent with Owen's teaching on apostasy and perseverance; it is the safeguard which allows a theological response to the phenomenon of ministers also falling from grace.

In the sense in which Owen thinks of ministry there are three necessary gifts. The *first* is wisdom, or knowledge, or

such a comprehension of the scope and end of the Scripture, of the revelation of God therein; such an acquaintance with the systems of particular doctrinal truths, in their rise, tendency, and use; such a habit of mind in judging of spiritual things, and comparing them one with another; such a distinct insight into the springs and course of the mystery of the love, grace, and will of God in Christ, – as enables them in whom it is to declare the counsel of God, to make known the way of life, of faith and obedience, unto others, and so instruct them in their whole duty to God and man thereon.[3]

The *second* is an ability rightly to handle the Scriptures.[4] For this, not only the knowledge of Scripture, but also a knowledge of the people is required, with an appreciation of the patterns by which God may work in their lives; an acquaintance with the nature of temptation; and a right understanding of spiritual diseases.[5]

Thirdly, there must be the presence of the gift of utterance from God, which is an amalgam of an enlarged heart, boldness, gravity of expression, and authority.[6] These are all to be

[1]IV.494–5.   [2]IV.508.   [3]IV.509.   [4]IV.510; 2 Tim. 2.15.
[5]IV.511.   [6]IV.512.

exercised pre-eminently in worship. Over against these ordinary gifts, and in the context of discussing them, Owen affirms any claim to the extraordinary gifts is simply 'an enthusiastic delusion'.[1]

[1] IV.518.

∞ 9 ∞

Sacraments and Prayer

As a theologian standing in the reformed tradition, it was inevitable that Owen's *soteriology* should be summarized in his teaching on the *sacraments* and *prayer*. This is particularly true in view of his emphasis on the covenant as the unifying principle of Scripture, the objective organizing principle of theology, and the pattern of the subjective experience of Christian life.

1. Sacraments

Sacraments for Owen are sacraments of the gospel, and therefore of the covenant of grace: 'These are the principal mysteries of our religion, as to its external form and administration, – the sacred rites whereby all the grace, mercy, and privileges of the gospel are sealed',[1] and it is by them that these privileges are 'confirmed unto them who are in a due manner made partakers of them.'[2] Here Owen brings together the two great elements of gospel and sacrament, namely, the objective content and presentation ('external form and administration') and the subjective experience and enjoyment ('unto them who are in a due manner made partakers of it'). There is a clear parallel here between Owen's doctrine of the Scriptures as the word of God, the gospel as the good news of God, and the sacraments as the mysteries of God. There is objective content in each: the Bible *is* God's Word; the gospel indicates that *God was in Christ* reconciling the world to himself; the sacraments *signify and seal* the gospel; and yet the work of the Holy Spirit is involved in each of these means of communication to ratify subjectively the objective message.[3] Undergirding this whole

[1]XV.168.   [2]*Ibid.*
[3]Cf. *Causes, Ways, and Means of Understanding the Mind of God*, IV.121–234.

[211]

emphasis is the doctrine of the covenant which, as we have seen,[1] is the structure within which the apparently disparate emphases of the Christian message are brought together in harmony.[2]

Owen confirms this by indicating that the sacraments are signs and seals of the promises of the covenant.[3] The action of God involved in them is unilateral, but beneficial only to faith. Hence Owen describes the operation of grace in the sacrament: 'in and by a visible pledge they contain a promise, and exhibit the thing promised unto them that believe.'[4]

How, then, are sacraments to be defined? They are 'Visible seals of God's spiritual promises, made unto us in the blood of Jesus Christ',[5] 'whereby God in him confirmeth the promises of the covenant to all believers, re-stipulating[6] of them growth in faith and obedience.'[7] Owen is careful to avoid any suggestion that faith *creates* the sacrament (it is *the word* which does this); but neither is faith made void by the sacramental principle. Rather, it is encouraged, indeed necessitated, by it. In this way Owen avoids either a mechanical (*ex opere operato*) doctrine while maintaining the objective content of sacraments, or a *memorialist* doctrine while maintaining the necessity of faith.

A sacrament is a *sign* of God's grace, in that it 'exhibits' the thing promised; but even more it is a *seal* of that grace and of the promises of God. In the covenants of God it is always his grace

---

[1]See above (pp. 31ff.) on Owen's covenant theology. See also, in this connection, his view that the security of the covenant is found, experimentally, in the presence of the risen Christ with the church. This, for him, is the sign whether the covenant is in operation or not. IV.501.

[2]The 17th century was the age in which the 'Hamlet' character hero emerged. It was in this context that the objective assurance which the covenant offered prevented the true Puritan from becoming a living illustration of the 'Hamlet syndrome'. In his self-examination, he was preserved from despair by the grace of God, revealed in the covenant, and experienced in the 'great chain' of the *ordo salutis*. Cf. Nuttall, *Holy Spirit*, p. 7.

[3]VII.441.   [4]XXIV.166.   [5]I.469.

[6]This is the language of the federal scholasticism of the Continent, e.g. Daniel Wyttenbach, who describes the covenant of works in terms of: *stipulatio; promissio; adstipulatio; restipulatio*. H. Heppe, *Reformed Dogmatics* (ed., E. Bitzer, trs. G. T. Thomson) 1950, p. 295.

[7]I.490.

that is authenticated by a sacrament. Furthermore, while the sacraments represent, exhibit and seal God's grace to faith, they do not contain *in themselves* the grace promised. It is found in Christ alone. Nor is this grace received by partaking but rather by believing, so that the grace represented is 'effectually exhibited'. It is no less effectual for *not* being *ex opere operato*.

The sacramental principle is as old as, and belongs to, the covenantal principle. Like many of his contemporaries Owen saw the 'original church state' formed in good order in the Garden of Eden 'by the *sacramental* addition of the two trees, – the one of life, the other of the knowledge of good and evil.'[1] Similarly in the period of the old covenant, circumcision was the initial seal of the covenant with Abraham, and the Passover was of a 'sacramental nature'.[2] 'This is expressed Exod. xii.11, where, speaking of the lamb to be slain and eaten, with all its rites and ceremonies, God adds, "It is the Lord's passover;" where the application of the name of the thing signified unto the sacramental sign of it is consecrated unto the use of the church.'[3]

This raises a question of some importance particularly in view of the reformed argument for the baptism of the children of believers. Is there a distinction to be drawn between sacraments according to the dispensation to which they belong? Owen answers: 'Accidentally only, in things concerning the outward matter and form, as their number, quality, clearness of signification, and the like, – not essentially, in the things signified, or grace confirmed.'[4] Clearly, as a paedobaptist, and

---

[1]XV.229. There were differences of opinion among the federal theologians as to the exact identification of the sacraments of Eden. Cocceius and Heidegger located them in the tree of life and Paradise itself. Mastricht, Amesius and others, along with most British contemporaries, located them in the two trees; Witsius located three or four sacraments, in Paradise, the trees, and the sabbath. Heppe, *op. cit.*, pp. 297–8, cf. Owen, *Works* XXIII.185.

[2]XXIV.165.

[3]XXIV.166.

[4]I.490. In this context Owen did not give special attention to the supposed *national* (and therefore *temporary*) aspect of the covenant with Abraham, although it is precisely here that much of the weight of the Baptist argument has rested.

in the midst of a rising tide of baptist teaching,[1] Owen had an interest in such an argument. He equated, so far as possible, the significance of the sacraments of the old and new covenants.

It is important to notice that while not a 'sacramentalist' in the ordinary sense of the term, Owen believed that true religion had always been sacramentally administered, and in this sense he held a high view of the sacraments.

What then do sacraments mean to the Christian? This question may be answered more fully in the separate examination of each sacrament, but Owen allows himself a general comment. Sacraments are of value only when the recipient sees through, or beyond them, as signs, to the reality which is communicated through them. This exercise of faith involves three things: the submission of the soul to the authority of Christ; trust in the veracity of Christ actually to accomplish that which is sacramentally exhibited; and an understanding of the mystical relation between the symbols and Christ himself.[2]

As far as the administration of the sacraments is concerned, Owen adopts the classical position. Those ordained to the pastoral office, alone, may administer baptism and the Lord's Supper: '*The administration of the seals of the covenant* is committed unto them, as the stewards of the house of Christ'.[3] The sacraments, regarded as appendages to the word, and given for its confirmation, should be in the hands of those who are called to minister that word. This, for Owen, involves delegating times and seasons for sacraments, following the institution of Christ in their administration, and taking care that only those '*who are meet and worthy*, according unto the rule of the gospel'[4] should partake.

The sacraments of the new covenant are two, since only two have been appointed by God. Baptism seals the believer's initiation into Christ, and the Supper confirms his participation in Christ.

[1] An appendix to his work on infant baptism (XVI.24off.) deals with the objections of John Tombes, who wrote *Examen of the Sermon of Mr. Stephen Marshall about Infant Baptism*, London 1645. He was 'reputed the most learned and able Anabaptist in England.' *Reliquiae Baxterianae*, ed. M. Sylvester, London 1696, I.137.

[2] VII.220–221.   [3] XVI.79.   [4] *Ibid*.

i. *Baptism: initiation into the covenant life*

Owen pointedly indicates that baptism is not regeneration[1] but represents the washing of regeneration.[2] It is 'An holy action, appointed of Christ, whereby being sprinkled with water in the name of the whole Trinity, by a lawful minister of the church, we are admitted into the family of God, and have the benefits of the blood of Christ confirmed unto us.'[3] It is significant that this definition is serviceable both for the baptism of adults on profession of faith, and of infants of believing parents – a matter of some importance which was on occasion forgotten in the later development of the doctrine of baptism within the tradition of Owen's theology.[4]

Baptism

giveth all the external rights and privileges which belong unto them that are regenerate, until they come unto such seasons wherein the personal performance of those duties whereon the continuation of the estate of visible regeneration doth depend is required of them. Herein if they fail, they lose all privilege and benefit by their baptism.[5]

While Owen adopted the principle of the 'gathered' church, he

[1]XXIII.39; cf. III.216.   [2]III.424; VI.465–6; XVI.12.   [3]I.491.
[4]J. Bannerman, *The Church of Christ*, Edinburgh, 1868, II, 108–9, maintains that 'The proper and true type of Baptism . . . is the Baptism of adults. . . . It is abundantly obvious that adult Baptism is the rule, and infant Baptism the exceptional case . . . it is an error . . . to make Baptism applicable in the same sense and to the same extent to infants and to adults'. This objection is rooted in his objection to any expression of sacramental theology which does not make room for the recipient's faith in the definition of sacrament: 'There are some theologians indeed who in their explanation of the Sacraments make them seals of the covenant in general, and not seals of the believer's own personal interest in the covenant. . . . This explanation of the Sacraments, however, is, I think, much too narrow and limited.' He goes on to distinguish the two kinds of baptism in terms of a 'right of property' and a 'right of possession'. But it becomes difficult, on these grounds, to avoid the inevitable charge of special pleading, which Owen, on the other hand, would seem to avoid. W. Cunningham, *The Reformers and the Theology of the Reformation*, Edinburgh, 1866, p. 246, adopts a somewhat similar position. It is 'quite plain to anyone who is capable of reflecting upon the subject, that it is *adult* baptism alone which embodies and brings out the full idea of the ordinance, and should be regarded as the primary type of it'. It was not obvious, it would appear, to Owen. He does not seem to have adopted this dichotomy.
[5]XVI.12–13.

believed that the children of believers were part of it. The supposed 'problem' of baptized children who later proved unfaithful to Christ was not a *theological* problem for him (however much it was a pastoral agony). He seems to have seen the biblical response to this situation lies in church discipline and ultimately excommunication – not in the denial of baptism as the sign and seal of the covenant. God remains true to his covenant (even in judgment) not least when men prove to be faithless (2 Tim. 2.13).

Baptism symbolizes two essential elements of the gospel. (1) It is a token of forgiveness. God 'appoints it to be such as to represent the certainty and truth of his grace in pardon unto their senses by a visible pledge. He lets them know that he would take away their sin, wherein their spiritual defilement doth consist, even as water takes away the outward filth of the body'.[1] (2) But baptism is also *a pledge of union with Christ*, for

Hereon we are said to be 'buried with him' and to 'rise with him,' whereof our baptism is a pledge, chap. vi. 3, 4;[2] not in an outward representation, as some imagine, of being dipped into the water and being taken up again (which were to make one sign the sign of another),[3] but in a powerful participation of the virtue of the death and life of Christ, in a death unto sin and newness of life in holy obedience, which baptism is a pledge of, as it is a token of our initiation and implanting into him.[4]

The value of baptism is not tied to the time of its administration, but is to be to the Christian a constant reminder and pledge of his being *constituted* a Christian, and of the basic elements in the 'new creation' which has come in Christ.

There is already an indication in Owen's words that he was unwilling to follow Calvin in allowing immersion to be the primary *mode* of baptism, and the one employed by the New

---

[1]VI.465–6.   [2]i.e. Rom. 6.3–4.

[3]Division on the interpretation, and implications, of Romans 6.1ff. for the mode of baptism in the New Testament continues, even among paedo-baptists. Dodd, Nygren, and others assume that the thought pattern expresses the mode of immersion.

For a contrary view (and one similar to Owen's) see J. Murray, *Christian Baptism*, Philadelphia, 1952, pp. 29–33.

[4]III.560–1.

Testament church.¹ *Baptismos*, Owen argues, is any kind of
washing, whether by dipping or sprinkling, but in Scripture
'the sense of dipping is utterly excluded'² from the meaning of
baptizein although it is an acceptable mode of baptism 'provided
the person dipped be naked'!³ His argument against immersion
is based on the Septuagint's use of *baptizein* to convey the sense
of washing⁴ and sprinkling.⁵ Further, in the New Testament it
signifies *pouring*⁶ and is used in parallel with *niptein*, to wash.
Owen's position is that there is no example of Scripture using
baptizein necessarily in the sense of either 'to dip' or 'to plunge'.⁷
Furthermore, in the passages of Scripture in which baptism is
explained, the fundamental idea is that of washing, and the
mode represented is sprinkling.⁸ The affirmations of Romans
6.3–5, and 1 Peter 3.21 leave Owen unshaken in his view. It
cannot be argued from these passages that immersion was the
mode of baptism in the New Testament since they neither
reflect on the question, nor do they speak of Christ's death and
resurrection as symbolized in baptism, but only of the Christian's *participation* in him.

This brings us to consider Owen's teaching on the baptism of
infants, and the implications of this for the Christian experience
of the children of believing parents.⁹ It is noteworthy that this
element was so strongly retained in Owen's theology even when
he increasingly emphasized the concept of the 'gathered
church'.

Owen's argument for infant baptism is along the following
lines:¹⁰

He finds that there is no explicit scriptural warrant for the
refusal of baptism to infants from believing homes,¹¹ and
further, that there is no instance, in the annals of the primitive

¹Calvin expresses himself thus: 'The word "baptize" means to immerse,
and it is clear that the rite of immersion was observed in the ancient church' –
but he argues that the mode is not compulsory. *Institutes* IV. xv. 19.
²XVI.267.   ³*Ibid.*   ⁴2 Kings 15.14 (Septuagint).
⁵Exodus 12.22 (Septuagint).   ⁶Acts 1.5.   ⁷XVI.266.
⁸Owen refers to Tit. 3.5; Eph. 5.26; 1 Pet. 3.21 with Tit. 2.14, Heb. 9.14, 19,
25.
⁹Cf. XXIII.354: 'It has been the way of God from the beginning, to take
children of covenanters into the same covenant with their parents'.
¹⁰XVI.258ff.   ¹¹XVI.258.

church, of such a person being baptized in later life.[1]

It has been argued against this view that 'It is striking that several prominent Christians like Gregory Nazianzen, Basil the Great, Chrysostom and Augustine, though all born of at least one Christian parent, were not baptized in childhood.'[2] Owen, however, was conscious that these examples come from a much later period, in which the *time* of baptism was postponed because of a mistaken view of the *efficacy* of the sacrament.

The principle which lay at the heart of the old covenant administration that God's grace was extended 'to you and to your seed after you' cannot possibly be regarded as abrogated (as the baptist apologists argued) without *specific* divine command, and this is absent from the Scriptures.[3] Again, those who possess the thing signified (regeneration, cleansing and union with Christ) must surely have a title to the sign itself,[4] and Owen is convinced that infants are to be regarded as possible objects of divine regenerating power, and that some at least (those who die in infancy)[5] are in fact regenerate. The repudiation of this radically alters the doctrine of covenant fulfilment. For if God should deny the *sign*, it can only be because he refuses to extend the *grace* signified. The implication of this would be the exclusion of infants from his saving mercy. Owen regards this as contrary in every respect to the fulfilment of covenant grace in Christ.

Owen's argument, however, is even more fundamental than this. What is implied in the baptismal controversy involves the doctrine of the church, and, for Owen, goes beyond that to the doctrines of grace and creation. It is here that his baptismal doctrine may be seen to merge with his theology in general.

For Owen, grace, operating within the covenantal administration of divine revelation, is essentially restorative and recreative.[6] In this limited sense he agreed with Aquinas: 'grace does not destroy nature, but instead perfects it.' Grace

---

[1]*Ibid.* Owen is here an interesting precursor of the argument of O. Cullmann, *Baptism in the New Testament*, trans. J. K. S. Reid, London, 1950, p. 26.

[2]P. K. Jewett, article 'Baptism (Believer's) in *Encyclopaedia of Christianity*, I, Delaware, 1964, p. 523.   [3]XVI.259.   [4]*Ibid.*

[5]XVI.260. Here the assumption appears to be that they are children of believing parents.   [6]XVI.259.

brings man, and his environment, back to God's original intention (and in a sense takes him even further by securing his status as a son). But God's creating grace made man in the context of family life, a context soon spoiled and wrecked by sin. The operations of covenant grace take place through the broken channels of creation, to mend, heal and restore. The whole principle of inheritance and seed in the old dispensation of the covenant was therefore not regarded by Owen as merely *a matter of the flesh*, as the baptist argument ran. It was a matter of *grace* working in the created order, restoring nature, not destroying it. If, under the old dispensation, children are reckoned to the covenant of their parents; in the operations of the new covenant that cannot be any less so.[1] This is not, for Owen, trusting in the flesh, but trusting in the covenant which God the Creator has made as Saviour.

The baptism of infants brings them within the fellowship of the church. But evangelical paedobaptists have sometimes felt a tension here. Are church and family membership received together? Baptists have sometimes argued that the paedobaptist position means that grace and faith are reduced to the level of natural inheritance. Does the paedobaptist doctrine mean that a person is always and under every circumstance a member of the church?

Owen finds the answer to this emerging naturally in the context of the discipline into which an infant is brought by baptism. To argue for infant baptism is only part of the matter in his view. The practice must be seen in the light of the encouragement and help which is later available to the child. *Children*, thus baptized, receive all the privileges appropriate to their capacities[2] and the responsibilities appropriate to their standing in the church.[3] *The parents* have a special ministry to them, and *the officers of the church* will have a special care for them, no less than for adult members. In the Puritan congregation this would be seen in prayer, catechetical instruction, visiting, advice to parents,[4] and encouragement to consider 'joining themselves unto the church in full communion'.[5] If all

---

[1] See Norman Pettit, *The Heart Prepared, Grace and Conversion in Puritan Spiritual Life*, New Haven, 1966, p. 12.   [2] XVI.24.   [3] XVI.23.
[4] Cf. Richard Baxter, *The Reformed Pastor*, London, 1657, many editions, *passim*.   [5] XVI.23.

this is fulfilled, then, says Owen, 'there is provision for church order, usefulness, and beauty, beyond what is usually to be observed.'[1]

ii. *The Lord's Supper: covenant seal*

The only material in Owen's *Works* on the Lord's Supper is gathered in his sacramental discourses, published posthumously from notes taken by members of his congregation, and three brief sermons anonymously written, but with good reason attributed to Owen.[2] His doctrine cannot be said to be given formal representation. This may be taken as further evidence that Owen was supremely concerned with the pastoral help his contemporaries needed to enable them to live fully Christian lives, and less so with polemics.

While no systematic treatment is given, it is clear from the content of the sermons that Owen's treatment, of which we have only a fractional representation, was serious and thorough. The Lord's Supper was to be celebrated weekly, or as often as was possible and convenient.[3]

In Owen's teaching, Jesus Christ *himself* is central in the supper. He explains that there is 'in the ordinance of the Lord's supper, an especial and peculiar communion with Christ, in his body and blood, to be obtained.'[4] In its celebration, faith is directed, not so much to the veracity of God in the Bible, nor to Christ in general terms as the Saviour, but to the '*human nature of Christ*, as the subject wherein mediation and redemption was wrought.'[5] In more particular terms, it is Christ's human

---

[1]XVI.24.

[2]Gould comments that 'It needs but a glance at the three discourses in order to feel assured, from internal evidence, that they belong to Owen.' XVII.595 (XVI.527). They were in fact published in 1798 as Owen's. Certain features constrain agreement with this judgment: 1. The emphasis on *representation* and *exhibition*, XVII.597, 598–9 (XVI.529, 530–1); 2. The anti-sacramentalist critique, in thought patterns and language employed elsewhere by Owen, XVII.597 (XVI.529). 3. The emphasis on the fact that *Christ* offers himself in the supper, rather than the Father or the Spirit offering him to men, XVII.597 (XVI.529).

[3]XV.512.   [4]IX.523.

[5]IX.524, cf. Calvin's emphasis in *The True Partaking of the Flesh and Blood of Christ*, trans. J. K. S. Reid, in *Calvin: Theological Treatises*, pp. 258–324.

nature 'as *distinguished into its integral parts, – into body and blood*', which 'are not only considered as *distinguished*, but as *separate* also.'[1] In this special sense, in the supper faith focuses on the 'violent separation of body and blood'.[2] This is its object because it is the ground of salvation. But here too, faith penetrates to the cause of this separation – the moving cause of the Father's love,[3] the procuring[4] and efficient[5] causes in the work of Christ. This leads to an understanding of the supper which is dependent upon an appreciation of the doctrine of the atonement, and the 'great exchange' of reconciliation, in which communion with God is gained through the separation of the body and blood of Christ on the cross, that is, his death and penal substitution. In this separation, and its representation in the bread and wine, lies the great confirmation of the covenant,[6] and this results in strengthened faith. Yet there remain depths of the meaning of the sacrament to be further explored and appreciated in Christian experience. Owen emphasizes that God 'gives out unto us the object of our faith in parcels',[7] not in the sense that believers do not receive all of Christ (*totus Christus*) in the supper (a thought which he would deprecate) but in the sense that there may be increased enjoyment and blessing in the supper, in keeping with growth in grace, faith, and understanding.

The communion of the supper is *commemorative* since it involves a profession and proclamation of Christ's death. It is *eucharistical*, and *federal*,[8] in that God *confirms* his covenant (*he* has no need to *renew* it) and believers renew themselves in covenant obligations.

But how is Christ present in the supper? Owen believes he is present '*in an especial manner*'.[9] There is not more of Christ, or another Christ, but the same Christ is represented in a particular way. Negatively, his presence is not corporeal. Employing John 16.7 and Acts 3.21.[10] Owen teaches that the body of Christ is in heaven, and therefore is neither *in* the

---

[1]IX.524. Owen will have nothing to do with the Roman doctrine of concomitance, 'that is, whole Christ is in every kind'.
[2]IX.525. [3]*Ibid.* [4]IX.525–6. [5]IX.526.
[6]Cf. The Abrahamic covenant, Genesis 17. [7]IX.527.
[8]IX.527. [9]IX.572, cf. p. 529, 573.
[10]IX.572. Cf. Calvin *Institutes* IV. xvii. 12, 26.

sacramental bread and wine (in the Roman sense), nor *ubiquitous* (in the Lutheran sense). Nevertheless, Christ *is present*, and not simply *remembered* (in the so-called Zwinglian sense) in *the supper*, not in *the elements*. This is the classical, dynamic doctrine of Calvin's theology. In particular, Christ is present by representation, exhibition and obsignation.

Representation is a favourite expression.[1] Christ is shown as the one who suffered for men's sins and as 'newly sacrificed'[2] is food for their souls. This representation is seen with respect to God's setting him forth; his passion; his exhibition in the promise; his incorporation with the believer in union; and his participation with Christ by faith.[3]

Christ is also *exhibited* in the supper. Here the important thing for Owen is that *it is Christ who exhibits himself*. He is not proposed as the object of faith by the Father or the Spirit, but by himself.[4] This makes the supper a 'peculiar' ordinance as Christ sets himself forth as Prophet, Priest and King.[5] 'It is himself, as accompanied with all the benefits of that great part of his mediation, in dying for us.'[6] The bread and the wine then are not empty signs;[7] nor are they carnal signs, for it is Christ himself (Owen refuses to separate Christ's person from his work) who is present, sacramentally and spiritually, to be received, not by eating, but by believing.

Christ is also present by *obsignation*: the covenant has been made and confirmed by the blood of Christ; 'he comes and seals the covenant with his own blood in the administration of this ordinance.'[8]

Christ then is received sacramentally, not by taking the elements, but by the observation of the whole ordinance. He is received spiritually, as the one who has made peace with God by his death. If he is thus received, 'we may go away and be no more sorrowful.'[9] He is received so that believers become 'partakers of him in his sacramental tender,' and this brings 'peace and rest in our own bosoms'.[10] This 'is so to receive him

---

[1] IX.563, 593, 595, 605, 606.
[2] IX.564, cf. III.440. The reference is to Hebrews 10.20.
[3] IX.540–1.   [4] IX.589.   [5] IX.621–2
[6] IX.590.   [7] IX.563, 584; cf. XV.473.   [8] IX.574
[9] IX.565.   [10] IX.566.

as to enable us to sit down at God's table as those that are the Lord's friends . . . there being now no difference between him and us.'[1]

Preparation for the Supper. Owen argues from Scripture[2] that a general spiritual disposition is not in itself a sufficient preparation for the supper. This is true of solemn worship in general,[3] for which preparation 'consists in the removal of that from us which stands in peculiar opposition to that ordinance, whatever it be.'[4] Conscious of excesses which may here mar evangelical liberty, he wisely cautions that 'It is not good to have carnal boldness in our accesses and approaches to him'.[5] There must then be not only a general disposition, but a genuine preparation if we are to worship aright.

With respect to God, our fundamental need is for a realization of his authority in the ordinances of religion. We also need to recognise his holy presence with a view to the purpose for which the particular act of worship has been instituted.[6] With respect to himself, the worshipper must refrain from treasuring iniquity in his heart, and turn to God in a spirit of humility and self abasement, cherishing a genuine affection for the sacrament.[7] With respect to the sacrament itself, he must be persuaded that God has appointed it, otherwise it is not a sacrament to him.[8] He should be anxious to share in it according to God's will: 'And, above all things, take heed of that deceit I mentioned (which is certainly very apt to impose itself upon us), that *where there is a disposition in the person there needs no preparation for the duty.*'[9]

Since self-examination is a *preparation* for the sacrament, it must take place antecedent to it.[10] Apart from this, no other rules for it appear to be established in Scripture.[11] Clearly, however, it should take place at a time which will most help in the actual ordinance. This may be influenced by providential events and circumstances, or by a gracious disposition, sovereignly bestowed by God.[12] In the matter of length of time,

---

[1]*Ibid.*
[2]He quotes Gen. 35.1–5; Ex. 19.10–11; 2 Chron. 30.18–20; Rom. 15.30–1; Ecc. 5.1; Ps. 26.6.
[3]IX.545.   [4]IX.546.   [5]*Ibid.*   [6]IX.548–50.
[7]IX.551–2.   [8]IX.552.   [9]IX.553.   [10]IX.554.
[11]IX.555.   [12]*Ibid.*

Owen counsels common sense and prudence, insisting only that it be sufficient for the preparation of mind and heart to be really accomplished,[1] and that, on extraordinary occasions, the time should be naturally prolonged.[2]

As for the preparation itself, he has comparatively little to say. It consists of several parts: *Meditation* on the guilt of sin, the holiness of God, and salvation in Christ;[3] *Self-examination* in a spirit of repentance (do we mourn over sin? do we repent for actual sin? have we kept alive previously received pledges of God's love?),[4] and faith (do I stir it up to meet Christ in the supper?);[5] *Supplication*, in which prayer is added 'which may inlay and digest all the rest in the soul';[6] and *Expectation* that God will keep his promise, and 'meet us according to the desire of our hearts.'[7]

In this way the Christian is made ready to be entertained at the table of Christ, and receive him, and the blessings of the covenant afresh.

2. *Prayer*

Owen gave the theme of prayer extended treatment in only one place,[8] in the context of his work on the Holy Spirit. It is therefore concerned particularly with the work of the Spirit in prayer, and is characterized by the vigour and strength of the doctrine of prayer elucidated in the reformed tradition of the previous century. In particular (although he makes no direct reference to him), its antecedents are to be found especially in the teaching of Calvin.[9]

Owen steers a course which avoids mysticism[10] on the one hand, and on the other, the pietism and quiescence of a later period in the Evangelical tradition, which was marred by an unhealthy subjectivism. For him it is axiomatic that theology finds its true expression in prayer, and prayer is the clearest reflection of theology.

---

[1]IX.556.   [2]IX.557.   [3]IX.559.   [4]IX.561.
[5]IX.562.   [6]*Ibid.*   [7]*Ibid.*   [8]IV.237ff.
[9]Cf. *Institutes* III. xx.

[10]See G. F. Nuttall, *The Holy Spirit*, pp. 1–19. Also R. M. Jones, *Spiritual Reformers in the 16th and 17th Centuries*, London, 1914, pp. 208ff.

Prayer is an activity to be engaged in by men according to the light of nature, since it is a 'natural, necessary, fundamental acknowledgment of that Divine Being which they did own.'[1] Men have a sense of deity by which they recognize the eternal power and deity of God.[2] In this sense, prayer is a creation ordinance. There is something 'natural' about the duty and obligation of prayer, even for the natural man who is at enmity with God and alienated from him.[3] This thought reappears in Owen's discussion on religious affections and emotions, in the context of written prayers. There he indicates that there is a difference (in his view) between natural devotion and evangelical affections. The former may follow from the 'general notion of a Divine Power' and not from the character of God revealed in Scripture.[4]

Prayer is to be made according to the tenor of the covenant of grace.[5] If a man's theology in general is the *formal* content of his view of prayer, then, in a truly biblical theology, the covenant will be its *material* content and provide the inner structure and dynamic for his prayers. This is important for Owen, because it immediately relates prayer to the whole of the Christian life. Prayer *is* the whole of the Christian life, in embryo and miniature, involving both the objective (what we believe) and the subjective (the act of believing) aspects of it.[6] In prayer the Spirit of God is simply 'copying' the pattern of his work in man in general:[7] '*Prayer at present I take to be a gift, ability, or spiritual faculty of exercising faith, love, reverence, fear, delight, and other graces, in a way of vocal requests, supplications and praises unto God*'.[8]

With this in view we can examine Owen's teaching under the divisions of prayer as a *covenant privilege* and then as a *scriptural duty*.

i. *A covenant privilege*

The privilege of prayer, and its validity depend upon the nature and character of God as a God of promise. This is of course the heart of the biblical doctrine of the covenant, in

---

[1]IV.251–2.   [2]Rom. 1.21.   [3]IV.252.   [4]IV.346.
[5]III.399.   [6]IV.315–6.   [7]III.398–9.   [8]IV.271.

which God is represented as a promise-making and promise-keeping Redeemer, in the light of which man is able to ask for help and grace with assurance. Thus the promises of God 'are the measure of prayer, and contain the matter of it'.[1]

This is a thought to which we must return in another context,[2] but for the moment we should consider how it sets the tone of the whole of Owen's thinking. The promise which God gives creates the objective possibility of prayer, while the Spirit (who is himself given within the scope of the divine promises) is the condition of its subjective realization. His work is vital, since prayer (in contrast to the *doctrine* of prayer) is 'a gift, ability or spiritual faculty'.[3] Scripture assures us of the Spirit's help since his office is that of the Spirit of 'grace and supplications'.[4] His divine help is available both in the *matter* and the *manner* of our praying.

(1) *The Matter of prayer*

The Spirit of God is directly promised in Romans 8.26 to guide and help the children of God in prayer. We do not know what to pray for as we should and so he comes to our aid. There are several aspects to this ignorance.[5] The Christian is not fully aware of his own needs;[6] he is certainly not aware of how these needs may be supplied by God; and he may be ignorant of the precise ends to which his prayers should be directed.[7] This lack the Spirit can supply. It is also his office to bring the believer to a sense of his need of grace as well as a confession of his creaturely ignorance. In this way he produces an awareness of

---

[1]IV.275. Cf. T. Goodwin: 'There is never a prayer but it includes and supposeth a promise as the ground and foundation of it.' *Works* IX.372. Also D. Clarkson: 'Believing the promise whereby God has engaged himself to give what he asks; so to ask in faith is to pray with confidence the Lord will grant the petition, because he has promised; to pray with David, "Do good to thy servant," etc., and to rest assured he will do it, because it is his word, his promise, 1 Kings viii.24–26.' *Practical Works*, Edinburgh, 1864, 1.199. Similarly, Clarkson sees the covenant and its promise as the foundation of prayer: 'Get assurance of your interest in the covenant. . . . If you be sure you are his favourites, you may be sure to have his ear.' *Works* I.202.

[2]See below, pp. 228ff. [3]IV.271. [4]Zech. 12.10.
[5]Cf. IV.271; XI.346. [6]IV.272–5. [7]IX.72.

his external, internal and spiritual needs as well. He impresses on him the great sin of unbelief, concerning which constant prayer is required,[1] and also the depravity of his nature, the extent of which is beyond understanding.

But the Spirit not only knows men's needs; he also knows the will of God.[2] So Owen indicates that the Spirit's help is given in connection with the promises of God, which contain the answer to our needs. This is what is involved in praying in faith, since faith always has respect to the promises of God, which 'are the measure of prayer, and contain the matter of it.'[3] It is indispensable for the believer to know what God has promised if he is to be able to pray – 'These are the things which he hath "prepared" for us, as the apostle speaks, 1 Cor. ii.9; and what he hath so prepared he declareth in the promises of the covenant, for they are the declaration of the grace and good pleasure which he hath purchased in himself.'[4]

(2) *The Manner of prayer*

The Spirit is a Spirit of *supplications*.[5] Owen traces the origin of this expression to 'a bough or olive-branch wrapped about with wool or bays, or something of the like nature, which those carried in their hands and lifted up who were suppliants unto others for the obtaining of peace or the averting of their displeasure.'[6] The Spirit of God is not formally the one who makes supplication. He works in and through the believer's prayers, creating a gracious inclination to the duty of prayer, and giving a similarly gracious ability to discharge it. Owen sees both aspects included in the statement of Romans 8.26 that the Spirit helps us in our weakness. For apart from this inner work even the child of God may suffer a 'secret alienation' from prayer and supplication.[7]

This help is commonly described as the 'grace of prayer', but in fact,

prayer absolutely and formally is not a peculiar grace distinct from all other graces that are exercised in it, but it is the way and manner

---

[1]IV.277.   [2]Rom. 8.27.   [3]IV.275.   [4]IV.282.
[5]Zechariah 12.10.   [6]IV.257.   [7]IV.259.

whereby we are to exercise all other graces of faith, love, delight, fear, reverence, self-abasement and the like, unto certain especial ends. And I know no grace of prayer distinct or different from the exercise of these graces.[1]

Here again, perhaps even more forcefully, prayer is directly related to the whole course of the Christian life, and regarded as inseparable from our total experience of God.

Beyond this gracious work Owen recognized a distinct 'gift' or 'ability' in prayer.[2] This is the work of the 'Spirit of adoption',[3] given by virtue of the covenant between the Father and the Son, so that through him the Christian 'cries Abba, Father'. Prayer then is not only an exercise of graces, but a response to our relationship and standing with God the Father as his adopted children. It is of interest in this context to note that the covenant ground of prayer, for Owen, extends into the very nature of the economic Trinity, and the character of the inter-Trinitarian relationship.

The Spirit works in our wills and affections enabling us to have a sense of the *value* of the Christian's needs.[4] This is followed by his inward enabling in the actual supplication. He gives a '*delight in God* as the *object of prayer*'[5] which involves 'A sight or prospect of God as on a *throne of grace*'.[6] He inspires *confidence* or *boldness* in prayer. This 'respects not the answer of every particular request, especially in their own understanding of it, but it consists in a holy persuasion that God is well pleased with their duties, accepts their persons, and delights in their approaches unto his throne.'[7] In this way God's goodness and power, promised to the church, in the covenant, may be experienced.

Prayer then, according to Owen is a *covenant privilege*, and draws its inspiration, both in content and manner from what the Christian learns of God as the God of promise in the covenant, and through the Holy Spirit.

ii. *A Scriptural duty*

We have already seen that the whole of the Christian life is the

---

[1] *Ibid.*   [2] IV.260.   [3] Rom. 8.15, Gal. 4.6.
[4] IV.287.   [5] IV.290.   [6] IV.291.   [7] IV.295.

work of God's grace and love, to which our thankful response is
fulfilment of our spiritual duties.[1] We have also seen that
prayer is a reflection of this. While discussing the weighty
scriptural objections he finds to the Arminian system of
soteriology, Owen brings both of these thoughts together – the
macrocosm of the Christian life and the microcosm of prayer –
by suggesting, 'We are to pray only for what God hath
promised, and for the communication of it unto us in that way
whereby he will work it and effect it.'[2]

The idea that the content of prayer should be held within
certain bounds is a scriptural one. It appears, for example in
the Epistle of James, when he suggests that men do not have
what they ask for because they ask for the wrong reasons, and
perhaps also for the wrong things.[3] In the history of theology
the formulating of this idea goes back at least as far as
Tertullian, whose distinction between 'legitimate' and 'illegitimate' prayer is developed in the teaching of Calvin.[4] For
Calvin, as for Owen, Scripture dictated the content and
inspired the activity of prayer. Calvin plainly states that we are
'not to ask any more than God allows. For even though he bids
us pour out our hearts before him, he still does not indiscrimin-
ately slacken the reins to stupid and wicked emotions.'[5] But
what is it that God allows? What is *legitimate* prayer? Calvin
answers in commenting on Psalm 119.38:

Here we have briefly set forth the sole end and legitimate use of
prayer, which is, that we may reap the fruits of God's promises. . . .
For we perceive the prophet allows not himself to wish any thing but
what God has condescended to promise. And certainly their presumption is great, who rush into the presence of God without call from
his word.[6]

There needs to be a 'call from his word' for prayer to be
legitimate.

Only what God has promised to do in the word can be the

---

[1]Above, pp. 67ff.   [2]III.312.   [3]James 4.3.
[4]See *Institutes* III. xx. 48.
[5]*Institutes* III. xx. 5.
[6]*Commentary on Psalms*, Edinburgh, 1843–55, IV, trans. J. Anderson,
pp. 428–9.

theme of true prayer. In a sentence reminiscent of Calvin, Owen affirms: 'What God hath promised, all that he hath promised, and nothing else, are we to pray for; for "secret things belong to the Lord our God" alone, but the declaration of his will and grace belongs unto us, and is our rule.'[1] Other statements[2] point in the same direction, and it is as a consequence of this that Owen echoes the ethos of prayers made under the old covenant. Since certain spiritual and material blessings have been *promised* 'so we may press God immediately about them.'[3] In this sense prayer is seen as a scriptural duty to Owen, because its exercise is both encouraged and governed by the teaching of Scripture. The promises of Scripture, properly understood and applied, are the grounds of all assurance in prayer.

It follows that one important aspect of truly scriptural prayer is that of waiting on God. True, the promises of God are the ground of assurance for answered prayer, but the purposes of God, and the providential government he exercises in the world frequently mean a temporal gap between the asking in prayer and the receiving of the answer to the petition. Under these circumstances, Owen issues the following advice (in a sermon on Habakkuk 2):

Wait for it believing, wait for it praying, – wait for it contending. Waiting is not a lazy hope, a sluggish expectation. When Daniel knew the time was come, he prayed the more earnestly, Daniel ix.2, 3. You will say, perhaps, What need he pray for it, when he knew the time was accomplished? I answer, The more need. Prayer helps the promise to bring forth. Because a woman's time is come, therefore shall she have no midwife? nay, therefore give her one. He that appointed their return, appointed that it should be a fruit of prayer. Wait, contending also in all ways wherein you shall be called out; and be not discouraged that you know not the direct season of deliverance.[4]

Elsewhere this seed thought is enlarged. It is the duty of the Christian to pray for the fulfilment of all unfulfilled promises of God in Scripture.[5]

---

[1]IV.275.   [2]Above, pp. 227–29.   [3]IX.379.
[4]VIII.85–6.   [5]XXI.498.

What then are the duties of prayer enjoined in Scripture?

Clearly the Christian must pray about every matter where he finds a command to do so. But Owen draws our attention to what he considers the salient features of such prayer. We have noted above the responsibility to pray for the fulfilment of prophecy; we have also seen that our needs, described in Scripture, will be impressed upon us by the Spirit. We will make these needs, especially our own sinfulness and unbelief, special matters of concern. In particular, Owen argues that the Lord's Prayer outlines the main material for prayer[1] and points us to the glory of God. This should be our highest and most important supplication.[2] It involves our blessing since it is to God's glory that we are to ask for the Spirit of illumination[3] and for the Spirit of prayer.[4]

As we follow through these principles, the gift of prayer will be developed in our lives. Few things are more important than this. Thus Owen writes with feeling: 'I press it the more, and that unto all sorts of prayer, in private in families, in assemblies for that end'.[5] He adds a reason that might well be found in any treatise on prayer:

the temptations and dangers of the days wherein we live do particularly and eminently call for it. If we would talk less and pray more about them, things would be better than they are in the world; at least, we should be better enabled to bear them, and undergo our portion in them with the more satisfaction. To be negligent herein at such a season is a sad token of such a security as foreruns destruction.[6]

In this way the Christian is to be exercised in prayer, knowing himself, as he searches his heart; knowing the Scripture as he searches its pages; meditating on the glory of God and the intercession of Christ; frequently and fervently in prayer through the ministry of the Spirit.[7]

[1]VI.468. [2]IX.315. [3]XXI.311. [4]III.155.
[5]IV.319. [6]*Ibid.* [7]III.320–4.

∾ IO ∾

Apostasy and its Prevention

The central theme which runs through Owen's teaching on the Christian life may be summarized as follows: The life of the believer in this world develops *positively*, in his regeneration and his subsequent growth in grace; the latter is the flower of which the former is the seed. But it also develops *negatively*. His new life is grounded in the fact that he has been raised to newness of life in Christ. But this newness of life is the fruit of union with Christ in his death. The Christian is 'born with' or 'united to' Christ in his death.[1] The deliverance from the reign of sin is something which also flowers in his life, as he battles against all that would prevent him from growing in the grace of God. The new life in Christ must be protected if the child of God is to persevere to the end and reach the goal of the Christian life in this world and the next. Any exposition of Owen's teaching must give attention to what he says about the pathway on which the Christian must go, and the goal to which he aims. To these we now turn in the closing chapters of our study.

1. *The Danger of Apostasy*

In 1676, conscious of a decline in contemporary religion, Owen published *The Nature of Apostasy from the Profession of the Gospel and the Punishment of Apostates Declared, in an exposition of Hebrews 6.4–6; with An inquiry into the causes and reasons of the decay of the power of religion in the world, or the present general defection from the truth, holiness, and worship of the gospel; also, of the proneness of churches and persons of all sorts unto apostasy. With Remedies and Means of*

[1] Rom. 6.5, *sumphutos*.

[232]

Prevention.[1] Characteristically, Owen's title page also serves as a table of contents!

The work is grounded in a painstaking exposition of Hebrews 6.4–6, which Owen knew had been a seed-bed of controversy since the days of the early church.[2] Within the context of Owen's teaching, the problem is whether the description of the blessings received by apostates before they commit apostasy is in fact a description of true Christians. It is the logic of his position that true believers cannot fall from grace in this way.

Owen notes that the author of Hebrews did not assume his readers were in the condition described in these verses, and quotes Hebrews 6.9 as evidence: 'Even though we speak like this, dear friends, we are confident of better things in your case –things that accompany salvation'. This statement controls the whole of his exegesis, and leads him to argue that whatever significance the description in vv. 4–6 may have it is not a *saving* significance. In fact the Hebrews had experienced 'better things', 'that is, such as salvation is inseparable from'.[3] Nevertheless, the privileges described are 'evangelical' according to Owen, in the sense that they are *peculiar to the gospel dispensation*. They are 'especial gospel privileges, which professors in those days were promiscuously made partakers of'.[4] He explains the five privileges which Hebrews describes.

They were once enlightened. Owen admits that in the early church baptism was described as *phōtismos*, illumination. But, he reasons, it was 'at least an age or two, if not more,'[5] before this expression was used in the church to denote baptism. In the Scriptures it is used in another sense 'denoting an inward operation of the Spirit',[6] and so the meaning is 'to be instructed in the doctrine of the gospel, so as to have a spiritual apprehension thereof'.[7] Owen also took this to be the meaning in 2 Peter 1.19. There is a knowledge of spiritual things which is merely natural; a further illumination, such as is spoken of

---

[1]VII.1–259.
[2]He refers to Cyprian, Novatian and Tertullian.
[3]VII.17.   [4]VII.18.   [5]VII.18.   [6]VII.19.
[7]*Ibid.*

here; and a *saving* light which goes beyond either of these. It is possible to be enlightened without being converted.[1]

They have tasted the heavenly gift. Owen holds that the Spirit is the referent in both this and the following statements, first of all in his work in bringing in the new dispensation as opposed to the old, and then with respect to his operations. More importantly, he interprets 'taste' as 'test' or 'experiment'. It does not include the eating and digesting always involved in food becoming nourishment.[2] Men may taste the truth of God and not know his power, may experience the worship of the church without its inward beauty, and share in the gifts of the Spirit without experiencing his graces.

They are made partakers of the Holy Spirit. This, for Owen, is the central statement and the fundamental one. In contrast to their former Judaism, 'the Holy Ghost is present with many as unto powerful operations with whom he is not present as to gracious inhabitation; or, many are made partakers of him in his spiritual gifts who are never made partakers of him in his saving graces'.[3]

They tasted the good word of God. They heard the preaching of the gospel but tasted it without digesting it. Owen draws on his earlier distinction to demonstrate that a man may be delighted with the preaching of the gospel, particularly by a skilled preacher, and yet be like Herod before John the Baptist; he may rejoice in what he hears, but be like the stony ground in the parable of Jesus.[4] He may even undergo a measure of moral

---

[1]This is the view adopted by Calvin: 'We must note in passing the terms by which he denotes knowledge of the Gospel. He calls it *enlightenment*'. *The Epistle of Paul to the Hebrews*, trans. W. B. Johnston, ed. D. W. & T. F. Torrance, Edinburgh, 1963, p. 75. Clarkson gives a similar view of this passage, *Works* II.247. Alford suggests that Owen treats the passage 'at great length and very perspicuously'. But he disagrees strongly with Owen's interpretation! *The Greek Testament*, IV, London, 1894, p. 112. This, however, forces him to the extraordinary conclusion: 'The regenerate may fall away, the elect never can' (*ibid.*, p. 113). It is worth noting that Owen does not adopt the interpretation which would (within the framework of his own theology) create less tension. He gives experimental content to the expression 'enlightened', and would seem to be unwilling to lessen in any way the ultimate '*mystery* of iniquity' (2 Thess. 2.7) working in even outstanding professing Christians.

[2]VII.24. [3]VII.26. Cf. above, pp. 202–3.

[4]VII.30.

reformation, and yet not truly mix the word heard with faith.[1]
A *mere* taste will not give strength to stand in times of trial and
temptation.[2]

They tasted the powers of the world to come. 'The world to come' is
taken as a reference to the times of the Messiah[3] in which the
gifts of the Spirit were spread abroad. Those who share in the
gifts do not thereby necessarily share in his grace.

Clearly Owen's exegesis of the idea of 'tasting' in these verses
in Hebrews also influences his whole interpretation. It has been
described as 'ingenious' but dubious even by those in sympathy
with his theological position.[4]

I. H. Marshall accuses Owen of failure to interpret Scripture
by Scripture, and points to Hebrews 2.9 where Christ is said to
have 'tasted death' in the most complete and total way.[5] Owen
himself admits that the expression there means 'really to die',[6]
but maintains that 'the event showeth that it was only a
thorough taste of it that he had; he neither was nor could be
detained under the power of it'.[7] In other words the expression
conveys the idea of reality but also of impermanency.[8] Owen
also points to the experience of Jesus on the cross, when he *tasted*
the vinegar mixed with gall, but would not drink it.[9]

What in fact Owen is anxious to maintain is that, whether
permanently or temporarily, really or falsely experienced, this
'tasting' does not have salvation itself as its object.[10] This is so
even if it is contended that his particular understanding of this
expression, 'taste' is not supported by the general use of the
New Testament.

---

[1]Heb. 4.2.   [2]VII.31.

[3]Owen refers to the exposition of Hebrews 2.4 in his Commentary,
XX.281ff.

[4]John Brown, *An Exposition of Hebrews*, Edinburgh, 1862, p. 285.

[5]I. H. Marshall, *Kept By the Power of God*, London, 1969, pp. 135–141.

[6]XX.358.   [7]*Ibid.*

[8]Cf. II.246; XX.359.   [9]VII.24.

[10]This is why not all reformed writers are in sympathy with Owen's
exposition, although they are concerned to maintain the same doctrine of
eternal security. George Smeaton, for example, writes that Hebrews 6 is an
instance 'of men receiving only the supernatural gifts, not true grace', and
adds in a note, 'we need not labour, as Owen and others have done, to meet
the arguments of those who contend against the perseverance of the saints
from this passage.' *Doctrine of the Holy Spirit*, Edinburgh, 1882, p. 85.

To whom then does the author of Hebrews refer? Owen's conclusion is that the reference is to those not long converted from Judaism who had obtained a share in the special (if external) privileges of the gospel era, experienced the gifts of the Spirit, and known his presence in their affections, and a degree of moral reformation. They may even be of 'great esteem among professors'.[1] 'But the least grace is a better security for heaven than the greatest gifts or privileges whatever.'[2]

It ought to be noted that Owen denies that what makes men apostates is one particular sin (e.g. denying Christ under the stress of persecution). What is involved in apostasy is 'a course of sin or sinning'. If we persist in a course of sinning we cannot then be brought to repentance. What then does the author of Hebrews mean when he says that this 'is impossible'? It is not an absolute or moral impossibility, Owen believes, in the sense of being contrary to God's power or character. It respects 'the *rule* and *order* of all things that God hath appointed'.[3] The church does not have at its disposal any means appointed by God to bring such to repentance. Owen emphasizes that this passage is not reflecting on restoration to a church fellowship *on repentance*. Novatian's refusal to do this was based on a misunderstanding of the passage.[4] The door of the church is 'shut only against those who shall never endeavour to turn by repentance.'[5]

The reason repentance is impossible (in Owen's sense) is because of the nature of the apostasy: it involves crucifying the Son of God to ourselves.[6] This is done by *'accession in suffrage'*[7] with those who first crucified the Lord of Glory, in the trial and rejection of the gospel. This sin is greatly aggravated in view of the identity of the person rejected. He has now been 'demonstrated to be the Son of God with power by the resurrection'.[8] No new 'crucifixion' can be alleviated by a plea of ignorance[9], for the power of Christ has been experienced and the purpose of his

---

[1]VII.24.   [2]*Ibid.*   [3]VII.37.
[4]VII.39.   [5]*Ibid.*
[6]Owen takes 'to themselves' rather than 'again' on MSS grounds but in meaning combines the two – 'They again crucify the Son of God, not absolutely, but in and to themselves' (VII.47).
[7]VII.48.   [8]Rom. 1.4.   [9]1 Cor. 2.8.

death clearly understood. Hence the rightness, and righteousness of withdrawing ordinances for repentance.

Owen did not go so far as to dogmatize that such would never repent; only that such an event is beyond the scope of the provisions God has made for the church. Such a repentance would depend entirely on his own exercise of sovereign grace and mercy. It has not been *promised*, therefore it is not something for which the church can legitimately pray.[1]

Why should Owen be so concerned to make these points? The question is the more relevant when we realize that the pages which follow in his work are not strictly a development of this initial exposition. The answer is not difficult to find. He was deeply concerned to show that a true Christian does not commit apostasy, and he is therefore obliged to show that Hebrews 6.4–6 does not refer to the genuine believer. He may stumble and fall, but by grace he perseveres to the end.[2] But the exposition is important for another reason in the context of the whole of Owen's theology. It helps to give scriptural backing and basis for Owen's frequent contention that *profession of faith* and *possession of Christ* are not the same thing. As we have already seen, much of his pastoral concern was motivated by the necessity to distinguish these things.

Owen now turns to consider the *nature* of apostasy from the gospel. It can be either *total* or *partial*. It is no part of Owen's purpose then to write off those who fall and fail, for that would be to transgress against Scripture and his own experience:

> I myself knew one, yea, was conversant with him, and assisting of him in the concerns of his soul, who in the Indies turned Mohammedan, was actually initiated by circumcision into their superstition, and lived in its outward practice a year or two, who yet was sincerely recovered unto repentance, and died in the faith of the Son of God.[3]

There may be extenuating circumstances which, while not affecting the outward expression of a man's sin, may alter the

---

[1]VII.37. Here again, Owen shares with Calvin and Tertullian this insight about prayer – that there is legitimate and illegitimate prayer, and that the former is governed by what the Scripture says God promises to perform; cf. *Institutes* III. xx. 5: 'We are not to ask any more than God allows.' Owen, III.312: 'We are to pray only for what God hath promised.' See above, p. 230.

[2]See his treatment of Perseverance in *Works* XI.

[3]VII.52.

inner nature of his sin. Partial apostasy, as distinguished from total apostasy, is therefore 'every crime against the gospel which partakes of the nature of the other in any measure or degree.'[1]

The character of apostasy is determined by the character of the gospel. This has three essential features, the mystery of its doctrine; the holiness of its precepts; and the purity of its institutions for worship.[2] Apostasy will have reference to each or all of these.

i. *Apostasy from gospel doctrine*

Scripture emphasizes the danger of apostasy from the *doctrine* of the gospel.[3] From apostolic days on there are countless examples of this kind of apostasy.[4] From them, a clear pattern emerges of the direction of apostasy. Members of the church speak 'perverse things'; others enter from outside, like wolves in sheep's clothing, to devour the flock; weariness of sound doctrine leaves room for their heresies, and coordinates with the 'mystery of iniquity' which is already at work.[5]

This apostolic teaching has a prophetic aspect to it for Owen. *Perverse things* were spoken, with sincere purpose by many of the early Fathers of the church: 'It is known how instances hereof might be multiplied out of the writings of Justin Martyr, Irenaeus, Clemens, Origen, Tatianus, Athenagoras, Tertul-

---

[1] *Ibid.* [2] VII.60.

[3] Owen cites 2 Tim. 4.6–8; 1 Tim. 6.20–1; Tit. 1.13–14; Jude 3.

[4] In XV.193ff., Owen gives an historical summary of the development of apostasy. He refers to the fact that so many New Testament letters were written to deal with teaching that tended to this danger. Speaking of the later period he says – 'For my part, I have as great a respect and reverence unto the primitive churches of the first, second, and third centuries, as I think any living man can justly do; but that they did in nothing decline from the grace, mystery, truth, or rule of the gospel, that they gave no admittance unto "vain deceit, after the tradition of men, after the rudiments of the world," there are such evidences unto the contrary as none can believe it but those who have a great mind it should be so, and [have] their credulity at their disposal.' VII.65.

[5] VII.66–7. Cf. Paul's words in the context of his concern for the church at Ephesus, Acts 20.28; Eph. 4.11–14; 2 Tim. 3.1–9.

lian, Lactantius and others'.[1] Thereafter follow *the wolves*, with explicit heresies of various kinds, Arianism, Pelagianism and so forth. Impatience with sound doctrine followed, flowering in medieval theology and practice, until finally the decay of the gospel 'came unto its height in the Papacy.'[2] At the Reformation the truth of God was re-established, although 'It is true, they arrived not therein at the purity and peace of the apostolical churches; nor was it by some of them absolutely aimed at.'[3] The message was scriptural and the testimony sealed with blood; but this work too has been thwarted. Such, then, is the Owenian interpretation of church history. It is characteristically Puritan, and helps explain why Owen regarded this subject as of great ecclesiastical as well as personal significance.

Owen lists no less than six general and six particular causes of real apostasy from the gospel. But they share a common foundation in the heart of man: 'That *rooted enmity* which is in the minds of men by nature *unto spiritual things*, abiding uncured under the profession of the gospel, is the original and first spring of this apostasy.'[4] When the gospel is presented to such, 'it proves irksome unto that enmity which is predominant in them'.[5] This underlines, for Owen, the heavy responsibility of the ministerial office.[6] Herein lies the guilt of the Roman

[1] VII.68. He instances their philosophical presuppositions and allegorical exegesis.
[2] VII.71.
[3] *Ibid.* This last phrase indicates Owen's belief that the church should be '*reformata et reformanda*'. He is thinking, especially, of the Anglican Reformation.
[4] VII.82.   [5] VII.84.
[6] It is only by the 'diligent ministerial dispensation of the word, with such an exemplary zeal and holiness in them by whom it is dispensed, and all other things requisite unto the discharge of that work, as may reconcile the hearts of the people unto evangelical truths, beget in them a delight in obedience, and implant the power of the word in their whole souls. Want hereof was that which lost the gospel in former ages, and will do so wherever it is, in this or those which are to come'. VII.91. This work is the one that God has ordained and promised to bless. The lack of it is such a cause of apostasy that Owen further stresses the importance of the work of the ministry – '*the well-being of the church depends on the right discharge of the office of the ministry*', VII.185. Their duties are as follows: To keep the gospel uncorrupted; to instruct the people with diligence; to set an example of holy living; and to attend to the discipline of the people. VII.185–191.

priesthood, that it has accommodated the gospel doctrines to the carnal minds of men (despite profession of the contrary), and, adds Owen, has introduced religion! – 'a device to satisfy sin and deceive conscience'.[1]

The second cause is 'that *spiritual darkness* and ignorance which abides in the minds of men under the profession of the truth'.[2] This includes an ignorance both of the things contained in the gospel, and of the 'doctrinal way of their declaration',[3] that is, of the transformation which takes place when biblical teaching is received by a mind illuminated by the Spirit.[4] The professing Christian needs therefore to pray for the Spirit of truth to lead him to understand spiritual things spiritually, and to learn the truth 'as it is in Jesus', and 'together with the knowledge of it, to have an experience of its power and efficacy in the mortification of sin, in the renovation of our nature, and transforming of the whole soul into the image of God in righteousness and the holiness of truth.'[5]

All truth is, for Owen, to be related to the knowledge of Christ as Saviour and Lord. Thus, the function and end of revelation is essentially practical: 'that it may put forth a *spiritual, practical power* in our souls'.[6] 'He who hath learned to be meek, humble, lowly, patient, self-denying, holy, zealous, peaceable, to purify his heart, and to be useful in his life, is indeed the person who is best acquainted with evangelical truth.'[7]

Apostasy's third cause is 'The innate *pride and vanity of the minds of men*'.[8] The gospel is given to deal with both the weakness of reason as finite, and the depravity of reason as fallen. It therefore contains truth which is beyond the scope of reason as finite, and contrary to carnal reason as perverted. But the vanity and pride of the human mind rejects what is above reason (the Trinity and the Incarnation) and seeks to 'deprave and wrest'[9] what is contrary to carnal reason. Only a 'humble subjection of mind and conscience unto the authority of God in his word . . . will be found to answer the experience of

[1]VII.101.   [2]VII.102.   [3]*Ibid.*
[4]Owen refers to 2 Cor. 3.8; Rom. 6.17.
[5]VII.113.   [6]VII.114.   [7]*Ibid.*   [8]VII.123.
[9]VII.131.

believers . . . is the only security against this distemper.'[1] Such willingness to submit the mind to the logic of Scripture is, for Owen, true spiritual reasoning.

The fourth general cause of apostasy is careless security and a trust in '*groundless confidences*'.[2] Scripture warns that a time of great apostasy may also be a time of false security among professing Christians, making them negligent of duty, indifferent to the truth and power of the gospel, and over-confident of their own ability to stand in the 'evil day'.[3]

The fifth cause is love of the world and the satisfaction it is able to provide. This is pre-eminently so in times of persecution and when superstition and doctrinal error reign unchallenged. But the seed of God's word is always falling among thorns, and there may be a Demas even in the apostolic camp.[4]

The sixth cause is the hand of Satan; he was the leader of the first apostasy from God; he constantly seeks to drag mankind down with himself.[5]

In the meantime, God himself is not idle, for he, 'in his holy, righteous judgment, gives them up unto *further delusions*'.[6] By removing their candlestick,[7] he deprives them of their means of light.[8] He may even send a strong delusion so that they believe a lie,[9] or smite them with blindness of mind and hardness of heart.[10] The fearful thing about such apostasy lies in its confirmation by God himself.

There is no easy formula, however, by which apostasy can be described and its signs recognized: 'Each especial defection in every kind hath reasons and causes peculiarly suited unto its rise and furtherance.'[11] Owen gives these briefer consideration: ignorance of the necessity of knowing Christ and the benefits he brings leads to apostatizing tendencies;[12] the person who is unaware of the nature of his sinfulness will not give himself to investigate the character of the Saviour,[13] nor will he find in Christ what the person conscious of sin discovers. A failure to draw on the power of Christ by the Spirit to deal with indwelling sin will lead to the same end, as will all efforts of man

---

[1]VII.134.   [2]VII.135.   [3]VII.137.   [4]VII.138–9.
[5]VII.139–40.   [6]VII.141.   [7]Rev. 2.5.
[8]VII.142.   [9]*Ibid.*, cf. 2 Thess. 2.11.
[10]VII.144; cf. Is. 6.9–10.   [11]*Ibid.*   [12]VII.146.   [13]VII.148.

to establish his own righteousness, not realizing that the doctrine of *grace* precludes this and his boasting in it.[1] Or, it may be that a person does not inwardly submit to or admire the sovereignty of God in the *way* of salvation. To despise the means is to despise the thing itself in this case.[2] Finally Owen mentions '*want of an evidence in themselves of the divine authority of the Scriptures*'.[3] Such are those who wrest the Scriptures to their own destruction.[4]

This, then, is the first way men fall from the church – by defection from the mystery and doctrine of the gospel.

ii. *Apostasy from the holiness of gospel precepts*

Gospel precepts are the rule of Christian obedience.[5] Owen's time was, he believed, marked by this second kind of apostasy. Yet even such times can bring strength to faith, because in them God's word is fulfilled in a remarkable fashion.[6]

The doctrine of the gospel requires a 'holiness without which no man will see the Lord'.[7] Holiness involves obedience, which in turn involves the fulfilment of duty.[8] Apostasy in this sphere may involve (1) the creation of man-made duties, or (2) a substitution of natural morality for spiritual duty, or (3) a pretence to fulfil the duties of sanctification.[9]

Of the first kind is the apostasy Owen sees in Rome. For her, *sanctitas*, holiness is one of the marks of the church,[10] and yet, her holiness is not that described in Scripture. The religion she upholds lacks the liberty and freedom which the gospel promises; the rule of her holiness is man-made law, not the God-given gospel. That law can be practised without faith in Christ, and is further corrupted by the teaching on merit and supererogatory works.[11]

Of the second kind is teaching which reduces gospel obedience to the level of ordinary morality,[12] and despises the work of supernatural grace as 'enthusiastical folly'.[13] Such living by the light of nature ignores that whatever is 'not

---

[1]VII.151ff.   [2]VII.157.   [3]VII.158.   [4]2 Pet. 3.16.
[5]VII.159.   [6]VII.161.   [7]Heb. 12.14.   [8]VII.161.
[9]VII.165.   [10]*Ibid.*   [11]VII.166–8.   [12]VII.168.
[13]*Ibid.*

wrought *in* us by the grace of God, as well as *by* us in a way of duty, is foreign unto evangelical obedience.'[1] It does not proceed from the renewal of the soul. But the rule of faith is that the tree must first be good if the fruit is to be good. Anyone who is seriously influenced by this erroneous teaching is, for Owen, destitute of the light of the gospel and a stranger to its power.

Of the third kind is any form of perfectionism.[2] Those who pretend to such attainments plainly contradict the teaching of Scripture, which stresses the constant warfare in which the believer is involved, because of the weariness of the flesh, the power of sin indwelling, and inexperience in spiritual things.[3] This is not to say that evangelical holiness is lax – it cannot exist alongside habitual sin. Those who are born of God do not commit sin,[4] that is they do not live in habitual omission of duties or satisfaction of lusts.[5] Evangelical obedience is universal in character, if not perfect in fulfilment, and it regards sin with horror. The Christian is not like those who

may be startled with sin in its first appearance, on their first convictions, or its first dangerous efforts; but when it is become their familiar, they suppose it a thing in their own power, which they can use or not use as they see occasion, though indeed themselves are the servants of corruption, being overcome thereby and brought into bondage.[6]

Owen seeks to strike the biblical balance avoiding antinomianism on the one hand, and perfectionism on the other. To depart from the biblical norm is to be in danger of forsaking evangelical holiness and committing apostasy.

There may follow a yet worse apostasy, into a 'profaneness

[1]VII.169.   [2]VII.171.   [3]VII.173–4.   [4]1 Jn. 3.9.

[5]VII.176. The interpretation of 1 Jn. 3.9 is fraught with difficulty. Owen's view draws on the use of the present tense to suggest habitual activity. This is all of a piece with Owen's interpretation of Romans 6, in which the Christian has *died* to sin, does not live under its dominion, does not 'continue in sin' but is not yet free from committing sins. Cf. David Clarkson: '1 John 3. Not that sin is not in him, or that he never is guilty of an act of sin; but it is not his delight, it is not his custom, he follows it not with full consent, he makes not a trade of it.' *Works* II.81–2. 'As he commits not sin like others, so he continues not committing it as others' *Works* I.34. For further elucidation of Owen's view see XI.561–578.

[6]VII.177–8.

and sensuality of life'.[1] For the second time in this treatise Owen emphasizes the great responsibility of the ministerial office, because he finds the first occasion of this kind of apostasy to be in the leaders of God's people, in the Old Testament and in the New Testament as well as in the history of the Church Catholic: *'the well-being of the church depends on the right discharge of the office of the ministry'*.[2]

But there are other causes such as *'a false appropriation of the justifying names and titles unto them, in ways of sin and wickedness.'*[3] Owen regarded the 'christianising' of the western world as a spiritual catastrophe. It permanently confused the difference between the church and the world, and buried the doctrine of the gospel, so that 'By these and like means, the generality of mankind were brought into an utter unconcernment with gospel holiness.'[4] The results were manifold: persecution of professing Christians by other professing Christians;[5] a lack of concern to guard against prevailing national vices;[6] a misplaced concern about the externals of public worship;[7] an increase in superstition. None of these could bring lasting peace to the consciences of men.[8] They led to scandal and the disgracing of the gospel, instead of the mutual love and respect which should characterize Christian witness and the usefulness which should be the hall-mark of every believer's life.[9] When the gospel is misrepresented to the world widespread and profane apostasy is inevitable.[10]

There is one final kind of apostasy to be considered.

iii. *Apostasy from gospel worship*

This serious spiritual decay is always marked either by a

---

[1]VII.182. [2]VII.185. See above, pp. 165ff.
[3]VII.196. [4]VII.201; *cf.* IX.311; cf. XVI.19; XVI.201.
[5]VII.203–205.

[6]VII.205–208. Owen quotes Paul's approval of Epimenedes' comments on the Cretans in Titus 1.12. He illustrates the point by reference to stubbornness among the Jews and, among the English, 'the sin of this nation hath been always esteemed *sensuality of life, in an excess of eating and drinking,* with the consequents thereof.' VII.207. Cf. XVII.548ff., (XVI.48off.). 'National Sins and National Judgments', a posthumously published sermon; also IX.294 for treatment of Christians.

[7]VII.208–211. [8]VII.211–213. [9]VII.215. [10]VII.217.

neglect of what God has appointed in his church or by adding to it. Thus, for example, some set aside the sacraments without realizing that in actual fact this is to denigrate the gospel itself.[1] In contrast to what is claimed (e.g. by the 'Inner Light' teaching) this shows a lack of spiritual illumination in an elementary failure to see into the heart of the sacraments and to grasp their inner significance.[2] On the other hand, Rome has added to the pure worship of the New Testament church: 'there is no one ordinance or institution of Christ which they have not corrupted'.[3] That these things should take place in the professing church suggests a mass apostasy from the gospel.

Owen now comes to the application of this teaching, discusses the dangers of apostasy (partial or total), and gives some directions to help the Christian avoid it.

The application of such teaching is illustrated by Paul's discussion of the apostasy of the Jews in Romans 9–11.[4] Although their fall was neither final nor total, Owen considers that the universality of it should act as a warning to all who profess faith. No Christian is so secure in himself that he can afford to be sanguine about his power to stand firm in the future. He must always trust only in the power and grace of God. The different ways in which apostasy has appeared in the world emphasize this,[5] and remind us that recovery from partial apostasy is uncertain. The situation may prove in the long term to be terminal. Its end is eternal ruin.[6]

The guilt of apostasy is greater than that of those who crucified Christ, because it presupposes a knowledge of the truth and a departure from it. Apostates first lose all taste of the goodness there is in Christ, and then their convictions about the truth of the gospel.[7] They begin to treat it with contempt, and substitute some other way of salvation for the grace of God in Christ.[8]

Apostates despise the witness of Christians. This despite is also directed against the Spirit of God, *because* the grand purpose of his ministry is to witness to Christ. It may even be that they will openly express their hatred of Christ and the

[1]VII.219.   [2]VII.220.   [3]VII.221.   [4]VII.222–3.
[5]VII.228.   [6]VII.229.   [7]VII.231.   [8]VII.233.

gospel.[1] All these are evidences that apostasy has already begun.

Could this teaching not be a stumbling block and a discouragement to weak and over-introspective Christians? Owen admits this could be so, and allows himself some comment. There may be those who feel that they have backslidden to such a degree that God has given them up to apostasy.[2] It is doubtless right and scriptural for them to examine themselves, but they must not forget that *decays of grace are recoverable*, so long as they retain a sense of the evil of them.[3] Christ expresses a provision for this condition in Scripture.[4]

Others may feel that, since they have fallen far short of the holiness described in the New Testament, they have virtually committed apostasy. Owen reminds us that there are various degrees of sin's power and prevalence:[5] its captivating power[6] when it conflicts with the will internally; its prevalence, when the will yields to it and sin gains dominion; and a third condition, between these two, when sin may bring a man into bondage for a period without gaining permanent dominion. Such is the condition of those described in 2 Peter 2.19. This is undoubtedly a situation of immediate and immense danger, but it *is* recoverable. It is not yet apostasy, and it may be remedied in three ways. Two of them, predictably, are prayerfulness and mortification. The third is a little unexpected and for that reason the more interesting: such a person should share his condition with 'some *able spiritual guide*'.[7] 'This sometimes hath broken, defeated, and scattered at once the forces of sin in the soul, where in its own wisdom and strength it was no way able to conflict with it.'[8] Owen cites James 4.16 as authority for this practice, and maintains it is an 'ordinance'[9] of God for this very purpose. It is, for Owen, a great loss that Roman *misuse* of this ministry has led to Protestant *disuse* of it.

How, then, should the professing Christian shape his life in order to avoid the danger of apostasy? He must focus his whole life to seek the glory of God,[10] not least when under the stress of temptations. He will then learn to mourn for sin, both his own

[1]VII.254. [2]VII.235. [3]VII.236. [4]Rev. 2.1–5; 3.1–3.
[5]VII.238. [6]Rom. 7.23. [7]VII.239. [8]*Ibid.*
[9]*Ibid.* [10]VII.241.

and that of the world. He will learn to pray and to witness for that glory day by day. He should keep a watch on his own heart,[1] since this is where any declension will begin; he will keep awake both to its deceitfulness,[2] and to the safety it will find in Christ;[3] he will keep it in a state of self-conscious awareness, so that even the imperceptible beginnings of sin will be noticed.[4] He should also guard against resting in the external privileges of the church;[5] he will not be content with the exercise of the gifts of the Spirit only and will look for his fruit;[6] nor will he have too high an estimation of one special form of worship.[7] He will strive to have his heart set on God, spiritual things made real, his own sensitivity to sin increased, and his resolve to suffer with and for Christ strengthened.[8] If he experiences these in public worship, he will be less concerned for outward forms. He should further *beware of the infection of national vices*.[9]

In Owen's day this meant that a Christian will not spend too much time in 'talking houses'![10] The reference is to the famous coffee houses of seventeenth-century London. So powerful was the public opinion expressed in them that the Government at one time tried to suppress them.[11] Owen's sentiments are directed, not against coffee (on health grounds) but against time-wasting (on spiritual grounds)! Finally the Christian should avoid all '*miscarriages of professors which alienate the minds of men from the gospel*',[12] such as a lack of love or usefulness to society, or pride and censoriousness in social behaviour. To the extent that a Christian contributes to the apostasy of another he has a share in the guilt himself. The only censure he should pass on the life of another is the testimony of his own life of grace and graciousness.[13]

The Christian is ultimately concerned to deal with the remnants of corruption in his life, not simply because of the apostasy to which they eventually lead, but because of the

---

[1]VII.245.   [2]VII.246.   [3]VII.247.   [4]VII.248.
[5]VII.249.   [6]VII.251.
[7]This work was published in 1676 by which time Owen was established as an Independent. He is here thinking of the liturgics of a Prayer Book form of worship.
[8]VII.254-5.   [9]VII.256.   [10]*Ibid.*   [11]*Ibid.*
[12]VII.257.   [13]VII.258-9.

nature of sin itself. All sin is lawlessness and godlessness; it represents an affront to the grace and majesty as well as the holiness of God. For this reason it is never sufficient for Owen to guard his readers from the dangers of apostasy only negatively. Positively, the believer is guarded and strengthened by the development of *spiritual mindedness*.

2. *Spiritual Mindedness the Preservative*

In his exposition of Romans 8.6, in *The Grace and Duty of Being Spiritually Minded* (1681), Owen stressed that there are only two categories of men, those ruled by the flesh, and those ruled by the spirit.[1] The one leads to death, formally, meritoriously and eternally; it is nothing less than enmity with God. But to be spiritually minded is the essence of experiencing life and peace.[2]

What does it mean 'to mind the spirit'? In Romans 8.9-11, *pneuma* refers to the Holy Spirit.[3] But in verse 6 Owen prefers to take it as the principle of spiritual life in the believer, animated by the Spirit of God. Paul ascribes *phronēma* to the spirit. It is the power of the mind in a practical sense, (in contrast to speculative reasoning conveyed by *dianoia* or *sunēsis*),[4] and hence it means to think, or to set the affections on something, or to mind.[5] Paul is speaking of 'the actual exercise of the mind as renewed by the Holy Ghost, as furnished with a principle of spiritual life and light, in its conception of spiritual things and the setting of its affections on them, as finding that relish and savour in them wherewith it is pleased and satisfied.'[6] Here three things are distinguished; there is the actual *exercise* of the mind, the *frame*, or inclination of it, and also the *affections* of it.

To be spiritually minded in this sense is the hallmark of the genuine Christian who alone enjoys life and peace. It is the antithesis of carnal mindedness,[7] in which the love of earthly things fills the mind and captures the affections.

Spiritual mindedness arises from an inner disposition.[8] The water that comes from a spring runs constantly unless it

[1]VII.267. [2]VII.268. [3]VII.269; cf. IV.387; XI.332.
[4]VII.269–70. [5]Col. 3.2; Phil. 3.9.
[6]VII.270. [7]VII.271–2. [8]VII.277.

encounters a dam; that which comes from periodic thunder showers runs for a season and then dries up. Owen's metaphor also indicates the possibility of counterfeit spirituality. There may be things resembling spiritual mindedness but are not so. They lack spontaneity. This may appear in our response to the preaching of the word, as Scripture suggests in the parable of the soils;[1] or it may appear in prayer, since we may continue this duty while living in known sin.[2] Prayer may be made by the exercise of *gifts* rather than *graces*;[3] spiritual thoughts in it may be only occasional.[4] Nor is fervency in prayer necessarily a mark of reality, since it may arise from our natural affections or the keenness of recent convictions of sin or need. The spiritual quality of others may have a similar effect on us, producing an interest in spiritual things, without actually making us personally spiritually minded.[5]

Further, spiritual thoughts must not only be present, naturally; they must abound. In the ungodly man, even when the appearances belie the truth, every imagination of his heart is evil continually.[6] The root principle of all his thoughts is contrary to God, and diverted towards self ends. There is therefore no greater evidence of spiritual renewal than 'a change wrought in the *course of our thoughts*.'[7] The forsaking of individual sins is not a sign of spiritual mindedness: 'The cure of a particular sin may leave behind it the seeds of eternal death'.[8] But the spiritual man is to be 'filled with the Spirit'[9] and this is the cause of the abundance of his spiritual thought.

But how can this abundance be measured? 'I answer, in general, among other Scriptures read over Psalm cxix with understanding'![10] Owen is thinking naturally of the psalmist's constant delight in the law of the Lord. But he provides further thoughts for self-examination:

(a) On the principle that 'Where your treasure is, there will your heart be also', how are our thoughts of spiritual things to be related to our thoughts about ordinary life?[11] We are not to allow the concerns of this world to engage our thoughts in the

---

[1]VII.281–2.   [2]VII.284.   [3]VII.288.   [4]VII.290.
[5]VII.296–8.   [6]VII.298.   [7]VII.299.   [8]*Ibid.*
[9]Eph. 5.18.   [10]VII.301.   [11]*Ibid.*

way that only God should; nor to engage in *vain* thought, or worse, thoughts that are formally evil.[1]

(b) A second test is: Do thoughts of spiritual things take possession of my mind at their *proper* seasons?[2] Do times of leisure find my mind turning to spiritual matters? 'If we cannot afford unto God our spare time, it is evident that indeed we can afford nothing at all.'[3]

(c) A final test is: How is my mind affected by disappointment and failure in these things?[4] Does it mourn over negligence? Only when we are spiritually minded will that be our response.

i. *The objects of spiritual thoughts*

We often discover that affections and will do not comply with the leading of the mind. Sometimes the real fault is that we are ignorant of the way in which spiritual meditation is to be practised.[5] In order to remedy this Owen furnishes further guidelines.

Genuine faith will take note of duties which arise in God's providence.[6] This is very important when the purpose of his working in the world is the chastisement of his people.[7] At such times we should search our own hearts and past life to discover any cause of the divine anger.[8] This is also an opportunity for us consciously to yield the whole of our life to the sovereign will and wisdom of the Father.[9]

Again, private trials and temptations demand the exercise of spiritual thought. Owen sees special difficulty in this because the power of temptation lies in its ability to stir and direct our thoughts towards a particular object, or what it will lead to, through the influence that lust has formerly had in our affections, or through the imagination to which that object is frequently represented with fresh pleasure.[10] So difficult is this spiritual work that 'There have been instances wherein persons have entered with a resolution to punish sin, and have been ensnared by the occasion unto the commission of the sin they

[1]VII.304.   [2]VII.305.   [3]VII.306.   [4]*Ibid.*
[5]VII.308.   [6]*Ibid.*   [7]*Ibid.*   [8]VII.369.
[9]VII.310.   [10]VII.312–3.

thought to punish.'[1] Under these circumstances we must give strict attention to bringing the mind to contemplate the guilt of sin, and its power, rather than the activity itself.[2] At such times we must direct our trust to *Christ*; this will be encouraged by a right view of sin.[3]

But even this experience is not outside the purposes of God. 'It is true, *God tempts none*, as temptation formally leads unto sin; but he *orders temptations* so far forth as they are afflictive and chastisements. Thus it is when he suffers an especial corruption within to fall in conjunction with an especial temptation without, and to obtain a prevalency thereby.'[4] Here the practical value of spiritual mindedness now comes into its own. Through it we come to know our own peculiar weaknesses and temptations, and the remedy for them by faith in Christ's strength and victory, by our contemplation of his love and compassionate care.[5] This brings new fortitude to faith, a new assurance of hope, and prepares us to bear the cross.[6] Our faith penetrates to the joy of an eternal weight of glory,[7] and thus, Christ-like, we endure the cross and despise the shame.[8]

Owen realized that it is this contemplation of spiritual and heavenly things that so many Christians find difficult to understand and practise. How is this to be done? In general, our minds must be exercised in the discipline of right thinking on heavenly and future things.[9] That future state is one of deliverance and freedom from evil; more especially it is a deliverance from the sin which is our greatest burden and sorrow. How men think of heaven is then a primary test of their spiritual mindedness. Everyone sees it as something glorious, but for many it means only the satisfaction of natural and sensual desires.[10] Scripture provides an altogether different picture, in which *faith shall be turned into sight, and grace into glory*'.[11] Therefore, 'No man who is not acquainted experiment- ally, in some measure, with the life, power, and evidence of faith here, hath any other heaven in his aim but what is erected in his own imagination.'[12] Of course, we see in a glass darkly, yet '*Faith* shall be heightened into vision, as was proved before;

[1]VII.313.　　[2]VII.314.　　[3]VII.315.　　[4]*Ibid*.
[5]VII.317.　　[6]VII.319–323.　　[7]VII.325.　　[8]Heb. 12.2.
[9]VII.332.　　[10]VII.336.　　[11]VII.337.　　[12]VII.338.

which doth not destroy its nature, but cause it to cease as unto its manner of operation towards things invisible.'[1] 'This is no heaven unto any others',[2] affirms Owen. With a stroke he demolishes the delusions of the carnal man: 'It is generally supposed that however men differ in and about religion here, yet they agree well enough about heaven. But it is a great mistake; they differ in nothing more; they would not all go to the same heaven.'[3]

So much then for the importance of right thinking. But once such conceptions have been properly formed, they must be further contemplated,[4] for this is the pathway of progress and the evidence that a man has a genuine share and interest in spiritual things.[5] This meditation finds its zenith in contemplating heaven's glory *by comparison* with the opposite state of death and misery.[6] Owen finds men little inclined to give much thought to judgment, to the point of denying it for its inconsistency with the goodness of Christ, 'Whereas there is more spoken directly of hell, its torments and their eternity, by himself[7] than in all the Scripture besides.'[8] The root of such thinking is an unwillingness to be troubled by a sense of sinfulness. That is a universal disease which can be remedied only by the most strenuous labours to discipline the mind to biblical truth.

This right thinking *about* spiritual things in general, is to be supplemented in particular by actual concentration of our thought upon Christ, and upon God.[9]

Christ should be central in our thoughts because he is the life and centre of heaven; our whole future destiny is described as being 'ever with the Lord' to behold his glory.[10] This is the focus of the faith which grasps the significance of Christ's active and passive obedience, and the hope of being with Christ in the future.[11] That hope in turn creates a sense of the duty and desirability of being with Christ *now*: 'It is a vain thing for any to suppose that they place their chiefest happiness in being forever in the presence of Christ, who care not at all to be with

[1]VII.339.   [2]VII.340.   [3]VII.341.
[4]2 Cor. 3.18; Col. 3.1.   [5]VII.341.
[6]VII.342.   [7]That is, by Jesus.   [8]VII.343.
[9]VII.344f., 351f.   [10]1 Thess. 4.17.   [11]VII.344.

him here as they may.'[1] Such thoughts of Christ now will be *'conceived and directed according to the rule of the word.'*[2] This is treasure to every Christian to be placed in the balances against the sufferings of this life, in order to appreciate the weight of the glory that is to be revealed.[3]

God himself must also be central in these thoughts. We are not only to rejoice in the hope of glory[4] and in the midst of sufferings,[5] but in God himself.[6] But what in God is to be contemplated?

God's existence 'is *the first object* of faith, and it is the *first act* of reason'.[7] But the believer who lives a life of constant spiritual warfare will discover *this* to be a fundamental focus for satanic attack.[8] Satan will try to undermine the foundation of his faith by inducing blasphemous thoughts into his mind. These must be rejected. Our defences should be strengthened from the testimony of Scripture. 'If a man have a grenado or fire-ball cast into his clothes by his enemy, he doth not consider whether it will burn or no, but immediately shakes it off from him. Deal no otherwise with these fiery darts.'[9] Only then should personal experience be used in defence.[10] So the devil, resisted, firm in the faith, will flee.[11] Then the practical value of such trials will become clearer, as God's past faithfulness is recalled and the heart is uplifted in praise to him.[12]

In God we are to see omnipotence, omnipresence and omniscience. The immensity of this thought may readily overwhelm the mind, but Owen urges us to admire when we cannot comprehend. For those who find themselves at a loss precisely in this, Owen gives some practical instruction.[13]

This sense of inability will, in turn, lead to humility in the presence of God.[14] In itself it may prove to be useful. Owen reminds us that he is speaking here of spiritual mindedness, and not of *'solemn stated meditation'*.[15] We are still in the lower echelons of Christian experience, and are not to aim immediately for mature spiritual powers. For stated meditation, 'there is required thereunto such an exercise of our natural faculties

[1]VII.344–5. [2]VII.345. [3]VII.348. [4]Rom. 5.2.
[5]Rom. 5.3. [6]Rom. 5.11. [7]VII.367. [8]VII.369.
[9]VII.370. [10]*Ibid.* [11]I Pet. 5.8–9. [12]VII.372.
[13]VII.379–80. [14]VII.380. [15]VII.384.

and abilities as some, through their weakness and ignorance, are incapable of.'[1] Nevertheless, whatever principle of grace we do have, we will not come to enjoy the exercise of it without a great deal of difficulty and effort.[2] It is an invariable rule with Owen that an understanding and recognition of attendant difficulties in the exercise of grace can prove to be a source of stability.

The Christian must be careful in this respect to fulfil his spiritual duties. The heart must be guarded against the thoughts which gain advantage over it; sources of temptation must be avoided, and a constraint in the mind towards duty fostered. The means of grace must be used to supply strength for an unwavering conflict with the devil. The growth of every corruption must be guarded against, desires for the world duly mortified, and moderation developed. To these duties a definite portion of the Christian's time must be dedicated to *prepare* his mind to reverence God, and to *renew* his sense of the presence of God.[3]

ii. *The nature of spiritual mindedness*

'*Spiritual affections, whereby the soul adheres unto spiritual things, taking in such a savour and relish of them as wherein it finds rest and satisfaction, is the peculiar spring and substance of our being spiritually minded.*'[4] God says to men, 'My son, give me your heart,'[5] implying that he strives for their affections, because it is only through the affections that man is able to give as well as receive, to 'give away *what we are and have*'.[6] This is what is involved in the total restoration of man to God. His affections are to be patterned after the image of Christ, to participate in crucifixion to the world and resurrection to God. This is the pattern by which man, in Christ, was restored to God; it is repeated in each individual's experience.[7] Therefore the world, which crucified Christ, will never be the object of the Christian's affections, and his stewardship of earthly things will be governed by 'the rule of the word'.[8]

For this to be so, the carnal and natural affections must be

---

[1]*Ibid.*   [2]VII.385.   [3]VII.386-9.   [4]VII.395.
[5]Prov. 23.26.   [6]VII.396.   [7]VII.407.   [8]VII.408.

changed and imbued with grace. What does this imply? Owen
remorselessly drives us back to consider the natural state of
man in order to indicate the significance of this change. By
nature the affections are depraved, as even the heathen
recognize, and man suffers from an evil heart, which is the
'spring, root, and cause of all actual sin in the world'.[1]

As Owen had shown elsewhere at length,[2] this is evidenced
in 'An *utter aversation from God and all spiritual things*', and 'An
inordinate cleaving unto things vain, earthly, and sensual'.[3] Such
affections may have temporary impressions made on them;
they may even be liable to habitual change,[4] through education, or the influence of environment, but this is not the
gracious renovation of which Scripture speaks. It does not cure
men of their antipathy towards God. It may alter the direction
of the affections, while leaving their nature untouched.[5] Conversely when a man is regenerated, his affections 'continue the
same as they were in their nature and essence; but they are so
cured by grace as that their properties, qualities, and inclinations, are all cleansed and renewed.'[6]

What is this change which takes place in the affections?
Owen indicates that it is really twofold:

Firstly, it is a universal change. This is true in reality, even
though it is not so clearly seen in the lives of some, since 'God is
pleased sometimes to leave somewhat more than ordinary of
the power of corruption in one affection, that it may be an
occasion of the continual exercise of grace in the other
affections.'[7] But, in principle, *all* the affections need to be
sanctified if *any* are to be so.

The universal nature of the change is seen objectively too,
and 'affections spiritually renewed do fix themselves upon and
cleave unto all spiritual things, in their proper places, and unto
their proper ends'.[8] There is an order to the objects of this
'fixing'. God himself, revealed in Christ is primary, in himself
and for his own sake; and then other things in so far as God is
present in them: 'God alone is loved for himself; all other things
for him, in the measure and degree of his presence in them.'[9]

[1]VII.411.   [2]VI.157–322.   [3]VII.412.   [4]VII.413.
[5]VII.414.   [6]VII.415.   [7]VII.418.   [8]VII.420.
[9]VII.421.

JOHN OWEN ON THE CHRISTIAN LIFE

The circumstances of life may cause certain truths or duties to be specially important to an individual; but even this must be brought into consistency with the universality here in view.

In the second place, this change in the affections brings pleasure in the duties of Christian worship.[1] Here self-deceit is always a possibility, and Owen stresses that it is important to penetrate beyond the outward manifestation of such pleasure into the grounds and reasons for it. Men can be affected by the outward trappings of worship, and the external duties involved in it;[2] unrenewed men are so because *they place their righteousness before God in them*.[3] For others a reputation for piety may bring a carnal diligence and even pleasure in their duties, as they secretly enjoy the praise of men rather than of God.[4] Superstition, that 'internal vice of the mind',[5] often has the same effect.

How then is a true delight of faith in duties to be recognized? It shows itself in the design and desire men have in coming to worship; they purpose to draw near to God in it, and through it find the stimulation of faith, love and delight in God, through Christ.[6] So David, in Psalm 84.1ff., longs for the house of God that he may come near to God. Owen rejects the view that it is more spiritual not to need and employ these ordinances; on the contrary, they are used by the Spirit, and the neglect of them issues 'in a great decay'.[7] True faith recognizes the divine appointment of worship, and the spiritual gifts that are exercised in it. It may be true that 'believers may have more delight and satisfaction in the ministry of one than of another' but this is only because 'they find the gifts of one more suited and more effectual to stir up faith and love unto a holy exercise in their minds and hearts than what they find in some others.'[8] This in no way detracts from the reality of delight in general though it may augment it in particular.

Changed affections also bring a sense of God's love and the power of his grace to us.[9] This in turn leads to an increased sense of delight in worship, and provides further encouragement to give glory to God.

Although this change is both universal and radical, it is not

[1]VII.423.   [2]VII.426.   [3]VII.427.   [4]VII.428.
[5]VII.429.   [6]VII.430.   [7]VII.434.   [8]VII.436.
[9]VII.437.

yet perfected in the whole of the Christian's life. There is room for development and growth.

iii. *The development of spiritual mindedness*

Growth comes in accordance with Owen's conviction that 'When affections are spiritually renewed in their exercise, or fixing of themselves on spiritual things, *there is an assimilation wrought in them, and in the whole soul, unto those spiritual and heavenly things, by faith.*'[1]

Spiritual affections develop by faith, for the Christian life is lived by faith, and not by sight; 'We can *love nothing sincerely with divine love* but what we *believe savingly with divine faith.*'[2] Faith penetrates to the inner nature of spiritual things, giving them substance, or reproducing them in the soul.[3] As the affections are fixed on heavenly realities they are renewed, 'becoming more and more to be what they are, – namely, spiritual and heavenly.'[4] In this way our affections become *through Christ,* what they essentially are *in* Christ. Thus the image of God, recreated in him and shared by the renewal of the Spirit, matures and develops in us into complete Christian humanity.

This progress is often slow, and liable to decay.

It may be slow, either because of our foolish contentment with our present growth, or forgetfulness that the kingdom of grace is marked by growth. These are symptoms of being 'wholly under the power of self-love.'[5] This condition is '*inconsistent with all solid peace of conscience*'.[6] But it is all too frequent. We may attribute this to the difficulty of being a Christian, but Owen maintains that the difficulty is very largely subjective. It lies in us, in ourselves rather than in the nature of consecration to Christ whose yoke is easy and whose burden is light. It is only difficult when we want to retain in our lives something which is inconsistent with following Christ. Some are 'always beginning at religion'[7] and 'do not attempt a thorough work in the mortification of any sin, but are hewing and hacking at it, as their convictions are urgent or abate, the wounds whereof in the body of sin are quickly healed'.[8]

Progress is liable to decay. For a variety of reasons men may lose

[1]VII.445.   [2]*Ibid.*   [3]VII.447.   [4]VII.448.
[5]VII.451.   [6]VII.452.   [7]VII.454.   [8]VII.454–5.

their first love. It is possible to judge oneself falsely in this respect, for example in a time of temptation when the Christian may feel that he has forsaken God, 'as a man in the night may apprehend he hath lost his way, and be in great distress, when he is in his proper road'.[1] It is possible too to mistake for a decay in affections what is actually a loss of a sense of them.[2]

This deceit and confusion may also work the other way. A man be convinced of his right standing in Christ when he has actually grieved the Holy Spirit and provoked the judgment of God. 'Nothing can be so ruinous unto our profession as once to suppose it is an easy matter, a thing of course, to maintain our peace with God.'[3] When we allow such decays to take place, it is easy to deceive ourselves: it is only one sin in which we are indulging; we can still love God even though we cannot shake off that sin; we will give some time in the future to deal with it; our condition is not as serious as is sometimes suggested, and arises from our present circumstances rather than our hearts; when restoration is *really* necessary, we will accomplish it – and so on. But this blinds us from seeing that 'Recovery from back-sliding is the hardest task in Christian religion'.[4]

How can restoration take place? Owen provides two directives; the first is to remember former spiritual experience.[5] If this provides no relief, no work of grace has ever taken place in the heart: 'You are *hardened through the deceitfulness of sin*, and there is no way left to give a sense or impression of spiritual things upon your minds. You have truly nothing left in religion but the fear of hell and trouble of duties.'[6] If such a consideration does help, then, secondly, the many severe warnings of Scripture against backsliding should be called to mind, as an incentive to spiritual duty. To this is added the simple advice, 'Be in good earnest'.[7]

The *pattern* of spiritual affections is to be found in the person of Christ, in the affections of his soul. Scripture supplies a full description of these with which every Christian should be conversant.[8] The *rule* of affections is the Scriptures themselves, both for the internal activity of these affections, and the external ways and means by which they are expressed. We are

---

| [1]VII.457. | [2]VII.458. | [3]VII.461. | [4]VII.463–4. |
| [5]VII.465. | [6]VII.466. | [7]VII.467. | [8]VII.468. |

to love God with heart, soul, mind and strength, so that every affection should be developed and exercised to the utmost for his sake. Here again is the essence of the Puritan understanding of the Christian life, and its affections in particular:

The rule of them also is the Scripture. The way marked out therein is the only channel wherein the stream of spiritual affections doth take its course unto God. The graces required therein are to act themselves by [them]; the duties it prescribes are those which they stir up and enliven; the religious worship it appoints is that wherein they have their exercise.[1]

Owen also indicates the *measure of their attainments*. Spiritual affections sense the appropriateness of spiritual things, and find a taste, or '*gust*'[2] for them. A simple test is this: where the affections are renewed, the person of Christ is the centre of them; where they are only diverted, they tend to focus on self.[3]

Spiritual affections are then those that have been renewed by grace. But affections are also spiritual because of their *object* as well as their *nature*. They are fixed on certain things: 'they comprehend God in Christ';[4] his goodness and love produce in us a love and fear for him. If our affections are thus to adhere to spiritual things, they must see 'a *goodness*, a *beauty*, and thence an *amiableness* and desireableness, in them'.[5] They must also see that love for Christ must exceed love for everything else (or it is not real love for him).

Spiritual affections will also be drawn to whatever makes known the divine wisdom in Christ.[6] This wisdom is foolishness to the unrenewed mind,[7] but when the renewed mind recognizes God's wisdom, the affections adhere to it. In this way the affections mature towards perfection, lifting us above our carnal capacity, preserving order in our souls, and quiet and security in our minds. This leads us to the great object of our affections: a present enjoyment of God in Christ, regarded as a preliminary to the full enjoyment of him in future glory.[8]

But having established that affections, renewed in principle, are directed towards spiritual objects for their nourishment,

[1]VII.469.   [2]VII.471.   [3]VII.473.   [4]VII.475.
[5]*Ibid.*   [6]VII.477–8.   [7]VII.479.   [8]VII.481.

Owen now indicates *'the way of the soul's application of itself unto those objects by its affections'.*[1] Our application must be firm and stable. The transient thoughts which rise out of a passing sense of God or sin are common to all men. But true spiritual affections have a measure of strength and regularity to them.[2] They also recognize an appealing quality in spiritual things which brings them satisfaction, so much so that spiritual things become a spring of spiritual thoughts and meditations.[3] When affections are thus applied to spiritual things they will not be allured by other objects or by the love of the world in general. Thus fixed, the affections bring to the Christian a measure of relief against indwelling sin.[4] In this way, the life and peace of Owen's text[5] become a reality.

The three privileges of Christian experience are justification, sanctification, and the comforts and blessings salvation brings,[6] to which spiritual mindedness contributes. Thus we retain a sense of the divine love, which 'God communicates by an act of sovereign grace, for the most part without any preparation for it in ourselves'.[7] The man who is spiritually minded is enabled to evaluate rightly the pledges he receives of that love. His spiritual frame also rejects the principal cause of trouble and dispeace: the sinfulness which naturally resides in the affections and creates disorder and disharmony in them.[8] In the same way the heart and mind will be guarded from an inordinate love of the world, and preserved in a suitable frame to perform every spiritual duty. Above all, such spiritual mindedness keeps the Christian's heart in close fellowship with heavenly reality and the blessing that accompanies it:

Nearness unto him gives us our initial conformity unto him, by the renovation of his image in us, as our presence with him will give us perfection therein; for when we see him, we shall be like unto him. He therefore alone, as he is in Christ, being the fountain of life and peace, by our drawing nigh unto him and by our likeness of him will they thrive and flourish in our souls.[9]

When we stand back from this mass of teaching from Owen

[1]VII.482.　　[2]VII.483.　　[3]VII.483–4.　　[4]VII.485.
[5]Rom.8.6.　　[6]VII.488–9.　　[7]VII.492.　　[8]VII.493.
[9]VII.497.

on the intricacies of Christian experience, and ask what the point of it is, two answers emerge. Since every Christian is a pilgrim and a stranger in this world, Owen sees himself as providing instruction for that pilgrimage, to secure the passage to the next world. This is what really matters. Only by knowing the route laid down in Scripture and following it can the individual be sure of reaching his destination. But Owen's theology is too biblical to infer from this that the only reason the Christian is in the world is to get out of it, and to help others get out too. Consequently his teaching is also given to help the Christian to glorify God in this world, particularly by perseverance and the development of a truly Christian life and character. These are the intermediate goals of the teaching, and to them we turn in the concluding chapter.

According to Owen's teaching, the whole of the Christian life is lived under the influence of the covenant of grace, and therefore the doctrine of the Christian life is worked out as an aspect of covenant theology. In this schematization, *perseverance* is the salt of the covenant.[1] For all his emphasis on divine sovereignty and the certainty of final salvation, Owen's teaching emphasizes that the means God normally employs are Christian duties. There is no room here for our security becoming an excuse for moral laziness or licence. For Owen, the Christian life demands the obedience of faith from start to finish.

[1] XI.78.

Perseverance and the Goal

If Owen had written a systematic theology, the doctrines of perseverance and the final goal of grace would have found their expected places in it. But – as we have repeatedly seen – Owen's interests were <u>primarily pastoral rather than systematic. He was a theologian *because* he was a pastor.</u> Consequently many of his lengthy works were called forth by circumstances in the church or the nation, and not because of a merely intellectual interest in theological systems.

It was in such a context that Owen wrote at length on the themes of perseverance and the goal of faith.

1. *Perseverance*

Owen's major discussion of perseverance is embodied in *The Doctrine of the Saints Perseverance Explained and Confirmed* (1654) directed against John Goodwin's (Arminian) *Redemption Redeemed*. Owen's work takes the form of a running commentary on Goodwin's study. It is a source of wonder in the present century, in every respect, that what amounts to an extended book review should digress to more than six hundred closely printed pages in the Goold edition, and still make its way into print.[1] From this somewhat unformed mass we are able to hew a more positive exposition of the key aspects of Owen's thought.

Owen's work was dedicated to Oliver Cromwell, and, perhaps as much for the relief of that busy man as for later readers, Owen outlines his thesis in the Dedicatory Epistle:

[1] XI.1ff. John Goodwin, *Redemption Redeemed*, London, 1651.

That you and all the saints of God may yet enjoy that peace and consolation which is in believing that the eternal love of God is immutable, that he is faithful in his promises, that his covenant, ratified in the death of his Son, is unchangeable, that the fruits of the purchase of Christ shall be certainly bestowed on all them for whom he died, and that every one who is really interested in these things shall be kept unto salvation, is the aim of my present plea and contest.[1]

The matter is therefore one of general 'concernment of the common people of Christianity'[2] and not simply fodder for the recondite arguments of theologians and scholars. In fact, for Owen, the very possibility of apostasy, whatever its true nature, tests believers in order to establish them in a greater maturity of faith. But should men commit apostasy 'He [John] lets them know that by their being apostates, they have proved themselves to have been but hypocrites'.[3]

On the other hand, assurance is a privilege promised to believers, and the Spirit of adoption[4] bears witness with the spirit of the weakest believer to give him an assurance of sonship. In this case, conscience not only reminds men of the weakness of their faith and their lack of grace (as Goodwin had argued[5]) but also of seasons when they have enjoyed God's gracious blessings. It is, to Owen, a crucial objection against Goodwin's view that all the arguments against perseverance are already accounted for by Scripture, and are consistent with 'this great truth of the gospel and grace of the covenant'.[6] Those who appear to 'fall away' have experienced only a temporary holiness, having been changed, not in their nature but only in their employment in the purposes of God.[7]

Rather than encourage loose living, the assurance of perseverance promotes truth and holiness in the Christian life. But this is to hurry to the conclusion of the matter, and we must first indicate the outline of Owen's thought.

Owen sets out five fundamental arguments for the consistency of the doctrine of perseverance with biblical teaching. (1) The first argument rests on the *immutability of the divine*

---

[1]XI.5–6.   [2]XI.16.   [3]XI.80.   [4]Rom. 8.15.
[5]*Redemption Redeemed*, pp. 109–110.   [6]XI.87.   [7]XI.90.

nature.[1] God has engaged himself *as Father,* to his people. Their relationship to him is irrevocable.

(2) Furthermore, it is strengthened by *the immutability of the divine purposes.* Since God himself is 'an infinite pure act' for Owen[2] and is also almighty, *his purposes* do not involve things which of themselves are necessary, but rather things which might not be.[3] Such is the perseverance of the saints. It is therefore positively grounded in his purposes, and involves the love he promises to all the saints.[4] This includes the divine decrees, which are not dependent upon the circumstances of their own outworking, but rather create them. Owen argues that God's foreknowledge, power, and the immutability of his purposes are all clearly taught in Scripture[5] as is the continuance of his love.[6] The great chain of salvation is presented as unbreakable, and Owen vigorously opposes *the importing of conditions,* other than those it creates itself, into the onward movement of the inner work of God in the Christian.

(3) The third theological pillar is *the argument from the covenant of grace* itself. 'The *principium essendi* of this truth, if I may so say, is in the decrees and purposes of God; the *principium cognoscendi,* in his covenant, promise, and oath, which also add much to the real stability of it, the truth and faithfulness of God in them being thereby particularly engaged therein'.[7] This covenant was externally administered to Abraham and his carnal seed, and internally and savingly administered to him and his spiritual seed.

This covenant, made new in Christ, is completely immutable, and is so described in Scripture. Every cause of alteration has been removed from it.[8] Unlike the covenant with Adam, 'God himself hath undertaken the whole, both for his continuing with us and our continuing with him.'[9] Thus, 'Though there be sundry persons in covenant, yet there is but one undertaker on all hands, and that is God himself.'[10] This covenant was also mediated and ratified by Jesus Christ, so that it is sound and certain because *he* has fulfilled both its divine and human requirements. The result is that, to the

---

[1]XI.131. Owen refers to Mal. 3.6. [2]XI.141. [3]XI.142.
[4]XI.143. [5]Is. 46.9–11. [6]Rom. 8.28. [7]XI.205.
[8]XI.21. [9]*Ibid.* [10]*Ibid.*

believer, this covenant is an unconditional *promise* of grace and perseverance. In this way, God reveals his special faithfulness as the God who keeps covenant.[1] It is of particular significance, as we have already suggested,[2] that, in reply to the argument of Goodwin that the very idea of covenant implies conditionality, Owen states that in Scripture *berith* is used 'for a single promise without a condition, Gen. vi.18, ix.9. . . . In a *testamentary dispensation* there is not in the nature of it any mutual stipulation required, but only a mere single favour and grant or concession.'[3] If we speak of conditions, then God himself promises to fulfil them in us.[4]

(4) The fourth argument is drawn from *the promises of God* which constitute the heart of the covenant of grace. It is objected that such gospel promises are conditional and dependent upon the recipient. But Owen demonstrates the concept of God's promises is far greater than this, for they are:

1. The free and gracious dispensations, and, 2. discoveries of God's good-will and love, to, 3. sinners, 4. through Christ, 5. in a covenant of grace; 6. wherein, upon his truth and faithfulness, he engageth himself to be their God, to give his Son unto them and for them, and his Holy Spirit to abide with them, with all things that are either required in them or are necessary for them to make them accepted before him, and to bring them to an enjoyment of him.[5]

These promises, Owen maintains, are 'often' confirmed by the assurance that God cannot lie.[6] So that the 'God who hath promised *life* upon *believing*, hath promised *believing* on no condition (on our parts) at all, because to sinners.'[7] To these promises God remains faithful. In the light of this, writes Owen with zest, Goodwin has taught no better than that 'God hath promised believers shall persevere in case they persevere'![8] Such teaching could never warrant the abounding confidence and hope which is the predominant spirit of the New Testament.

(5) The fifth and greatest argument for the perseverance of

[1]XI.211. [2]Above, p. 21. [3]XI.218.
[4]*Ibid.* [5]XI.227.
[6]XI.231. In fact the only references are in Hebrews 6.17–18 and Titus 2.2.
[7]XI.233. [8]XI.248.

the saints is *the mediatorial work of Christ*. He became a surety to us of the faithfulness of God, and of our faithfulness to him.[1] This surety consists in the High Priestly ministry of Christ, his oblation on the cross and his intercession at the right hand of God.[2] The first part of this ministry removes all cause of separation of believers from God both morally and efficiently. The effect of Christ's death is permanent.[3] He has atoned for the sins of all the elect.[4] By it Christ satisfied the requirements of divine justice,[5] fulfilled the law,[6] manifested the truth of God,[7] and evidenced the distributive justice of God,[8] by which his faithfulness is administered. No charge then can be brought against Christ's elect, for if the ransom price is paid, all the ransomed must be released. Christ is made sin for the elect, and they, by exchange, become his righteousness.[9]

Christ also deals in this capacity with the efficient cause of separation from God, in that he overcomes the devil.[10] He does so in two ways. Firstly, Christ takes away the right of rule which Satan enjoyed through sin.[11] It is by the entry of sin into the world that the devil could rule over men with the terrors and dread of hell.[12] It is, incidentally, this dread which Owen sees as lying at the root of all false ways of salvation, and all misplaced efforts to atone for sin. But Christ also takes away the actual exercise of Satan's power, and binds him, for 'What exercise of power is left to a conquered, bound, wounded, captived, triumphed-over, trodden-down, destroyed caitiff?'[13]

Christ has also procured the gift of the Spirit for believers,[14] and this is of primary significance in the doctrine of perseverance. It is part of what Owen elsewhere designates 'purchased grace'.[15] It is striking to notice the parallel here, by which Christ not only procures privileges for his people, but also the sending of the third person of the Trinity into their lives. It is significant that this great theme of the sending of the Spirit is taken up by Jesus in the discourses of the Upper Room, in

---

[1]XI.289.   [2]XI.290.   [3]XI.292–3.   [4]XI.294.
[5]XI.293.   [6]XI.295.   [7]*Ibid.*   [8]XI.296.
[9]Rom. 8.33; 2 Cor. 5.21.   [10]XI.304.
[11]XI.305.   [12]*Ibid.*   [13]XI.307.   [14]XI.308.
[15]Above, pp. 86ff.

which one of his great aims is to encourage the disciples in their perseverance.[1] The coming of the Spirit for Owen secures perseverance. If it is argued that if the Spirit can come to a man, he may also leave him, Owen maintains that the covenant of grace makes this impossible.[2] It gives a promise to the contrary, as in Isaiah 59.21: 'in a covenant there are two things, – 1. What is stipulated on the part of him that makes the covenant; 2. What of them is required with whom it is made (which in themselves are distinct, though in the covenant of grace God hath promised that he will work in us what he requires of us)'.[3] The teaching of Jesus, therefore, is that the Comforter dwells for ever with the elect.[4]

It is also the office of the Spirit to bear witness to Christ, and he does so in what Owen terms 'a real work of performance'[5] in which he seals believers, and thus provides them with an assurance of forgiveness and their corresponding security. Furthermore, since his presence with his people involves his personal indwelling, this contributes to perseverance, because it implies a bond of union with Christ,[6] eternal life, his guidance and support in infirmity[7] and his restraint from sin,[8] as well as the inward renewal of sanctifying grace.[9] This is but glory begun, and through it the believer is enabled to persevere to the end.

A further function of Christ in his office of Mediator is *intercession*. He is one who is able to 'save to the uttermost' all who come to God through him.[10] This intercession is given a 'preface', says Owen, in John 17 'being a manifest declaration on earth of that which Christ lives in heaven to do'.[11] A focal point in that prayer was the preservation of the disciples,[12] with the logical conclusion:

That which the Lord Jesus, as mediator, requesteth and prayeth for continually of the Father, according to his mind, in order to the accomplishment of the promises made to him and covenant with him (all his desires being bottomed upon his exact, perfect perform-ance of *the whole will of God*, both in doing and suffering), that shall certainly be accomplished and brought to pass; but thus, in this

---

[1]XI.309.   [2]XI.310.   [3]*Ibid.*   [4]XI.315; cf. Jn. 14.16.
[5]XI.322.   [6]XI.336.   [7]XI.346.   [8]XI.348.
[9]XI.350.   [10]Heb. 7.25.   [11]XI.367.   [12]John 17.11.

manner, upon these accounts, doth the Lord Jesus intercede for the perseverance of believers, and their preservation in the love of the Father unto the end: therefore, they shall undoubtedly be so preserved.[1]

The same argument is found elsewhere in the New Testament: Who can condemn the child of God? Christ has died for him, has risen again, is at the place of authority by the right hand of God, and *intercedes* for him.[2]

What are the practical repercussions of this teaching? Owen shows that it brings consolation and obedience.[3] The latter comes through the former, inasmuch as it removes the discouragements which produce disobedience, or render such obedience as is offered slavish and servile, and therefore unacceptable to God.

Goodwin's objection had been the common one that this doctrine makes men careless. But Owen resolutely maintains that God's love cannot be the cause of such conduct. Indeed that love can only produce obedience, since the Spirit of Christ in the gospel cuts sin's throat and destroys its power.[4] The rest of the debate is predictable. Goodwin maintained he upheld the evangelical doctrine of grace;[5] Owen replied that his doctrine was neither evangelical nor gracious. Goodwin affirmed that strict Calvinistic teaching leads to the view that men may be justified by faith irrespective of the lives they live, whereas the exhortations of the New Testament argue for the reverse.[6] This, according to Owen is utterly fallacious and misleading. Did not Augustine say 'Da, domine, quod jubes, et jube quod vis' (Give what you command, Lord, and command what you will)?[7] Furthermore, the very nature of prayer itself should have brought Goodwin to a clearer understanding of this teaching.[8] Exhortations are the means which God uses to preserve his people. It is true that grace may work apart from them, but that is not the rule for our conduct.[9]

Goodwin had further maintained that the fruit of such a doctrine would be harmful to true godliness. Owen replies with a long list of outstanding Christians who have held his teaching: Calvin, Zanchius, Beza, Perkins, Preston, Bolton,

[1]XI.369. [2]XI.370, cf. Rom. 8.31ff. [3]XI.380. [4]XI.393.
[5]XI.407. [6]XI.391. [7]XI.441. [8]*Ibid.* [9]XI.442.

Sibbes, and others,[1] who, Goodwin had maintained, had never come to a settled judgment on the matter, and whose godliness was really the result of other doctrines they did truly hold from Scripture! But Owen will not have this. Jewel, Abbott, Manton, Ussher, Hall, Davenant and Prideaux, all held to this teaching,[2] and 'not one of the ancients, much less Austin,[3] did ever maintain such an apostasy of saints and such a perseverance as that which Mr. Goodwin contendeth for.'[4]

It is true that some men, in response to the doctrine of grace have said 'Let us go on in sin that grace may abound!' But Owen is right to suggest that such an objection may be the sign that it is *free grace* which is proclaimed, and not some amalgam of gospel and law. But grace always reigns through righteousness, and this is a truth of which Owen never lost sight. The believer is never promised salvation *in sin* but *from sin*. How can he who has died to sin live in it any longer? – 'in plain terms, to have sin reign is to be unconverted; and to have sin not to reign is to be converted'.[5] Goodwin has done no more, in Owen's view, than borrow the arguments of the Remonstrants. They are no more successful in his hands than they were in theirs.

2. *The Goal*

Perseverance leads to the final, heavenly goal of the Christian life, but it is also productive of Christian character which is *shaped* here and now, and perfected hereafter.

i. *Christian character*

In Owen's teaching, the character of a genuine Christian is marked by various features:

Walking with God. The Christian life is set out in Scripture as a pilgrimage and the Christian is identified by a lifestyle[6] of fellowship with God.[7] Owen illustrates this from the story of

[1]XI.487.   [2]XI.497.   [3] Augustine.   [4]XI.498.
[5]XI.513, cf. Rom. 6.1ff.
[6]XVII.539 (XVI.471).
[7]IX.98.

Enoch's life. Although he was a great prophet, a patriarch, and a preacher, he is singled out for none of these things, but for personal character, in that he walked with God.[1] This implies peace with God[2] and a desire to share in his purpose and seek his glory: 'Our living unto God as our chief end consists in two things:– (1) Our doing of all things unto his glory; and, (2) Our aiming in and above all things at the enjoyment of him.'[3] This involves a number of graces: the Christian will value God's glory above all else, and will order his life to minister to it,[4] complying with nothing that may be to the contrary, and making constant prayer for its exaltation in the world, acting on it as the only motive of life. This is the reason for the Christian's subsequent enjoyment of God.[5]

This, then, is a basic dimension of the Christian life. It is the heart of Christian character and explains its quality. It develops in another dimension from natural character, namely in the presence of God, and this leads to its purity. It receives its contentment from another world, since it finds its joy primarily in God, and this explains its stability in the world and its attitude to it. Owen is essentially saying the same thing as Paul, that while living on the earth, the Christian's life is hid with Christ in God.[6] He lives in obedience to the covenant of grace,[7] constantly and progressively.[8] Walking thus with God 'is the only way to preserve and deliver any from the calamities of general apostasies, in wickedness, violence, and destruction'.[9]

Humility. Because the Christian life is a walk with *God* it cannot but be marked by humility. The rule of walking with God is his 'revealed will'[10] which is known in two ways: by the law of his grace (the way of salvation revealed in Scripture) and the law of his providence (the circumstances of the Christian's *own* life, unfolded in history).[11] The presence of both of these laws produces the grace of humility. If we are to walk by the law of grace, then we must be persuaded of our own helplessness and inability, and 'believe and accept of a righteousness that is

[1]XVII.570 (XVI.502).
[2]IX.87; XVII.540 (XVI.472), cf. Amos 3.3.
[3]XVII.576 (XVI.508), cf. IX.90.
[4]IX.90. [5]IX.97. [6]Col. 3.3. [7]IX.94.
[8]IX.97. [9]XVII.571 (XVI.503).
[10]XVII.580 (XVI.512). [11]IX.103.

not our own'.¹ Again, no one understands the great mystery of God's providence, and many aspects of it cause the heart to bow in humility before God. It is marked by visible confusion and great variety, by sudden changes and deep distresses, but in all this the Christian fixes his trust on the promise of God's sovereignty, wisdom and righteousness:

Let us lay our mouths in the dust, and ourselves on the ground, and say 'It is the Lord; I will be silent because he hath done it. He is of one mind, and who can turn him? He doth whatever he pleaseth. Am not I in his hand as clay in the hand of the potter? May he not make what kind of vessel he pleases? When I was not, he brought me out of nothing by his word. What I am, or have, is merely of his pleasure. Oh, let my heart and thoughts be full of deep subjection to his supreme dominion and uncontrollable sovereignty over me!'²

God's work here and now is recognized by the Christian as preparatory and indeterminate. When he realizes this, it 'unties all knots, and solves all difficulties whatever.'³

Such humility is clearly the product of a third aspect of Christian character.

Faith and trust. Faith grasps God's faithfulness in his providence. Faith is not philosophical or historical for Owen. It is *assensus, consensus*, and *fiducia*, a '*looking* or *seeing, hearing, tasting, resting, rolling* ourselves, *flying for refuge, trusting*, and the like.'⁴ And since the Christian life is a walk in faith, there must be degrees of faith and development and progress in it. All faith is doubtless equal in sincerity, but, for example, steadfastness of faith is a further degree of it.⁵

Every Christian lives by faith. The Christian character is not recognized by the degree of faith, but by its presence. The growth of character will, however, inevitably be related to and dependent on the growth of faith. Weak faith will carry a man to heaven, '*yet it will never carry him comfortably nor pleasantly thither . . . the least true faith will do its work safely, though not so sweetly*',⁶ since 'A little faith gives a whole Christ', 'Others may be more holy than he, but not one in the world is more righteous than he.'⁷ 'The most imperfect faith will give present justifica-

---

¹IX.106.   ²IX.116–7.   ³IX.118.   ⁴IX.23.
⁵IX.27.   ⁶IX.28.   ⁷IX.29.

tion, because it interests the soul in a present Christ. The lowest degree of true faith gives the highest completeness of righteousness, Col. ii.10. You, who have but a weak faith, have yet a strong Christ.'[1] But according to the example of Abraham, strong, or developed faith brings glory to God.[2] The *character* of the Christian therefore develops in proportion to his faith. And faith works by love.

Love. Love is the bond of perfection. In the context of Christian fellowship Owen thinks of this in terms of an illustration: the church is like a bundle of collected sticks, of different shapes and sizes. They can all be carried if tied with a band, but if the band is broken, 'every one's crookedness will appear, one to be too long, one to be too short; one too big, one too little; one crooked, and one straight; there is no keeping them together.'[3] The Christian character will be marked by an increase in love as faith develops, for '*Love . . . is the principle grace and duty that is required among, and expected from, the saints of God, especially as they are engaged in church-fellowship.*'[4]

Love is not only a fruit of faith, it is 'the second great duty that was brought to light by the gospel.'[5] It is the means of communion among Christians, as faith is their means of communion with God; hence the frequent joining of faith and love in the New Testament.[6] But what is this love?

It is a fruit of the Spirit of God, an effect of faith, whereby believers, being knit together by the strongest bonds of affection, upon account of their interest in one head, Jesus Christ, and participating of one Spirit, do delight in, value, and esteem each other, and are in constant readiness for all those regular duties whereby the temporal, spiritual, and eternal good of one another may be promoted.[7]

Again Owen stresses that Christian character is *not natural*, but is a fruit of the Spirit and an effect of faith.

The world opposes Christian faith, but it also opposes Christian love. Love will be most clearly seen, not in the world, but in the context of particular churches.[8] This is love's testing

---

[1]*Ibid.*   [2]Romans 4.20.
[3]XVII.547 (XVI.479). '*Love* is the fountain and foundation of all mutual duties, moral and ecclesiastical', XXIV.381.
[4]IX.257.   [5]IX.258.
[6]On seven or eight occasions in Paul, according to Owen's estimate (IX.258); but in fact about twenty times.
[7]IX.259.   [8]IX.262.

ground and the Christian's school of character-development. Love is itself a testimony to the gospel.[1] Owen suggests an interesting reason why this is so, putting love in a cosmic as well as personal context. He believes that sin, or self-love, shattered the *unity* of creation. The restoration of this unity, even in embryo in the church, is a testimony to the world that such a unity has been brought from another realm and dimension of being.[2] From this men should learn that God sent Christ into the world, to recapitulate all things in himself, since it is clear that the restoration of unity in Christians stems from him.[3]

This love is but one aspect of character that is marked also by consistent godliness.

Holiness, or godliness is the essence of the Christian's character. We have seen that he is united to God in Christ, and thereby increasingly participates in the personal grace of Christ. He is also in the world, and lives in it as one whose true identity is found in Christ. This is holiness. It means Christ- likeness on the one hand, and a consequent dissimilarity to the life of the world on the other.

Christ calls for five basic differences between the Christian's character and that of the world, according to Owen: the possession of the Holy Spirit; the principle of life, which is faith working by love; the conversation, or life-style; the goal of life, which for the Christian is the glory of God; and the object of worship. These are deeply rooted in the believer, as he fulfils his obligation to increase in godliness.[4] That obligation is impressed upon him by Scripture, and, as Owen often asserts, by the providences of God.[5]

[1]IX.263.   [2]IX.264.   [3]*Ibid.*, cf. Jn. 17.20–23; Col.1.19–23.
[4]XVII.537–42 (XVI.469–474).
[5]Owen based this on his exegesis of 2 Peter 3.10–12, which he takes to refer to these *providential* changes rather than eschatological ones, IX.131ff. Later in XVII.524 (XVI.456) he takes a slightly less definite view of the passage. He refers the cosmic disturbances to the judgment of God on the Jewish nation. This interpretation is based on an examination of the Scriptures which lie behind the thought of Peter, and the parallel thought of Jesus in Mark 13, Matthew 24. There Owen, again on the grounds of the Old Testament imagery, takes Jesus' references to be to the Fall of Jerusalem, which will be preceded by signs, and then to his final return, which will be without warning. In this latter respect he has found support in J. A. Alexander, *The Gospel of Mark*, 1858, r.i. London, 1960, pp. 342–368; R. T. France, *Jesus and the Old Testament*, London, 1971, pp. 227–239 (but not for the 2 Peter passage).

By such a godly, humble walk with God through faith that works by love, the Christian brings pleasure and glory to God, bears witness to the world, and enters the full enjoyment of Christian experience.

Worship. The mature fruit of grace is *worship*, which is 'nothing but the ascription of divine excellencies unto what is so worshipped'.[1] It is a rational duty[2] because these 'excellencies' are consistently to be ascribed to none but *God*. Man is made in his image, and therefore has fellowship and worship written into his very constitution.[3] Thus, 'No man, therefore, ever doubted but that by the *law of nature* we were bound to worship God, and *solemnly to express* that worship: for else wherefore were we brought forth in this world?'[4] It is therefore the essence of God men are to worship[5] as Owen writes in almost lyrical vein:

The principal and adequate reason of all divine worship, and that which makes it such, is what God is in himself. Because he *is*, – that is, an infinitely glorious, good, wise, holy, powerful, righteous, self-subsisting, self-sufficient, all sufficient Being, the fountain, cause, and author of life and being to all things, and of all that is good in every kind, the first cause, last end, and absolutely sovereign Lord of all, the rest and all-satisfactory reward of all other beings, – therefore is he by us to be adored and worshipped with divine and religious worship. Hence are we in our hearts, minds, and souls, to admire, adore, and love him; his praises are we to celebrate; him [are we] to trust and fear, and so to resign ourselves and all our concernments unto his will and disposal; to regard him with all the acts of our minds and persons, answerably to the holy properties and excellencies of his nature. . . . This is to honour, worship, fear God for himself; that is, on the account of what he is in himself. Where the divine nature is, there is the true, proper, formal object of religious worship, and where that is not, it is idolatry to ascribe it to or exercise it towards any.[6]

The *rule* of such worship is defined by the revelation of God,[7] that is, for all practical purposes, the Scriptures.[8] But from this Owen draws a further deduction, namely that New Testament worship is to be distinguished from that of the Old, by its spirituality: '*it is an eminent effect and fruit of our reconciliation unto God and among ourselves, by the blood of Christ, that believers enjoy the*

---

[1]I.104.   [2]XIX.338.   [3]XV.447; XIX.332, 347.
[4]XIX.332.   [5]II.269.   [6]III.65.   [7]III.65.
[8]*Ibid.* Cf. XV.448; 498f.

privileges of the excellent, glorious, spiritual worship of God in Christ, revealed and required in the gospel.[1] Here he stresses the fact that this worship involves communion with and through the Trinity, and distinctly with each of the persons.

Owen also maintains that three things are necessary for the performance of right worship; light and knowledge, to discern the will of God; grace in the heart, for spiritual access and communion with God; and an ability to fulfil and perform the duties prescribed by God.[2] In the New Testament dispensation, the spirituality (as opposed to the externality) and greatness of this worship is evidenced by the fact that it is performed really in heaven[3] and in the temple of the Spirit of God (i.e. among the people whom he indwells).[4] This new covenant form of worship will never change and remains until the end of the world. If it is suggested, as some of Owen's contemporaries did, that men may yet be freed from the external obligation of the institution of worship, he replies that it is inseparably annexed to the covenant of grace.[5]

It is then for worship that spiritual gifts are given and received[6] in all their diversity of operation; yet men have access in *one* Spirit to the Father, so that the many gifts given to the church together promote the unity of the faith as the church grows to the measure of the stature of the fulness of Christ.[7]

ii. *Eternal glory*

The covenant into which we enter through faith in Christ is an everlasting covenant, in that it is rooted in the eternal purposes of God the Father, and extends to the eternal enjoyment of the believer. Our appreciation of Owen's concept of the Christian life would be diminished without some kind of consideration of his view of the Christian's destiny, and the effect of this on the manner in which he lives and dies in the faith of Christ.

Owen wrote comparatively little on the future prospects of the church in this world. He shared with other Puritan writers the hope that the Jews would be converted, and that this, according to the teaching of Paul in Romans would lead to a

[1]IX.55.   [2]IX.70.   [3]IX.77.   [4]IX.78.
[5]V.467.   [6]III.75.   [7]Eph.2.18; 4.13.

world-wide period of expansion and blessing.[1] But he emphatically rejected any chiliastic interpretation of the kingdom of God, regarding all such views as little more than a 'dream'.[2] Owen attributed the rise of this view in the Fifth Monarchy men to the influence of Joseph Mede,[3] and set his face against it.[4] The Christian's best hope, therefore, must lie beyond this world in the next, when he will be with Christ in glory.

In this life, the believer knows Christ as in a mirror,[5] seeing only his likeness and image, as he appears, like the Shepherd-Lover of Canticles,[6] through the lattices of the ordinances of the gospel. But in glory the barriers of sin and the limitations of earthly experience will be broken down, and believers will be changed into his likeness. This final transformation and last crisis which brings the Christian from sanctification to glorification, involves a number of aspects which Owen outlines.

Firstly, the *mind* will be freed from all its natural darkness, through sin, and its incapacity through present creaturehood characterized by fleshly existence.[7]

Secondly, a new light, the light of glory will be implanted in him.[8] What Paul calls the change 'from one degree of glory to another' is of special interest here, and Owen says, 'as the *light of grace* doth not destroy or abolish the *light of nature*, but rectify and improve it, so the *light of glory* shall not abolish or destroy the *light of faith and grace*, but, by incorporating with it, render it absolutely perfect.'[9] Just as we cannot appreciate the light of grace by the light of nature, we do not yet appreciate the light of glory by the present light of grace; we only believe that it will form the soul into the image of Christ, so that as 'Grace renews nature; glory perfects grace'.[10]

Thirdly, the body of the believer will also be glorified through union with Christ in the body of his glory.[11] The sum of this is that 'Heaven doth more excel the Gospel state than that state doth the Law.[12] Owen is not describing the manner or means of

---

[1]IX.134, 151; XXIV.87. See I. H. Murray, *The Puritan Hope*, London, 1971, *passim*.

[2]I.380.　　[3]XX.152.　　[4]VIII.259; XII.34; XX.154.

[5]1 Cor. 13.12.　　[6]Song of Sol. 2.9.

[7]I.381.　　[8]I.382.　　[9]*Ibid*.　　[10]I.383.

[11]*Ibid*.　　[12]I.387.

dwelling in Christ, but only of the measure of enjoyment and experience of him. His glory knows three degrees of manifestation; the shadow, known through the law; the perfect image, known in the gospel; and the substance itself, known only in the glory.[1] It follows, according to Owen, that whatever we see here of Christ is to make us long to see him more clearly and fully in the future.[2] The Christian life, then, is simply the planting of the seed and the growth of the stock and bud. The flowering takes place in the future.

It is a characteristic of Puritan teaching that this most heavenly doctrine is regarded as among the most practical in its implications and application.[3] This is also the New Testament teaching.[4] Owen believed that the steady contemplation of Christ's glory, though an exercise of considerable spiritual difficulty, brings a lively experience of grace and of the manifestation of Christ to the believer. But the experience that awaits him is different again. For his faculties will then be made perfect, freed from the 'clogs of the flesh'[5] and its restraint upon spiritual powers. Because of the union of the soul with the body of sinful flesh it is arduous for us now to contemplate Christ's present glory.[6] But in glory Christ will be seen, not by the insight of faith, but with the immediacy of sight,[7] and he will no more withdraw from the church.[8] We will see him with vision that is no longer liable to defects or the assaults of external temptations. While we are here, we can but gather 'parcels' of Christ;[9] there we will see him at once, and for ever. The transformation will no longer be the gradual influence of faith, but the radical and immediate transformation of heaven, through the beatific vision which brings perfect rest.[10] Yet, even so, there will be a continual operation on and communication to the glorified, of the love of Christ. Everything will still depend on his mediation: 'We shall no more be self-subsistent in glory than we are in nature or grace.'[11]

It is of great interest that Owen turned to this theme during the last days of his life. Indeed his meditations on the Christian's share in the glory of Christ really represent his

[1]I.387–8.   [2]I.388.   [3]I.388–9.   [4]Col. 3.1ff.
[5]I.405.   [6]I.406.   [7]*Ibid*.   [8]I.407.
[9]I.408.   [10]I.410.   [11]I.414.

ministry to his own congregation.[1] It is natural therefore that they should contain a special strain of application to the attitude of the child of God to death. For contemplation of the glory of Christ *'will carry us cheerfully, comfortably, and victoriously through life and death, and all that we have to conflict withal in either of them.'*[2] At such a time God acts in sovereign wisdom with his children, and disposes their circumstances as he thinks fit. But certain duties are called for in every believer, and all believers will share in a common pool of experiences.

Firstly, special faith requires exercise, for committing the soul to God. The Christian cannot go to the world beyond in comfort without recognizing what awaits him. So it was with Christ, and with the first martyr, Stephen. This is the 'last victorious act of faith, wherein its conquest over its last enemy death itself doth consist.'[3] There is no greater sign of faith than this affirmation of the future presence of God. There is no greater encouragement to it than the knowledge that it is Christ himself who receives us.

Secondly, the Christian must be willing and ready to part with the flesh.[4] This requires an appreciation of the purposes of God, for the fact is that the body-soul union is unparalleled. Neither angels nor beasts know it. Only man can experience this great convulsion of being. And he, by nature, has a 'fixed aversation from a dissolution'.[5] It can be regarded with equanimity only through a sure knowledge of entrance into Christ's presence, and the promise of a future union in the resurrection.

He, therefore, that would die comfortably, must be able to say with himself and to himself, 'Die, then, thou frail and sinful flesh: "dust thou art, and unto dust thou shalt return." I yield thee up unto the righteous doom of the Holy One. Yet therein also I give thee into the hand of the great Refiner, who will hide thee in thy grave, and by thy consumption purify thee from all thy corruption and disposition to evil.'[6]

Thirdly the believer needs to learn a readiness to comply with the times and seasons that God has ordained for his departure.[7]

Fourthly, since the ways and means by which death approaches bring special trials, long illnesses, severe treatment,

[1]I.275. [2]I.277. [3]I.281. [4]*Ibid.*
[5]I.282. [6]I.283. [7]*Ibid.*

even persecution, the child of God must learn to resign himself to the gracious will of God and to the utter holiness of his decree, with its ultimate purpose that Christ should be the first-born of the many brethren who are predestined to be conformed to his image.[1]

And thus,

if our future blessedness shall consist in being where he is, and beholding of his glory, what better preparation can there be for it than in a constant previous contemplation of that glory in the revelation that is made in the Gospel, unto this very end, that by a view of it we may be gradually transformed into the same glory?[2]

Here our study of Owen's teaching on the Christian life comes appropriately to an end. But Owen himself would have wished that our study of the glory of Christ himself should continue, until (in his own words) we see that glory 'in another manner than we have ever done' or were 'capable of doing in this world.'[3] This, as we have seen, was the aim of all of his teaching. Like his life, it is a 'burning and a shining light' and, as David Clarkson said, 'we may rejoice in it still.'[4]

[1]I.284, Rom. 8.29.   [2]I.275.   [3]I.ciii.   [4]Above, p. xiii.

Postscript

What am I the better if I can dispute that Christ is God, but have no sense of sweetness in my heart from hence that he is a God in covenant with my soul? What will it avail me to evince, by testimonies and arguments, that he hath made satisfaction for sin, if through my unbelief, the wrath of God abideth on me, and I have no experience of my own being made the righteousness of God in him, – if I find not, in my standing before God, the excellency of having my sins imputed to him and his righteousness imputed to me? Will it be any advantage to me, in the issue, to profess and dispute that God works the conversion of a sinner by the irresistible grace of his Spirit, if I was never acquainted experimentally with the deadness and utter impotency to good, that opposition to the law of God, which is in my own soul by nature, with the efficacy of the exceeding greatness of the power of God in quickening, enlightening, and bringing forth the fruits of obedience in me? It is the power of truth in the heart alone that will make us cleave unto it indeed in an hour of temptation. Let us, then, not think that we are anything the better for our conviction of the truths of the great doctrines of the gospel, for which we content with these men, unless we find the power of the truths abiding in our own hearts, and have a continual experience of their necessity and excellency in our standing before God and our communion with him.

John Owen, *Works* XII.52

NAMES AND SUBJECTS INDEX

BIBLICAL REFERENCES

OLD TESTAMENT

Genesis

3:15	27,104
6:12–13	136n
6:18	265
9:9	265
15:17	113
17	221n
35:1–5	223n
37:24	136n
37:26–7	137n

Exodus

12:11	213
12:22	217n
15:9–10	136n
19:10–11	223n
31:18	187

Deuteronomy

15:11	169
29:4	44
30:6	44, 64n

1 Samuel

14:45	136n
23:27	136n

2 Samuel

11–12	129
23:5	83n

1 Kings

8:24–6	226n
17:18	112n

2 Kings

15:14	217n
18:35	136n
19:28, 35	136n

2 Chronicles

30:18–20	223n

Nehemiah

9:17	106n

Job

1:6	90n
13:23–7	112n

Psalms

2:8–9	27n
16:2	26n
16:10–11	27n
18:23	139n
22	27n
22:1	26n
26:6	223n
31:16	147n
32:3–5	113n
38:5	139n
40:8	26n
45:7	26n
50:21	101n
51:3	150n
51:5	151
51:8	147n
51:12	121
58:3	39
72:8	27n
73:26	111
84:1ff	256
89:28	27n
110:6	27n
119	249
119:38	229
119:67	137n
130	16, 100, 103, 108, 109, 110, 112
130:4–5	103n

NEW TESTAMENT